D0975240

Wall Street Lingo

Lingo

Thousands of Investment Terms Explained Simply

By

Nora Peterson

Wall Street Lingo: Thousands of Investment Terms Explained Simply

Copyright © 2007 by Atlantic Publishing Group, Inc.
1210 SW 23rd Place • Ocala, Florida 34474 • 800-814-1132 • 352-622-5836–Fax
Web site: www.atlantic-pub.com • E-mail: sales@atlantic-pub.com
SAN Number: 268-1250

REF
H G
4513
. P48
2007

ISBN-13: 978-1-60138-038-8   ISBN-10: 1-60138-038-0

Library of Congress Cataloging-in-Publication Data

Peterson, Nora.
   Wall Street lingo : thousands of investment terms explained simply / Nora Peterson.
      p. cm.
   Includes bibliographical references and indexes.
   ISBN-13: 978-1-60138-038-8 (alk. paper)
   ISBN-10: 1-60138-038-0 (alk. paper)
   1. Investments--Dictionaries. 2. Securities--Dictionaries. 3. Finance--Dictionaries.
   I. Title. II. Title: Wall Street terms and lingo.

   HG4513.P48 2007
   332.603--dc22
                              2006031404

EDITOR: Marie Lujanac • mlujanac817@yahoo.com
PROOFREADER: Angela C. Adams • angela.c.adams@hotmail.com
ART DIRECTOR: Meg Buchner • megadesn@mchsi.com
INTERIOR LAYOUT DESIGN: Studio 6 Sense • info@6sense.net

Printed in the United States

Contents

Part I: Market Mechanics

Part II: Who's Who

Part III: Market Forces

Part IV: Asset Classes

Part V: Analysis Strategies: Identifying a Good Investment When You See It

Part VI: Investment Mechanics

Part VII: Additional Resources

We recently lost our beloved pet "Bear," who was not only our best and dearest friend but also the "Vice President of Sunshine" here at Atlantic Publishing. He did not receive a salary but worked tirelessly 24 hours a day to please his parents. Bear was a rescue dog that turned around and showered myself, my wife Sherri, his grandparents  Jean, Bob and Nancy and every person and animal he met (maybe not rabbits) with friendship and love. He made a lot of people smile every day.

We wanted you to know that a portion of the profits of this book will be donated to The Humane Society of the United States. *–Douglas & Sherri Brown*

The human-animal bond is as old as human history. We cherish our animal companions for their unconditional affection and acceptance. We feel a thrill when we glimpse wild creatures in their natural habitat or in our own backyard.

Unfortunately, the human-animal bond has at times been weakened. Humans have exploited some animal species to the point of extinction.

The Humane Society of the United States makes a difference in the lives of animals here at home and worldwide. The HSUS is dedicated to creating a world where our relationship with animals is guided by compassion. We seek a truly humane society in which animals are respected for their intrinsic value, and where the human-animal bond is strong.

Want to help animals? We have plenty of suggestions. Adopt a pet from a local shelter, join The Humane Society and be a part of our work to help companion animals and wildlife. You will be funding our educational, legislative, investigative and outreach projects in the U.S. and across the globe.

Or perhaps you'd like to make a memorial donation in honor of a pet, friend or relative? You can through our Kindred Spirits program. And if you'd like to contribute in a more structured way, our Planned Giving Office has suggestions about estate planning, annuities, and even gifts of stock that avoid capital gains taxes.

Maybe you have land that you would like to preserve as a lasting habitat for wildlife. Our Wildlife Land Trust can help you. Perhaps the land you want to share is a backyard—that's enough. Our Urban Wildlife Sanctuary Program will show you how to create a habitat for your wild neighbors.

So you see, it's easy to help animals. And The HSUS is here to help.

2100 L Street NW • Washington, DC 20037 • 202-452-1100
www.hsus.org

Foreword

We've decided to create a poison pill!" If stated by an evil scientist in a pharmaceutical lab, everyone would immediately understand the implications of this statement. However, if spoken by the CEO of a retail firm, many people might not understand its implications – though they would probably guess that no one should die as a result!

Many professions employ language that is understood only by those who practice it, and the finance profession is no exception. Like other professionals, those in finance developed their own lingo as a means of conveying ideas succinctly. Unfortunately, this language can serve as an initial barrier to those interested in learning more about the economy and our financial markets.

With the eclipse of defined benefit retirement plans individuals are increasingly in control of their own investments. In turn, as more people desire a greater awareness and understanding of financial market products and trading mechanisms, more are increasingly confronted by the barrier created by finance lingo.

Wall Street Lingo is an excellent dictionary through which everyone can learn the language used by finance professionals. The book is an ideal reference for people who want to gain a deeper understanding of finance from outlets ranging from *The Wall Street Journal* to *CNNfn* broadcasts. This book's greatest appeal is derived from its organization. The unique arrangement by subject area will help readers link related concepts; thus providing context for the words in addition to their literal meaning. Therefore, from the novice trying to understand the difference between the NYSE and an ECN, to those considering the implications of investing in a firm with a *poison pill*, everyone will find this book to be helpful and stimulating.   — *Jay F. Coughenour*

Jay Coughenour is an Associate Professor of Finance at the University of Delaware, Lerner College of Business & Economics. Professor Coughenour's research has been presented at the National Bureau of Economic Research, the New York Stock Exchange, the Securities and Exchange Commission, and at over 35 academic conferences or seminar programs. Professor Coughenour has published in the *Journal of Finance*, *Journal of Financial Economics*, *Journal of Derivatives*, and *The Financial Review*; additionally his research has been cited in the *CFA Digest*, *Dow Jones Newswires*, and *The Wall Street Journal*.

Author Biography

Nora Peterson has been actively involved in the financial and real estate markets for more than three decades. A retired computer industry analyst and business writer, Ms. Peterson trades the stock market and writes both fiction and nonfiction from her home on the outskirts of Phoenix, Arizona. She is the author of *Retire Rich With Your Self-Directed IRA: What Your Broker and Banker Don't Want You to Know About Managing Your Own Retirement Investments*, also from Atlantic Publishing Company, and *Past Imperfect*, a mystery from Cambridge Books. For more information about Ms. Peterson, visit her Web site at **www.norapeterson.com**.

Author Dedication

Introduction

Wall Street

1. A street in New York City bounded by Broadway on the northwest and South Street on the southeast.

2. The address for the largest stock exchange in the world.

3. A reference to the banks, stock exchanges, and commodities markets in New York City's financial district.

4. The financial capitol of the world.

What happens on Wall Street does *not* stay on Wall Street. In fact, it's been said that if the U.S. economy catches a cold, the rest of the world's economies get the flu. Intel's earnings matter as much on the street of New Delhi and Brussels as they do in mid-town Manhattan. And they matter where you and I work, shop, and play—right here on Main Street, U.S.A.

In a country where capitalism is king and free enterprise his queen, jobs depend on corporate profitability: our jobs. The cereal boxes above the refrigerator, the bananas dangling on a hook on the kitchen counter, the running shoes under the bed, the gasoline we pump into the SUV and the ready-made dinner we pick up on the way home from work all make their way into our lives because companies see an opportunity to make a profit by providing them.

Bringing products to our doorsteps also requires people like you and me to design, produce, market, and deliver them. Jobs mean paychecks. Paychecks empower consumers. Robust consumer spending ultimately translates into more profits for corporate America. But what about you and me?

Paychecks rarely pave the road to financial freedom. It's what we do with the money we pay ourselves (our savings) that sets us on one of the many different paths to that destination. That's where *Wall Street Lingo* enters the picture – and hopefully your life.

Of course, not everyone is wired for building wealth by aggressively investing in securities or buying and selling oil and gas futures or index options. That said, experience has convinced me that more people could be shoring up their financial security by incorporating them to some degree into their overall financial plan if they could simply get over the intimidation hump. I'm well acquainted with how formidable the foreign world of Wall Street can appear because I started my journey from the very same square.

Overcoming the language barrier is always a good place to begin when embarking on a journey to a new land. Learning the language of finance is much the same – except that it might be a tad easier than becoming fluent in a completely unfamiliar tongue. It is based on English after all. Think of it as English in a different context. Here's a short example.

Consider the word *leg*, which has a number of different meanings when we're bellied up to the dining room table for Thanksgiving dinner.

1. One of two sumptuous turkey limbs that we also call drumsticks.

2. The chair and table supports that make it possible for us to sit comfortably as we survey the feast.

3. One part of the trip from Omaha that Uncle Frank made to join us.

4. The way the fine Cabernet he brought with him grabs the side of the wine glass.

5. One side of the straddle cousin Helen initiated on Wednesday afternoon.

"A straddle?" you say. "Isn't that the way you sit on a horse? And what's that got to do with a leg?" Everything, because a straddle is an investment strategy comprised of two legs – one long leg and one short. And, no, that doesn't mean Helen's been hiking a Colorado mountainside too long. It means you need to turn to Chapter 23, "Investing Your Way: Brokers, Strategies, and Tools that Match Your Style" to satisfy your curiosity.

In the pages that follow, you'll find definitions for the terminology that so intimidated me in the beginning that my husband had to drag me kicking and screaming into the terrifying world of investing. Looking back, I think I would have become a willing participant early on if I'd have had a book like *Wall Street Lingo* at my elbow.

Not Just For Novices

I wrote *Wall Street Lingo* for investors like me. Investors who know a little or know a lot, but know for sure they need to continue expanding their knowledge of finance and investing; investors who don't yet and probably never will need a vocabulary of 4,000 financial terms; investors who want clear, concise explanations for the words they encounter when speaking with their brokers, reading the financial pages, doing their research, and listening to the business channels on TV.

Organization

Most dictionaries start at A and end with Z. I'm not knocking them. They have their place. My desk is simply not one of them. *Wall Street Lingo* takes a different approach. It's designed to stimulate the reader's curiosity, not overwhelm it.

To that end, *Wall Street Lingo* includes an exhaustive index that points to the definitions which are grouped by subject matter and divided into sections and chapters, the way any good reference book is organized. That way, when you look in index for *relief rally*, for example, you'll notice that *primary market trend* is listed a few lines above it and *Santa Claus rally* is included just a few lines below it. My hope is that your curiosity will get the better of you and you'll end up reading all three definitions and maybe a few others as well and then sit back and say, "Ah ha! I didn't know that."

Some terms could have rightly been included in more than one chapter. For example, the term *Redemption* relates to bonds, mutual funds, and preferred stock. In each case where I was forced to make a decision as to where it should go, I chose the placement that seemed most reader-friendly. In some instances that meant including it in each chapter. In other instances, particularly where no clear advantage seemed to be gained by duplicating it or choosing one location over another, I made an arbitrary decision as to which chapter it most rightly belonged.

Pronunciation

A handful of the terms included beg for a little pronunciation help. In keeping with the goal to make Wall Street Lingo simple to use and easy to read, for those terms alone I've included a basic, self-explanatory pronunciation key along with the definition.

Errors and Omissions

Finally, a few words about the definitions themselves; the list of terms is necessarily shorter than most finance dictionaries. This choice was made by design to allow for the latitude to include further explanations on certain topics.

Each term included was checked against multiple sources to confirm its most common usage. As with most disciplines, I found that financial terms sometimes have more than one meaning, depending on the source. This is particularly true in regard to technical analysis, which resembles an art more than a science. So, while every attempt has been made to relate the most common definition for each term accurately, errors or differences of opinion are possible.

Market Mechanics

CHAPTER ONE

The Exchanges:
At Home and Abroad

STOCK EXCHANGE A marketplace where securities are bought and sold on the secondary market.

FUTURES EXCHANGE A marketplace where forward contracts on commodities, currencies, and other financial instruments are traded.

AMERICAN STOCK EXCHANGE (AMEX or ASE) One of the oldest U.S. stock exchanges and innovator of the Exchange Traded Fund (ETF), now a specialty of the AMEX. The AMEX also claims bragging rights for being the first stock exchange to establish a presence on the Internet. Located in New York City, it incorporates both open outcry auctions that are conducted on the floor of the exchange and electronic trading. Each auction is facilitated by a specialist whose job is to match up buyers and sellers and to make a market in one or more securities. See Hybrid Market. On the Web at **www.amex.com**.

ARCAEX A fully automated stock exchange, formed by the union of the Pacific Stock Exchange and Archipelago and which later became NYSEArca when the two companies merged with the New York Stock Exchange. On the Web at **www.nysearca.com**.

ARCHIPELAGO A division of NYSE Group. Archipelago originated in 1996 as an electronic communication network (ECN) serving the NASDAQ marketplace. In 2000, it joined forced with the Pacific Stock Exchange to introduce ARCAEX, the first fully automated stock exchange. In 2002, Archipelago and the Pacific Stock Exchange merged with the New York Stock Exchange to form the NYSE Group. On the Web at **www.nysearca.com**.

BIG BOARD, THE Another name for the New York Stock Exchange (NYSE). On the Web at **www.nyse.com**.

BOSTON EQUITY EXCHANGE (BeX) An electronic stock exchange formed as a joint venture between the Boston Stock Exchange (BS) and CitiGroup, CSFB, Fidelity Brokerage Company, and Lehman Brothers in 2005. On the Web at **www.bostonstock.com**.

BOSTON OPTIONS EXCHANGE (BOX) An electronic options exchange formed as a joint venture between the Boston Stock Exchange (BSE) and Credit Suisse First Boston, JP Morgan, UB, and Citigroup in 2004. On the Web at **www.bostonoptions.com**.

BOSTON STOCK EXCHANGE (BSE) A regional stock exchange located in Boston, Massachusetts. The third-oldest stock exchange in the United States, the BSE was established in 1834. It is owned by its 200 members, each of whom has a seat on the exchange. The BSE trades approximately 2,000 securities in a hybrid trading system that combines an open outcry auction and electronic trading. On the Web at **www.bostonstock.com**.

BOURSE DE MONTREAL, INC. (MX) Canada's primary options and futures exchange where currency, equity, index, and interest rate products are traded. On the Web at **www.m-x.ca**.

CANADIAN DERIVATIVES EXCHANGE See Bourse de Montreal, Inc.

CANADIAN VENTURE EXCHANGE See TSX Venture Exchange.

CBOE FUTURES EXCHANGE (CFE) An all-electronic futures exchange owned by the Chicago Board Options Exchange (CBOE), where index futures and Gas at the Pump Futures are traded. On the Web at **www.cfe.cboecom**.

CHICAGO BOARD OF TRADE (CBOT) An exchange where futures and option contracts are traded on agricultural commodities, financial products, and industrial and precious metals. The CBOT was established in 1848 as an open outcry auction for agricultural products. Today it incorporates both a live auction system and fully electronic trading for more than 50 different products. On the Web at **www.cbot.com**.

CHICAGO BOARD OPTIONS EXCHANGE (CBOE) The futures and options exchange where contracts on securities, indexes, and financial products are traded. The CBOE uses a hybrid system that combines an open outcry auction with electronic trading. It also operates the all electronic CBOE Futures Exchange (CFE). On the Web at **www.cboe.com**.

CHICAGO MERCANTILE EXCHANGE (CME) The largest commodity and futures exchange in the U.S. Trading pits at the CME conduct open outcry auctions on equity, currency, agricultural, and interest rate products. The CME also operates the all-electronic Globex exchange. On the Web at **www.cme.com**.

CHICAGO STOCK EXCHANGE (CHX) A regional stock exchange, founded in 1882 as an open outcry auction system. At this writing, the CHX is in the process of obtaining approval from the Securities & Exchange Commission (SEC) for a plan to migrate to a totally electronic trading system. On the Web at **www.chx.com**.

CINCINNATI STOCK EXCHANGE (NSX) See National Stock Exchange.

COFFEE, SUGAR, AND COCOA EXCHANGE (CSCE) A futures exchange formed by the 1979 merger of the original Coffee and Sugar Exchange and the Cocoa Exchange. In 2003 the CSCE merged with the New York Cotton Exchange to form the New York Board of Trade (NYBOT). On the Web at **www.nybot.com**.

COMEX See Commodities Exchange, Inc.

COMMODITIES EXCHANGE INC. (COMEX) A division of the New York Mercantile Exchange where futures and option contracts on gold, silver, copper, and aluminum are traded.

COMMODITIES FUTURES EXCHANGE An exchange on which derivative contracts such as futures and options are traded on agricultural products, securities, indexes, and debt instruments.

EUREX An electronic futures and options exchange that is jointly operated by Deutsche Börse Ag and SWX Swiss Exchange. Eurex has offices in Chicago, Frankfurt, London, Paris, and Zurich. On the Web at **www.eurex.com**.

EUREX US A Chicago-based futures exchange established in 2004 by Deutsche Börse AG. On the Web at **www.eurexus.com.**

EURONEXT An Amsterdam, Holland-based international stock and derivatives exchange. Euronext was formed in 2000 with the merger of the Amsterdam, Brussels, and Paris exchanges. In 2000 it acquired the London International Financial Futures and Options Exchange (LIFFE) and the Bolsa de Valores de Lisboa e Porto exchange of Portugal.

FRANKFURTER WERPAPIERBORSE (FWB) The largest German stock exchange and an important international marketplace. Also known as the Frankfurt Stock Exchange, the FWB is operated by Deutsche Börse Group. On the Web at **http://deutsche-boerse.com.**

FRANKFURT STOCK EXCHANGE See Frankfurter Werpapierborse.

FUTURES EXCHANGE A marketplace where forward contracts on commodities, currencies, and other financial instruments are traded. See Derivative; Futures; Futures Contract.

INTERNATIONAL SECURITIES EXCHANGE (ISE) A New York City-based stock exchange providing an international market for equity options. On the Web at **www.iseoptions.com.**

KANSAS CITY BOARD OF TRADE (KCBT) A Kansas City, Missouri-based exchange on which grain futures are traded, founded in 1856. On the Web at **www.kcbt.com.**

LONDON INTERNATIONAL FINANCIAL FUTURES AND OPTIONS EXCHANGE (LIFFE) See Euronext. On the Web at **www.liffe.com.**

LONDON METAL EXCHANGE (LME) A London, England-based futures exchange for non-ferrous metal and plastics. The LME's roots go back to 1571 with the establishment of the Royal Exchange, London's first stock exchange. On the Web at **www.lme.co.uk.**

LONDON STOCK EXCHANGE (LSE) An international stock exchange located in London, England, with a regional office in Hong Kong. More than 400 international companies from more than

60 countries are currently traded on the LSE. On the Web at **www. londonstockexchange.com.**

MERC See Chicago Mercantile Exchange.

MIDWEST STOCK EXCHANGE See Chicago Stock Exchange.

MONTREAL EXCHANGE See Bourse de Montreal, Inc. On the Web at **www.m-x.ca/accueil_en.php.**

NASDAQ The largest U.S. electronic stock exchange, it was founded in 1971 by the National Association of Securities Dealers (NASD) as a bulletin board trading system. In 2000, NASDAQ members voted to spin off the New York-based company to a shareholder-owned company, and in 2006 it announced its intention to conduct an initial public offering of its stock. See American Stock Exchange; New York Stock Exchange; Regional Stock Exchange. On the Web at **www. nasdaq.com.**

NATIONAL STOCK EXCHANGE (NSX) A regional stock exchange founded in 1885 as the Cincinnati Stock Exchange. In 1980 the exchange closed its trading floor and became the first all-electronic stock exchange and subsequently moved its operations to Chicago. In 2003 it changed its name to the National Stock Exchange. On the Web at **www.nsx.com.**

NEW YORK BOARD OF TRADE (NYBOT) A futures and options exchange for agricultural products, currency, and indexes. The New York Board of Trade was formed by the 2004 the merger of the New York Cotton Exchange and the Coffee, Sugar & Cocoa Exchange. On the Web at **www.nybot.com.**

NEW YORK COTTON EXCHANGE (NYCE) See New York Board of Trade.

NEW YORK MERCANTILE EXCHANGE (NYMEX) The world's largest commodities futures exchange and one of the most active options exchanges for the precious metals and energy markets. The NYMEX is comprised of two divisions: NYMEX, where energy, platinum, and palladium are traded and COMEX, where gold, silver, copper, and aluminum are traded. On the Web at **www.nymex.com.**

NEW YORK STOCK EXCHANGE (NYSE) The world's largest stock exchange and the de facto center of the U.S. financial markets. Founded in 1792, the New York Stock Exchange merged with Archipelago (Arca) and the Pacific Stock Exchange (PCX) in 2006 to form the NYSE Group. NYSE Group operates two separate exchanges, the New York Stock Exchange and NYSEArca. The New York Stock Exchange operates from the floor of its Wall Street location as a hybrid system that combines an open-outcry auction with electronic trading. NYSEArca is a fully electronic exchange. On the Web at **www.nyse.com**.

NYMEX A division of the New York Mercantile Exchange, where energy, platinum, and palladium options and futures are traded. On the Web at **www.nynex.com**.

NYSEARCA A division of the NYSE Group, formed by the merger of Archipelago (Arca), the Pacific Stock Exchange, and the New York Stock Exchange.

NYSE GROUP The publicly traded parent company of the New York Stock Exchange (NYSE) and NYSEArca. On the Web at **www. nyse.com**.

ONECHICAGO, LLC. An all electronic futures and options exchange for Single Stock Futures (SFF), Exchange Traded Funds (ETFs), and indexes. OneChicago is a joint venture of the Chicago Board Options Exchange, Chicago Mercantile Exchange, and the Chicago Board of Trade. On the Web at **www.onechicago.com**.

OVER-THE-COUNTER BULLETIN BOARD (OTCBB) An electronic quotation system introduced as a result of the Securities Enforcement Remedies and Penny Stock Reform Act of 1990. See Bulletin Board Stock. On the Web at **www.otcbb.com**.

OVER-THE-COUNTER MARKET (OTC) A negotiated market for the trading of unlisted stocks. Not all over-the-counter stocks are required to file financial reports with the Securities & Exchange Commission (SEC), making it difficult to secure reliable information on which to base investment decisions. See OTCBB.

PACIFIC STOCK EXCHANGE (PCX) A regional stock exchange, originally founded as the San Francisco Stock and Bond Exchange in 1882. Over the next 124 years, it expanded and reorganized a number of times before it merged with the New York Stock Exchange and Archipelago to form the NYSE Group in 2006. On the Web at **www.nysearca.com**.

PHILADELPHIA STOCK EXCHANGE (PHLX) A regional stock exchange, located in Philadelphia, Pennsylvania. Founded in 1790, the PHLX was the nation's first organized stock exchange. It is the home of the some of the most closely followed industry indexes. On the Web at **www.phlx.com**.

REGIONAL STOCK EXCHANGE A stock exchange that is not located in a country's financial center. In the United States, any exchangethat is located in a city other than New York City is considered a regional exchange. Regional stock exchanges add liquidity and competition to the financial markets by increasing market participation.

A Closer Look at U.S. Regional Stock Exchanges
Boston Stock Exchange
Chicago Stock Exchange
Philadelphia Stock Exchange
National Stock Exchange*
*(Formerly the Cincinnati Stock Exchange)

SAN FRANCISCO STOCK AND BOND EXCHANGE See Pacific Stock Exchange.

STOCK EXCHANGE A marketplace where securities are bought and sold on the secondary market.

SWISS EXCHANGE (SWX) Switzerland's stock exchange. SWX is an electronic marketplace for trading securities and derivatives. On the Web at **www.swx.com**.

TOKYO STOCK EXCHANGE (TSE) Japan's primary stock and derivative exchange. TSE also has offices in New York, London, and Singapore. The TSE traces its roots back to the 1878 founding of the Tokyo Stock Exchange Co., Ltd. On the Web at **http://www.tse.or.jp/english/index.shtml**.

TORONTO STOCK EXCHANGE (TSX) A Canadian equities exchange located in Toronto, Ontario. TSX is owned and operated by TSX Group which also owns the TSX Venture Exchange. On the Web at **www.tsx.com**.

TSX GROUP The parent company of the Toronto Stock Exchange and TSX Venture Exchange. TSX Group has offices in Vancouver, Calgary, Winnipeg, Toronto, and Montreal. On the Web at **www.tsx.com**.

TSX VENTURE EXCHANGE A regulated marketplace where Canadian mining, oil and gas, manufacturing, technology, and financial services companies raise capital from investors. TSX Venture Exchange is part of the TSX Group which also includes the Toronto Stock Exchange. On the Web at **www.tsx.com**.

CHAPTER TWO

Exchange Operations: Bringing Order to the Markets

AUCTION A market system in which buyers bid against each other to establish the selling price of the item offered for sale.

ACCESS A New York Mercantile Exchange (NYMEX) after-hours trading system. See Electronic Trading System; Extended Hours Trading.

AFTER THE BELL A term that refers to the time after the close of the regular trading session. Certain news releases and earning announcements are delayed until after the bell. See Before the Bell; Embargo.

AFTER-HOURS TRADING Electronic trading that takes place after the close of the regular trading session. Compare to Pre-Market.

A Closer Look at The Risks Associated with Trading in the After-Hours Market

Whether you're buying and selling securities, real estate, or snails, price stability depends on a balanced supply of both buyers and sellers. In the often thinly traded after-hours market it's not at all uncommon for that balance to skew in one direction or the other, resulting in widening spreads between the bid and ask price for a security. The result? Buyers or sellers who are anxious to get in or out of the market during post-market trading may be forced to raise or lower their bid or ask price in order to get their orders filled, which can eat away at profit or increases the loss on a bad trade.

NOTE: Market orders are not accepted for execution during extended trading hours, again because the potentially large spreads can result in adverse order fulfillment and further increase trading volatility.

AUCTION A market system in which buyers bid against each other to establish the selling price of the item offered for sale. Some stock exchanges conduct live open outcry auctions on the floor of the exchange. Participants in these auctions include a specialist, who serves as the auctioneer, floor brokers who represent their clients, and registered traders who trade their own accounts. Live auctions are employed at some commodity and futures exchanges also.

AUTOMATED BOND SYSTEM (ABS) The electronic bond trading system used at the New York Stock Exchange.

AUTOMATED SEARCH AND MATCH (ASAM) An automated system employed at the New York Stock Exchange to examine public information and cross reference it with trading data to identify possible trading irregularities.

BEFORE THE BELL A term that refers to the time before the start of the regular trading day. Certain news releases and earning announcements are scheduled before the bell. See After the Bell; Embargo.

BLUE ROOM One of three trading rooms at the New York Stock Exchange. The Blue Room was opened in 1969 and expanded in 1988, at which time it became known as the Extended Blue Room.

BOOK A list maintained by a specialist that tracks unfilled buy and sell. The term refers to the notebooks that specialists used before the advent of computer-based order tracking systems. See Buy the Book; Specialist Display Book.

BUTTONWOOD AGREEMENT The 1792 agreement among 24 New York stockbrokers and businessmen to form an investment community that later became the New York Stock Exchange. The agreement was named for the buttonwood tree under which it was signed.

BUY THE BOOK A market order to purchase all available shares (the book) of a given security from one specialist and all other broker dealers. Buy the book orders are typically generated by institutional investors.

CASH MARKET A term that refers to the actual purchase and sale of a commodity or financial product for immediate delivery, as opposed to trading on the futures price for the same product. See Cash Price, Spot Price.

CLEARPORT eACCESS A New York Mercantile Exchange (NYMEX) after-hours trading system. See Electronic Trading System.

CIRCUIT BREAKER Rules that trigger a trading halt on an exchange or individual security to prevent panic buying and selling that might destabilize the market. Circuit breakers give investors and traders a chance to pause and appraise the market with a cool head before trading resumes. See Imbalance of Orders; Maximum Price Fluctuation.

CLOSING BELL An audible signal indicating the end of the regular trading day on an exchange. Representatives of public corporations, celebrities, and newsmakers often celebrate notable events by performing the honor of ringing the closing bell of an exchange. Compare to Opening Bell.

COMMODITIES EXCHANGE CENTER Located at the World Trade Center until the September 11, 2001, attack.

COMPETITIVE MARKET MAKER SYSTEM A system in use at some exchanges in which any member of the exchange can make a market in any stock traded on that exchange. See Registered Competitive Market Maker.

CONSOLIDATED QUOTE SYSTEM (CQS) An electronic system that collects and disseminates the volume, bid, ask, and size price quotations for each security and for each exchange on which it is traded. The CQS is administered by member exchanges and is overseen by the Consolidated Tape Authority (CTA). See Consolidated Tape System (CTS).

CONSOLIDATED TAPE ASSOCIATION (CTA) The policy-making and operating authority for the systems that collect, process, and disseminate trade data. See Consolidated Quote System and Consolidated Tape System. See Consolidated Tape Plan.

CONSOLIDATED TAPE PLAN (CTP) A body of policies and procedures that govern the collection and dissemination of trading data. The CTP is developed and overseen by the Consolidated Trade Association and filed with the Securities & Exchange Commission (SEC). Member exchanges administer the plan. See Consolidated Quote System; Consolidated Tape System.

CONSOLIDATED TAPE SYSTEM (CTS) An electronic data feed for collecting and disseminating last trade information for exchange-listed securities from all of the markets in which they trade. Sometimes referred to as the Consolidated Trade System.

CONSOLIDATED TRADE SYSTEM See Consolidated Tape System (CTS).

CONTRACT MARKET An exchange that is registered with the Commodity Futures Trading Commission (CFTC) to trade specific commodity or option contracts. See Commodity Futures Exchange; Derivatives.

CURBS Temporary trading restrictions imposed by an exchange to even out dramatic price swings of a volatile market. Curbs are typically triggered by a large drop in the broader market and may include a complete halt in trading. In some situations, the restrictions may prohibit program trading or limit acceptable trades to those placed only on an uptick. See Circuit Breaker; Trading Halt.

DISPLAY BOOK (DBK) A New York Stock Exchange electronic filing system that displays limit orders until filled or canceled. Also referred to as the specialist display book, the DBK also records and reports transactions to other systems in use at the exchange. It receives its information from the Limit Order Processing System.

DUAL TRADING A situation in which a floor broker or a brokerage firm executes trades on behalf of a client and for his or her own benefit on the same day.

ELECTRONIC COMMUNICATION NETWORK (ECN) Any one

of several computer-based order matching systems that provides investors with direct access to the market, bypassing the middleman (broker) for order placement. With ECN access, investors can see quotes for the best bid and best ask and enter orders directly into the system. As a result, the ECN can speed up the order entry and execution process as well as making it possible for investors to participate in extended trading hours. Each brokerage firm is free to decide which ECN it chooses to include in its order flow system and how much access to the ECN it will provide to its customers.

ELECTRONIC TRADING SYSTEM A computer-based system that allows for the entry and execution futures and options orders after the close of open-outcry auction trading.

EXTENDED BLUE ROOM A 1988 expansion to the New York Stock Exchange to accommodate increased trading activity.

EXTENDED HOURS TRADING A period of electronic trading that takes place before or after the regular trading session for an exchange. At one time, only orders placed by institutional investors could be placed and filled during extended hours trading. Today electronic communications networks (ECNs) make it possible for market makers and brokerage firms participate in pre-market and after-market trading on a voluntary basis. Individual investors can also buy and sell stocks during extended trading hours by choosing a broker that provides access. See Pre-Market; After Hours Trading (AFT).

FLOOR The trading area of an exchange where buyers and sellers meet face-to-face to participate in an open outcry auction. Compare Electronic Trading System.

FOREX Short for the Foreign Exchange Market. See Foreign Exchange Rate.

GLOBEX The Chicago Mercantile Exchange electronic trading platform for futures and option contracts. Globex provides a virtually continuous worldwide market, opening Sunday evening and remaining open for trading roughly 23 hours a day until it closes each Friday. See Electronic Trading System.

HYBRID MARKET An order fulfillment system that combines an open outcry auction with an electronic order handling system. Hybrid trading systems are in use, to some degree, at every U.S. exchange that continues to conduct live auction trading.

INTERMARKET TRADING SYSTEM (ITS) An electronic system that connects the multiple stock exchanges, allowing floor brokers to see the current bid and ask for any security and to place orders with any participating exchange.

LIMIT ORDER INFORMATION SYSTEM An electronic system that stores and displays information on limit orders and feeds the data to the specialist display book. Orders that are entered as good, until cancelled, remain in the system until filled or cancelled; all other orders are deleted from the system at the close of the trading session.

MAKE A MARKET To manage an inventory of a given stock from which shares are bought and sold to other market participants for the purpose of ensuring market liquidity. On the New York Stock Exchange (NYSE) and American Stock Exchange (AMEX), the individuals responsible for making a market are called specialists. On NASDAQ, they are referred to as market makers.

MARKET CLOSE Time at which the regular trading session ends on an exchange. See Closing Bell.

MARKET HOLIDAYS U.S. exchanges are closed in observance of nine holidays, annually.

A Closer Look at U.S. Market Holidays

- New Year's Day
- Martin Luther King, Jr. Day
- Washington's Birthday
- Good Friday
- Memorial Day
- Independence Day
- Labor Day
- Thanksgiving Day
- Christmas Day

NATIONAL SECURITIES TRADING SYSTEM (NSTS) An automated trading system in use at the National Stock Exchange.

NEGOTIATED MARKET A market in which buyers and sellers negotiate on price via posted bid and ask prices. NASDAQ is an example of a negotiated market, as opposed to the New York Stock Exchange and American Stock Exchange where traders bid against each other in an open outcry auction.

NETWORK A The Consolidated Tape System (CTS) data feed that disseminates quotation and last sale data for securities traded on the New York Stock Exchange. Compare to Network B.

NETWORK B The Consolidated Tape System (CTS) data feed that disseminates quotation and last sale information for securities traded on all U.S. exchanges other than the New York Stock Exchange. Compare to Network A.

OPENING AUTOMATED REPORTING SYSTEM (OARS) An electronic system that reports the opening price for each security to the originating broker.

A Closer Look at OARS

On a typical day, between 15 and 20 percent of all orders are executed at the market opening. Through SuperDOT, market orders to buy or sell, routed to the specialist post prior to the market opening, are automatically paired with opposing orders. The specialist, after matching buy and sell market orders and checking outstanding *limit orders* and larger opening orders, sets an opening price for the stock. The specialist then executes all paired orders at one price and sends confirmation notices to originating brokers within seconds of the market opening, through the Opening Automated Reporting System (OARS).

Source: *Electronic Bulls and Bears: U.S. Securities Markets and Information Technology*

U.S. Congress, Office of Technology Assessment, *Electronic Bulls & Bears: U.S. Securities Markets & Information Technology, OTA-CIT-469* (Washington, DC: U.S. Government Printing Office, September 1990).

OPENING BELL An audible signal indicating the start of the regular trading day on an exchange. Representatives of listed companies, celebrities, and newsmakers often celebrate notable events by performing the honor of ringing the opening bell at an exchange. See Trading Hours.

PINK SHEETS A privately owned company that provides a real-time quotation system listing bid and ask prices for over-the-counter stocks. The term Pink Sheets originated when the National Quotation Bureau issued daily and weekly lists of quotations for small domestic and foreign stocks on pink paper. Since 2000, investors have been able to access Pink Sheets online at **www.pinksheets.com**.

PIT An area on the trading floor where futures and options are traded in an open outcry auction.

POSIT An electronic trading system that matches buy and sell orders from institutional investors.

POST See Trading Post.

POST EXECUTION REPORTING SYSTEM (PERS) An electronic order entry and reporting system in use at the American Stock Exchange (AMEX or ASE).

PRE-MARKET A period of electronic trading that takes place prior to the start of the regular trading session. See Extended Hours Trading. Compare to After-Hours Trading.

REAL TIME QUOTE A bid and ask price quotation that is reported with no time delay. Compare to Delayed Quote.

RUNOFF The end-of-day process by which an exchange prints the closing price for every security traded onto ticker tape.

SEAT (Exchange Seat) A term that refers to membership in a stock, futures, or options exchange. Membership represents an ownership interest in the exchange, a role in the decisions governing its operation and a share in the operating profits.

A Closer Look: Exchange Seats

The reference to exchange seats dates back to the beginnings of the New York Stock Exchange. At that time, the members assembled in assigned seats for the daily roll call of stocks offered for sale.

The seats were removed in 1871 when the exchange moved to a continuous trading system. Although it lost its literal meaning, the term "seat" lingered as an expression of membership in what might be viewed as one of the world's most exclusive clubs.

With the 2006 NYSE/Archipelago merger, the New York Stock Exchange eliminated its membership seats but retained its practice of issuing a maximum of 1366 licenses to trade on the floor of the exchange. The American Stock Exchange (AMEX) has 834 seats and roughly 40 more specialized seats that can be bought, sold, and leased either through the exchange or from the individual owners.

SECONDARY MARKET A market in which a security or derivative is bought or sold by someone other than the original issuer. Stock exchange transactions are an example of a secondary securities market. Compare to Primary Market.

SMALL ORDER EXECUTION SYSTEM (SOES) A NASDAQ automated electronic order matching and execution system for NASDAQ-listed securities for orders of 1,000 shares or less.

SPECIALIST DISPLAY BOOK See Display Book.

STOCK WATCHER A computer program employed by certain exchanges to monitor transaction and detect possible illegal activity.

STREAMING QUOTES A computer-based quotation system in which security and/or futures prices are continuously updated in real time. Compare to Delayed Quote.

SUPERDOT An electronic order entry and reporting system in use at the New York Stock Exchange.

SUPERMONTAGE An integrated electronic order entry and execution system used at NASDAQ.

TERMINAL MARKET A term used in the United Kingdom to refer to the market on which commodities and futures contracts are traded.

TICKER A term used to refer to a narrow strip of paper or an electronic display where streaming quotes are reported. Before the advent of computers, prices were stamped on ticker tape. Today tickers are displayed on televisions, computer monitors, or any other electronic display device.

Table 1

A Closer Look at a Stock Ticker
QQQQ◄38.18 -0.82 2.10%   MSFT◄23.36   -0.34 -1.43%   RMBS◄24.42 +1.65 +7.25%

TICKER TAPE A computerized stock price quotation system. Before the age of computers, stock prices were broadcast over desktop devices that spewed thin streams of paper (called ticker tape) on which the stock prices were stamped. The device was called a ticker because of the ticking noise it made.

TICKER TAPE PARADE A celebration during which massive amounts of shredded paper shower paraders. The October 29, 1869 dedication of the Statue of Liberty gave birth to the first ticker tape parade when office workers spontaneously tossed miles of ticker tape to the parade below.

TIME AND SALES A record of each trade that takes place on an exchange. If an investor questions the execution of a trade, the brokerage firm can access the time and sales report to clarify the exact time and price of its execution. Many direct access trading platforms include a time and sales report window.

TRADING HALT A temporary pause in trading on a particular security or futures contract. For securities, a trading halt is sometimes issued pending the release of news but may also occur due to an imbalance of buy and sell orders. On a futures exchange, a trading halt may be called when the bid or ask for a given contract exceeds the maximum price fluctuation. In either case, the purpose of the halt is to prevent irrational buying or panic selling and repair market liquidity by giving investors a chance to pause and appraise the situation. See Circuit Breaker.

TRADING HOURS Trading commences at U.S. stock exchanges at 9:30 a.m. and closes at 4 p.m. Eastern Time, Monday through Friday. ECNs extend the trading day by providing limited trading before and after the regular trading hours. The trading hours for futures and options exchanges vary by product and exchange. See Extended Hours Trading; Pre-market.

TRADING PIT An area on the trading floor of a futures and options exchange where contracts are bought and sold in a live open outcry auction.

TRADING POST An area on the trading floor of a stock exchange where a specialist conducts a live open outcry auction.

TRADING SESSION A term that references the normal trading day, but excludes trading that takes place before the opening bell or after the closing bell. The trading session does not include the pre-market or extended hours trading.

WATCH LIST A list of securities that a brokerage firm or exchange believes may be the target of trading irregularities.

XETRA The electronic trading platform in use at the Frankfurt Stock Exchange.

YELLOW SHEETS A daily listing of bid and ask price quotes for over-the-counter bonds. Yellow Sheets are a product of the National Quotation Bureau. On the Web at **www.pinksheets.com**.

CHAPTER THREE

Playing Fair:
Rules and Regulations

REGULATION FD The Securities & Exchange Commission (SEC) regulation that prohibits the selective release of material information about a company. Reg FD, as it is also called, attempts to level the playing field for all market participants by making it mandatory for companies to release information to all investors simultaneously. Sometimes referred to as the Fair Disclosure Regulation.

ABUSIVE TAX SHELTER A form of tax fraud in which a company intentionally uses inappropriate accounting practices to cheat on their taxes. Overvaluing depreciating assets and incorrectly recognizing certain types of income are two examples of abusive tax shelters.

AGGRESSIVE ACCOUNTING The sometimes fraudulent practice of incor-rectly recognizing income or expenses to make a company's financial picture appear more favorable than it actually is.

ANTITRUST LAWS Legislation intended ensure fair trade and consumer protection by blocking monopolistic practices and unlawful trade restraints. In other countries they are referred to as competition laws. See Monopoly.

ARBITRATION A voluntary process for dispute resolution in which an impartial person or group, called an arbitrator, hears arguments by opposing sides and issues a decision. Arbitration can be binding or non-binding. The decision in binding arbitration is final and enforceable. By contrast, the arbitrator in a non-binding arbitration case can recommend a resolution, but neither party is obligated to accept it.

ATTESTATION A statement attached to an audit report that contains the opinion of the auditor regarding the accuracy of a financial statement.

BANKING ACT OF 1933 Legislation that provided for regulation of the banking industry and insurance on account funds deposited banks and thrift institutions, through the establishment of the Federal Depository Insurance Corporation (FDIC). Also known as the Glass-Steagall Act.

BEAR RAID A prohibited practice in which a group of traders work together to drive down the price of a security. See Prearranged Trading.

BLANKET FIDELITY BOND Insurance against loss of money or other assets due to employee dishonesty. The Securities & Exchange Commission (SEC) requires brokerage firms to carry a blanket fidelity bond to protect clients' assets.

BLUE SKY LAW State laws enacted to prevent securities fraud. Blue sky laws require companies to disclose their true financial condition prior to issuing stock to the public. See National Market System.

CEO/CFO CERTIFICATION A written statement signed by the chief executive and chief financial officers of a publicly traded company that attests to their control over and acceptance of responsibility for internal controls relating to financial reporting. The CEO/CFO certifications are required under the Sarbanes-Oxley Act of 2002 and are a means of holding executives accountable for fraudulent financial statements.

CHANNEL STUFFING A fraudulent practice in which a company inflates its sales revenues by enticing wholesalers and/or retailers to order more product than they realistically expect to sell in the normal course of business. This is typically accomplished through extra-deep discounts and an understanding that the unsold product can be returned at a later date.

CHINESE WALL A set of ethical procedures that separates the internal operations of an organization to prevent a conflict of interest. For example, a sell-side analyst might be influenced to inflate earnings estimates for a company if he or she is aware that it generates revenue for her employer.

CHURNING The unethical practice of executing excessive trades on a managed account to generate commission revenue.

CLASS ACTION SUIT Litigation in which a single plaintiff represents a group of individuals with a common claim against the defendant.

CLAYTON ACT A 1914 amendment to the Sherman Antitrust Act that prohibits business practices that impair fair competition.

COMPETITION LAW See Antitrust Law.

CORPORATE AND CRIMINAL FRAUD ACCOUNTABILITY ACT A provision within the Sarbanes-Oxley Act of 2002 that provides for criminal penalties for securities fraud and protects employees of publicly traded companies from punitive actions from their employers for reporting Securities & Exchange Commission (SEC) violations and/or shareholder fraud. See Whistleblower.

CORPORATE FILING Any one of a number of forms the Securities & Exchange Commission (SEC) requires every publicly traded company to submit, disclosing its financial condition and material changes in the operation of the organization. See Form 8Q; Form 10K; Form 10-Q; Form S-1; Form S4.

EMBARGO A restriction on the release of economic or business data until a specific date and time. Federal agencies often release economic data with the stipulation that it must be held until the embargo is lifted.

ENTITY A thing that exists it its own right. The law recognizes corporations and people as entities with rights and legal obligations.

FAIR DISCLOSURE REGULATION See Regulation FD.

FEDERAL TRADE COMMISSION ACT OF 1914 The legislation

that created the Federal Trade Commission, which administers and enforces U.S. antitrust laws and fair trade practices.

FINANCIAL AND OPERATIONAL COMBINED UNIFORM SINGLE REPORT (FOCUS REPORT) A financial and operational report that stock exchanges are required to submit to the Securities & Exchange Commission (SEC).

FINANCIAL INSTITUTIONS REFORM, RECOVERY, AND EN-FORCEMENT ACT OF 1989 (FIRREA) The legislation that increased regu-latory authority and oversight for thrift institutions. FIRREA was prompted by the savings and loan scandal of the 1980s.

FOREIGN CORRUPT PRACTICES ACT (FCPA) Legislation signed into law in 1977 that prohibits U.S. firms from engaging in bribery and other unlawful and fraudulent practices when conducting business in foreign countries. The legislation assigned responsibility for FCPA enforcement to the U.S. Department of Justice with supporting roles played by the Securities & Exchange Commission (SEC) and the Office of General Counsel of the Department of Commerce.

GENERAL SECURITIES REGISTERED REPRESENTATIVE EXAM-INATION See Series 7 License.

GLASS-STEAGALL ACT Legislation passed in 1933 that prohibited commercial banks from owning or offering services relating to stocks or bonds. The anti-affiliation provisions of the Glass-Steagall Act were repealed in 1999 by the Gramm-Leach-Bliley Act.

GRAMM-LEACH-BLILEY ACT Legislation passed in 1999 that repealed the anti-affiliation provisions of the Glass-Steagall Act, opening the door for consolidation of the banking and securities industries.

INSIDER TRADE A sale or purchase of a company's stock by an individual with access to confidential company information. An insider trade may be legal or illegal, depending on when and under what circumstances it is executed. An illegal insider trade is one in which the transaction is initiated on the basis of material information that has not been released to the public. See Insider.

INSIDER TRADING AND SECURITIES FRAUD ENFORCEMENT ACT OF 1988 An amendment to the Securities Exchange Act of 1934 that expands the Securities & Exchange Commission (SEC) authority to enforce insider trading laws and to pay a bounty to informants.

INSIDER TRADING SANCTIONS ACT OF 1984 A House bill enacted in 1984 that laid out civil and criminal penalties for participating in an illegal insider trade.

INVESTMENT COMPANY ACT OF 1940 Legislation that regulates firms whose primary business is investing or trading in securities with money collected from individual investors. The act was passed to protect investors from conflicts of interest by requiring the company to disclose its organizational and financial information and its investment policies.

INVESTMENT COMPANY AMENDMENTS ACT OF 1970 An amendment to the Investment Company Act of 1940 that prohibits investment companies from engaging in deceptive incentive compensation practices and requires the filing of an ethics policy with the Securities & Exchange Commission (SEC) and proxy voting disclosure to investors.

LATE DAY TRADING The illegal practice of making a transaction that took place in after-hours trading appear to be executed during the regular trading session for the purpose of securing a better price. Late-day trading is prohibited by the Securities & Exchange Commission (SEC), but is sometimes carried out by certain funds.

LEGAL LIST A list of securities approved by a state for certain institutional investments, such as some pension funds, banks, and insurance companies.

MALONEY ACT An amendment to the Securities Exchange Act of 1934 that assigned oversight responsibility for the over-the-counter market to a Self-Regulatory Organization (SRO) registered with the Securities & Exchange Commission (SEC). See NASD.

MATERIAL INSIDER INFORMATION Confidential company information that is likely to affect the perceived value of a security when it is disclosed to the public. It is illegal for an individual who

MEDIATION A voluntary, non-binding process for dispute resolution in which a neutral third party listens to both sides of the argument and suggests an equitable settlement. Compare to Arbitration.

MONOPOLY A company that has no competition. In the United States we refer to legislation intended to stimulate competition and prevent unfair business practices that become possible when a company is the single-source for a product or service as antitrust laws. In other countries they are referred to as competition laws.

NATIONAL MARKET SYSTEM (NMS) A system of federal laws governing the licensing, regulation, and enforcement of securities traded on a stock exchange. See National Securities Market Improvement Act of 1996.

NATIONAL SECURITIES MARKETS IMPROVEMENT ACT OF 1996 (NSMIA) Legislation passed by Congress in 1996 that created the Securities & Exchange Commission (SEC) as the sole licensing, registration, and regulatory authority for securities traded on national markets. States retained the right to prosecute fraud and to license and regulate activities restricted to an individual state.

OVER-TRADING See Churning.

PENNY STOCK REFORM ACT OF 1990 See Securities Enforcement Remedies and Penny Stock Reform Act of 1990.

PIGGYBACKING An unethical practice of a broker making a trade in his or her own personal account immediately after executing the same trade for a client. If the broker has reason to believe that the customer is making the trade on the basis of inside information, piggybacking (also known as tailgating) can be illegal as well as unethical.

PORTFOLIO PUMPING The fraudulent and illegal practice of bidding up the price of securities in a fund's portfolio to inflate the its performance artificially right before the end of the quarter.

PREARRANGED TRADING An illegal practice in which trading takes place in a manner agreed on between market participants. For example, if a floor broker agrees to buy a security from another trader at an inflated price, the arrangement would be considered prearranged trading.

PROSPECTUS A legal document that makes an official offer to sell a security, mutual fund, or Unit Investment Trust (UIT) product. The Securities & Exchange Commission (SEC) establishes the rules regarding what information each type of prospectus must contain, but in general it must include sufficient information for an investor to make an informed evaluation about the risks associated with an investment. A prospectus typically describes the enterprise and its management, provides details about the product offering such as voting rights and anti-dilution provisions, and it discloses the financial state of the company and risks associated with the enterprise. The mutual fund's prospectus will also disclose information such as its fee structure, investment objectives and strategies, and performance history. See Final Prospectus; Red Herring Prospectus.

PROXY STATEMENT An official document, filed with Securities & Exchange Commission (SEC) and provided to every shareholder that discloses all pertinent information to be voted on at a shareholder meeting. The proxy statement also includes a request for the shareholder to authorize the company's management to vote the shareholder's shares at the meeting. See Proxy; Proxy Fight.

PRUDENT MAN RULE A principle that requires a trustee or other fiduciary to invest entrusted funds in the manner that a reasonable, informed individual would invest his or her own assets. See Discretionary Account; Managed Account.

PUMP AND DUMP A stock manipulation scheme in which one or more investors promote (pump) a security they own with the express intent to sell (dump) it at an artificially inflated price.

QUIET PERIOD A waiting period between the time a company submits a registration filing with the Securities & Exchange Commission (SEC) and the time when the company can publicly disclose the information contained in the filing. See Form S-1.

REGISTRATION APPROVAL Official Securities & Exchange Commission (SEC) acceptance of the registration statement, typically after one or more rounds of comments and requests for more information from the company.

REGISTRATION STATEMENT Documents filed with the Securities & Exchange Commission (SEC) by a privately held company, declaring its intent to offer shares of its stock to the general public. See Form S-1; Initial Public Offering.

REGULATION D The Securities & Exchange Commission (SEC) regulation that spells out the rules for limited offer and sale of a security without registering it under the Securities Act of 1933.

REGULATION FD The Securities & Exchange Commission (SEC) regulation that prohibits the selective release of material information about a company. Reg FD, as it is also called, attempts to level the playing field for all market participants by making it mandatory for companies to release information to all investors simultaneously. Sometimes referred to as the Fair Disclosure Regulation.

REGULATION Q The Federal Reserve regulation that establishes a limit on the interest rate a bank can pay on deposits held in savings accounts.

REGULATION T A Federal Reserve regulation that governs loans made by brokerage firms to fund stock purchases. See Margin.

REGULATION U A Federal Reserve regulation that governs loans made my companies other than brokerage firms (a bank or credit union) to fund stock purchases.

RISK DISCLOSURE DOCUMENT A document disclosing potential risks associated with options and futures trading. The Commodity Futures Trading Commission (CFTC) requires that a risk disclosure document be provided to all prospective options or futures investors.

RULES OF FAIR PRACTICE Code of conduct rules developed by NASD for broker dealers when doing business with the public.

SAFE HARBOR A legal protection for companies that mitigates or eliminates liability for statements made about future prospects and expectations, provided the company can demonstrate that the remarks were made in good faith.

SAFETY AND SOUNDNESS EXAM An Office of Thrift Supervision examination of the financial condition and operating policies and procedures of a thrift institution. See Federal Thrift Regulator; Thrift Administration Review Program; Thrift Financial Report.

SARBANES-OXLEY ACT OF 2002 (SOX) Market reform legislation sponsored by Senator Paul Sarbanes and Representative Michael Oxley in the wake of a series of Wall Street corruption scandals, including Enron and WorldCom. The primary focus of Sarbanes-Oxley was to improve the accuracy of financial information disclosed by U.S. public companies and foreign companies with a U.S. presence. SOX also provided for civil and criminal penalties for violations of the Act.

SCHEDULE 13D A Securities & Exchange Commission (SEC) filing required when a person or group of persons acquires beneficial ownership of more than 5 percent of the stock in a publicly traded company.

SECURITIES ACT OF 1933 Legislation passed in the wake of the stock market Crash of 1929 that required registration of certain publicly traded securities, disclosure of financial information of registered securities, and penalties for securities fraud.

SECURITIES ENFORCEMENT REMEDIES AND PENNY STOCK REFORM ACT OF 1990 An amendment to the Securities Act of 1933 that expanded enforcement remedies for Securities & Exchange Commission (SEC) violations and mandated the development of an electronic quote system that would provide greater transparency to OTC transactions. Sometimes referred to as the Penny Stock Reform Act of 1990.

SECURITIES EXCHANGE ACT OF 1934 Legislation that created the Securities & Exchange Commission (SEC) and charged the agency with providing oversight and enforcement of the securities industry.

SECURITIES INVESTOR PROTECTION ACT OF 1970 An amendment to the Securities Exchange Act of 1934 that governs the administration of the Security Investor Protection Corporation

(SIPC), which insures investor accounts held by member brokerage firms.

SERIES 7 LICENSE Certification obtained by passing the Series 7 examination administered by NASD. A Series 7 license is required to solicit the purchase and sale of securities products. See Registered Representative; Self-Regulatory Organization (SRO).

SHAREHOLDER COMMUNICATIONS IMPROVEMENT ACT An amendment to the Securities Act of 1933 that increased proxy and financial disclosure requirements for certain investment companies.

SHERMAN ANTITRUST ACT Legislation enacted in 1890 and amended in 1914 by the Clayton Act that prohibits monopolistic business practices intended to restrict interstate or foreign trade.

SHORT SALE RULE A Securities & Exchange Commission (SEC) rule that prohibits initiating a short sale at a lower price than where the previous trade took place. The purpose of the short sale rule is to prevent runaway panic selling, which is generally believed to be responsible for the stock market Crash of 1987. It is also known as the uptick rule because it requires that orders to sell short be submitted only on an uptick.

SPECULATIVE POSITION LIMITS Restrictions imposed by the Commodity Futures Trading Commission (CFTC) to prevent large price swings associated with excessive speculative trading. The number of commodity futures positions or option contracts a trader can hold in single product varies by product and contract month. See Aggregation; Commitment of Traders Report; Reportable Positions.

STOCK MANIPULATION A form of fraud that employs deception to artificially inflate or deflate the price of a security.

SUSPENDED TRADING See Trading Halt.

TAILGATING See Piggybacking.

THRIFT ADMINISTRATION REVIEW PROGRAM A program administered by the Office of Thrift Supervision that helps thrift institutions improve their recordkeeping and internal controls.

THRIFT FINANCIAL REPORT A quarterly operating and financial report that thrift institutions must provide to the Office of Thrift Supervision.

TRANSPARENCY In finance and economics, a term used to describe conditions under which facts are fully and accurately disclosed in a timely manner. Securities & Exchange Commission filing regulations, the Sarbanes-Oxley Act of 2002, and government reporting on economic conditions are examples of measures intended to improve market transparency.

UNIFORM COMMERCIAL CODE (UCC) A set of state laws governing the conduct of commercial transactions.

UNIFORM PRACTICE CODE (UPC) Rules established by NASD for the handling of over-the-counter (OTC) transactions.

UNIFORM SECURITIES ACT Legislation to address securities fraud at the state level, drafted in 1956 by the National Conference of Commissioners on Uniform State Laws and recommended for adoption by all states.

UNIFORM SECURITIES AGENT STATE LAW EXAMINATION A NASD certification examination required by some states. See Blue Sky Law.

UNLISTED TRADE A trade in an unlisted stock that takes place on an exchange. Unlisted trading must be approved by the Securities & Exchange Commission (SEC).

UPTICK RULE See Short Sale Rule.

WAITING PERIOD The period between the filing of Form S-1 and its acceptance by the Securities & Exchange Commission (SEC). See Quiet Period.

WHISTLE BLOWER A person who discloses improper or criminal activity within an organization.

WILLIAMS ACT Legislation that regulates tender offers.

Who's Who

CHAPTER FOUR

The Big Wheels:
Wall Street Professionals

BROKER An individual or company that acts as an agent and charges a fee to buy or sell stock on behalf of account holders.

ACTIVE BOND CROWD Members of the New York Stock Exchange who trade a large number of bonds.

AGENT An individual or company who acts on behalf of another party in a transaction. For example, a brokerage firm acts as an agent when it issues buy or sell orders for its account holders.

ANALYST An investment professional who specializes in acquiring and analyzing data on a single company or industry and issuing future earnings and stock price performance estimates, and in some instances buy, sell, or hold recommendations. Analysts are most often employed by a brokerage firm, investment bank, or other financial institution, but sometimes are affiliated with an independent consulting or research firm. See Buy Side Analyst; Sell Side Analyst.

AUTOMATED CLEARING HOUSE (ACH) An electronic payment system operated by the National Automated Clearing House Association, through which banks and other financial institutions transfer funds between accounts. On the Web at **www.nacha.org**.

BROKER An individual or company that acts as an agent and charges a fee to buy or sell stock on behalf of account-holders. See Broker Dealer; Floor Broker; Stockbroker.

BROKER DEALER A broker who buys and sells stocks as a principal to the transaction. Some brokerage firms maintain an inventory of stock holdings from which it attempts to fill clients' orders before submitting the orders to a specialist or market maker. In this case, the broker acts as both an agent for the client and a principal to the transaction.

BUY-SIDE ANALYST An analyst who is employed by a firm that buys stocks for the company's own holdings mutual funds, insurance companies, and pension funds, for example. A buy-side analyst's recommendations remain in-house for use by staff money managers and are not typically disseminated to investment community at large. Compare to Sell-Side Analyst.

CLEARINGHOUSE A financial services organization employed by an exchange to acts as a third-party agent for recording and reporting security, options, and futures transactions, collecting margin funding and attending to the end-of-day settlement of trading accounts.

COMMISSION BROKER A floor broker who acts as an agent for a brokerage firm and who receives compensation on a commission basis for executed trades.

DEALER See Broker-Dealer.

DEEP DISCOUNT BROKER A brokerage firm offering very low fees, typically in exchange for little more than order execution and do-it-yourself investor resources. Deep discount brokers are most often Internet-based services, although a few brick-and-mortar stockbrokers also offer a deep discount option. Compare to Discount Broker; Full Service Broker.

EUROCLEAR A clearinghouse and central depository for European and international bonds and securities transactions. On the Web at **www.euroclear.com**.

FLOOR BROKER A member of a stock exchange or futures exchange who trades securities or derivatives on the trading floor on behalf of other investors. Compare to Floor Trader. See Pit Broker.

FLOOR TRADER A member of a stock exchange or futures exchange who trades securities or derivatives on the trading floor for his or her own account. Compare to Floor Broker; Pit Broker.

FOREIGN CROWD A term used to refer to New York Stock Exchange foreign bond traders.

FULL SERVICE BROKER A stockbroker who provides a portfolio of investment services, such as financial advice, market research, stock recommendations, and order execution. A full-service broker will typically charge higher fees than a discount broker. Compare to Deep Discount broker.

FUTURES COMMISSION MERCHANT (FCM) An individual or organization that acts as a broker for futures contracts and issues margin loans to secure the transactions. Futures Commission Merchants are required to register with the Commodity Futures Trading Commission (CFTC).

GUARANTEED INTRODUCING BROKER A broker with a contractual agreement and a single Futures Commission Merchant (CFM) who maintains floor operations and agrees to accept liability for the Introducing Broker's obligations under the Commodity Futures Trading Act, including order execution. See Independent Introducing Broker.

INDEPENDENT INTRODUCING BROKER An Introducing Broker (IB) who maintains minimum financial requirements prescribed by the Commodity Futures Trading Commission (CFTC) and retains the right to introduce orders to any FCM for execution.

INTRODUCING BROKER (IB) A broker who acts primarily as a sales and customer service representative for futures investors. An introducing broker is not registered with the Commodity Futures Trading Commission (CFTC), does not maintain floor operations, is not required to maintain minimum financial standards, and does not accept margin deposits used to secure clients' futures and options transactions. Instead, an introducing broker introduces customer accounts and orders to a Futures Commission Merchant (FCM) for execution. See Guaranteed Introducing Broker; Independent Introducing Broker.

MARKET MAKER A broker/dealer responsible for improving liquidity and market depth by managing their own inventory of a given set of securities out of which they fill both buy and sell orders as necessary. See Registered Competitive Market Maker; Specialist.

ODD LOT DEALER A dealer who combines odd lot orders and fills them as round lots. Brokers sometimes charge a higher commission to execute odd lot orders.

ONLINE BROKER A brokerage firm that interfaces with its customers over the Internet rather than face-to-face at a brick and mortar office location. Online brokers tend to offer lower fees and do-it-yourself investor resources. Compare to Full Service Broker.

PIT BROKER A member of a futures exchange who trades options and futures on behalf of other investors. Compare to Floor Trader. See Floor Broker.

REGISTERED COMPETITIVE MARKET MAKER A member of the New York Stock Exchange who is obligated to improve market liquidity by using his or her own inventory to buy and sell stock for a given security at prices that narrow the spread or increase market depth. Compare to Specialist. See Make a Market; Market Maker.

REGISTERED INVESTMENT ADVISOR (RIA) A firm or individual who is registered at the state level and/or with the Securities & Exchange Commission (SEC) to give investment advice and manage the investments of individual investors.

REGISTERED OPTIONS TRADER A floor trader who monitors options trading to ensure a fair market. A registered options trader may trade his or her own account, but is not required to serve as a market maker, unlike a registered competitive market maker or registered trader.

REGISTERED REPRESENTATIVE A person who holds a Series 7 license from NASD. Registered representatives are typically employed by brokerage firms as account representatives and serve as the primary contact for account holders.

REGISTERED TRADER A member of a stock exchange who buys and sells securities from his or her own account.

RETAIL BROKER A brokerage firm that offers account services to individual investors.

SELL-SIDE ANALYST An analyst employed by a brokerage or research firm and who develops earnings estimates, price targets, and buy-sell-hold recommendations that are passed on to the investment community at large. Compare to Buy-Side Analyst. See Initiate Coverage.

SPECIALIST A member of an exchange who facilitates trading in a security by conducting an open outcry auction at a trading post on the floor of an exchange, posting bid and ask prices, and matching up buyers and sellers. If a shortage of either buyers or sellers develops, the specialist is also obligated to make a market in the security by buying or selling shares from his or her own inventory. See Market Maker.

The Money Machines: Bankers, Economists, and World Trade

CENTRAL BANK A country's chief banking authority, responsible for issuing currency, establishing monetary policy, and regulating and overseeing a nation's banking system.

BANK An enterprise that is licensed by a state or federal government to receive deposits and extend loans. See Commercial Bank; Consumer Bank; Cooperative Bank; Farm Bank; Investment Bank; National Bank; Regional Bank.

BANK INSURANCE FUND (BIF) The fund that insures monies on deposit at a commercial bank. The Bank Insurance Fund is administered by the Federal Depository Insurance Corporation (FDIC).

BANK OF ENGLAND The central bank of the United Kingdom. Compare to Federal Reserve. On the Web at **www.bankofengland.co.uk**.

BANKING SYNDICATE A group of investment banks that act together for a specific purpose, such as to underwrite an initial public offering (IPO) or to loan money to a borrower.

BERNANKE, BEN Chairman of the Board of Governors of the Federal Reserve. He was sworn in on February 1, 2006. His four-year term as chairman will expire on January 31, 2010 and his 14-year term as a member of the Board of Governors will expire on January 31, 2020. See Central Bank; Federal Reserve System.

BOARD OF GOVERNORS OF THE FEDERAL RESERVE The seven-member board that administers the Federal Reserve System. Board members are appointed by the President of the United

States and confirmed by the Senate to serve a 14-year term. The Chairman and Vice Chairman are appointed by the President and confirmed by the Senate to serve four-year terms. On the Web at **www.federalreserve.gov.**

BRITISH BANKING ASSOCIATION (BBA) A not-for-profit trade association for the banking industry in the United Kingdom. On the Web at **www.bba.org/uk.**

CENTRAL BANK A nation's chief banking authority, responsible for issuing currency, establishing monetary policy and regulating and overseeing a nation's banking system. See Federal Reserve; Deutsche Bundesbank; European Central Bank; Bank of London.

COMMERCIAL BANK A full service bank for both individuals and business clients. Compare to Investment Bank.

COMMON MARKET A group of nations that cooperate to remove trade barriers between participating countries.

CONFERENCE BOARD, THE A not-for-profit membership organization that conducts business and economic research and publishes reports and forecasts for use by business executives. The Conference Board releases the monthly Consumer Confidence Index, the Help Wanted Index, and the Leading Indicators Index.

CONSUMER BANK A bank whose primary focus is accepting deposit from and making loans to individuals. Compare to Business Bank; Commercial Bank; Investment Bank.

COOPERATIVE BANK A bank that holds deposits, makes loans, and provides other financial services to cooperatives and member-owned organizations. Also known as Banks for Cooperatives.

CREDIT UNION A financial cooperative that is owned and operated by its depositors.

DEUTSCHE BUNDESBANK The central bank of Germany.

ECONOMIST An individual who studies and interprets the data concerning the factors that influence supply and demand, such as inflation and unemployment.

EUROPEAN CENTRAL BANK (ECB) The central bank for the European Union and issuer of the Euro.

EUROPEAN UNION (EU) An alliance of European states that works together to address mutual concerns.

EXPORT-IMPORT BANK OF THE UNITED STATES An agency of the U.S. government that facilitates the export of U.S. goods and services by providing pre-export business financing. On the Web **www.exim.gov**.

FARM CREDIT BANK Any one of four federally chartered thrift institutions that provide financial services to the farming industry. Farm Credit Banks are regulated by the Farm Credit System.

FARM CREDIT SYSTEM An agency within the Administrative Branch of the U.S. government that regulates and oversees the financial institutions that provide banking services to the farming industry. On the Web at **www.fca.gov**.

FED A commonly-used nickname for the Federal Open Market Committee (FOMC) or the Federal Reserve System. On the Web at **www.federalreserve.gov**.

FEDERAL DEPOSIT INSURANCE CORPORATION (FDIC) A federal agency that provides insurance on funds deposited with banks and thrift institutions. Established in 1933 for the purpose of instilling confidence in the nation's banking system, the FDIC insures deposits for up to $100,000 per account-holder per financial institution. It was created by the Banking Act of 1933. On the Web at **www.fdic.gov**.

FEDERAL HOME LOAN BANK One of 12 regional banks that comprise the Federal Home Loan Bank System. On the Web at **www.fhlbank.com**.

FEDERAL HOME LOAN BANK SYSTEM (FHLBS) A system of 12 regional banks established to extend loans and other services to member institutions. On the Web at **www.fhlbank.com**.

FEDERAL OPEN MARKET COMMITTEE (FOMC) A 12-member committee within the Federal Reserve that administers U.S. monetary policy. The committee is comprised of the seven members of the Federal Reserve Board of Governors and five of the 12 presidents of the Federal Reserve Banks. The president of the Federal Reserve Bank of New York holds a permanent seat on the FOMC, and the remaining 11 presidents sit on the committee on a one-year rotating basis. See Central Bank. On the Web at **www.federalreserve.gov/fomc**.

FEDERAL RESERVE As the central bank of the U.S. government, the Federal Reserve (or Fed) establishes monetary policy. It also regulates and oversees member institutions and international banks. The Federal Reserve is comprised of 12 Federal Reserve Banks. The agency is administered by a seven-member Board of Governors. Board members are appointed by the President of the United States and confirmed by the Senate to serve a 14-year term. The Chairman and Vice Chairman are appointed by the President and confirmed by the Senate to serve four-year terms. On the Web at **www.federalreserve.com**. See Bernanke, Ben; Greenspan, Alan.

A Closer Look at the Federal Reserve Banks		
Atlanta, GA	Dallas, TX	Minneapolis, MN
Boston, MA	Kansas City, MO	New York, NY
Chicago, IL	Richmond, VA	Philadelphia, PA
Cleveland, OH	San Francisco, CA	St. Louis, MO

GREENSPAN, ALAN The former chairman of the Federal Reserve. Greenspan was appointed to the position in 1987 by President Ronald Reagan and re-appointed every four years until his retirement in 2006. He is considered by many to be an unparalleled expert on monetary policy and economic matters. See Bernanke, Ben.

GROUP OF FIVE (G5) A group comprised of the six (not five) leading industrialized countries, including France, Germany, Italy, Japan, the United Kingdom, and the United States. State representatives from the G5 meet periodically to address international economic and monetary issues.

GROUP OF FIVE EURO (G5) A group of five European Union countries, including France, Germany, Italy, Spain, and the United

Kingdom that meet periodically to discuss matters of common importance.

GROUP OF SEVEN (G7) The G7 is a group of the seven leading industrialized nations that gathers for an annual summit meeting to discuss economic and political concerns. In 1997, the G7 was expanded to become the G8 with the acceptance of Russia as an official member.

A Closer Look at the Group of Seven (G7/G8)

It was formed as an outgrowth of a 1975 summit of the leaders of France, West Germany, Italy, Japan, the United Kingdom, and the United States. The meeting was held in France, at the invitation of French President Giscard, to discuss issues pertaining to the oil crisis. The following year, President Gerald Ford hosted a second summit in Dorado Beach, Puerto Rico, where the addition of Canada brought the member nations to seven. In 1994, Russia began attending portions of the G7 meetings and in 1997 was accepted as an official member, when the group became known as the G8. Russia, as the smallest economy of the member nations, is excluded from financial and economic discussions, which remain the purview of the G7.

GROUP OF EIGHT (G8) A group of the eight leading industrialized nations that gathers for an annual summit meeting to discuss economic and political concerns. See G7.

GROUP OF TEN (G10) A group of eleven (not ten) industrial nations: Belgium, Canada, France, Germany, Italy, Japan, the Netherlands, Sweden Switzerland, the United Kingdom, and the United States. Finance ministers and central bank governors from the G10 meet annually to address international economic and monetary issues.

GROUP OF TWENTY-FOUR (G24) A group of developing countries that meets twice a year to discuss economic and development issues effecting member nations.

A Closer Look at International Economic Cooperation

G5-Euro	G5	G7	G8	G10
France	France	Canada	Canada	Belgium

A Closer Look at International Economic Cooperation				
G5-Euro	**G5**	**G7**	**G8**	**G10**
Germany	Germany	France	France	Canada
Italy	Italy	Germany	Germany	France
Spain	Japan	Italy	Italy	Germany
U.K.	U.K.	Japan	Japan	Italy
	U.S.A	U.K.	Russia	Japan
		U.S.A.	U.K.	Netherlands

A Closer Look at the Group of 24 (G24) Countries		
Region I: Africa	**Region II: Latin America and the Caribbean**	**Region III: Asia and Developing Countries of Europe**
Algeria	Argentina	India
Cote d'Ivoire	Brazil	Iran
Egypt	Columbia	Lebanon
Ethiopia	Guatemala	Pakistan
Gabon	Mexico	Phillipines
Ghana	Peru	Sri Lanka
Nigeria	Trinidad	Syrian Arab Republic
South Africa	Tobago	
Democratic Republic of Congo	Venezuela	

HOUSE OF ISSUE An investment bank that underwrites an Initial Public Offering (IPO).

INSTITUTE FOR SUPPLY MANAGEMENT (ISM) An industry association for supply management professionals. The ISM produces two monthly supply management reports: the Manufacturing Report on Business and the Non-Manufacturing Report on Business. Both reports are viewed by economies and investors as important tools for predicting economic growth or contraction because the data on which they are based reflect business purchasing trends. On the Web at **www.ism.ws**. See Economic Indicator; Leading Indicator.

INTERNATIONAL MONETARY FUND (IMF) An international organization established to foster world-wide monetary stability, facilitate international trade, and reduce poverty. It was established in 1944 and has 184 member nations.

INVESTMENT BANK A bank that specializes in providing financial services to corporations, including serving as the underwriter for an initial public offering and corporations issuing securities. Investment banks typically maintain broker dealer operations and employ investment professionals who facilitate mergers and acquisitions.

LENDER OF LAST RESORT A bank that loans money to an organization unable to obtain any other financing. Typically such a loan takes place when the borrower's credit or financial standing does not meet minimum underwriting criteria. In the United States, the Federal Reserve is the lender of last resort and steps in when failure to obtain funding will adversely affect the national economy.

MUTUAL SAVINGS BANK A bank that is owned by its depositors.

NATIONAL ASSOCIATION OF PURCHASING MANAGERS (NAPM) The former name for the Institute for Supply Management (ISM).

NATIONAL BANK A bank that is federally chartered, a member of the Federal Reserve, and whose deposits are insured by the FDIC.

OFFICE OF THRIFT SUPERVISION (OTS) An agency of the U.S. Treasury Department that serves as the primary regulator of federally chartered savings banks, savings and loans, and some state banks. Institutions belonging to the Savings Association Insurance Fund (SAIF) fall under the jurisdiction of the Office of Thrift Supervision.

PRIVATE BANKER A provider of personalized banking services to depositors with a high net worth.

REGIONAL BANK A bank that operates in a limited area of the country, rather than nationwide or internationally.

SAVINGS AND LOAN ASSOCIATION See Savings Bank.

SAVINGS ASSOCIATION INSURANCE FUND (SAIF) An

insurance system for thrift banks and savings and loans. The SAIF is administered by the Federal Deposit Insurance Corporation (FDIC).

SAVINGS BANK A financial institution whose primary function is to hold deposit in savings accounts. Also known as a Savings and Loan Association.

SELLING GROUP A banking syndicate of formed to underwrite an Initial Public Offering (IPO).

THRIFT INSTITUTION A financial institution that holds deposits for individuals. Compare to Investment Bank.

UNDERWRITER An investment bank that acts as an intermediary between the issuing company and the investors who purchase the company's debt instruments and/or stock at the Initial Public Offering (IPO). The underwriter buys the newly issued securities from the company and sells them to investors on the secondary market through a stock exchange. See Book Running Manager; Co-Underwriter; Lead Underwriter; Primary Market.

UNDERWRITING SYNDICATE See Banking Syndicate; Underwriter.

WORLD BANK An international association formed to reduce poverty and improve living standards in the world's poorest countries. It is comprised of two entities, the International Bank for Reconstruction and Development and the International Development Association, which are owned by 174 member countries. On the Web at **www.worldbank.com**.

WORLD ECONOMIC FORUM A Geneva, Switzerland-based organization that strives to solve global problems through international cooperation. In addition to the annual World Economic Summit in Switzerland, the forum hosts events throughout the year that focus on issues pertaining to specific geographic regions.

WORLD TRADE ORGANIZATION (WTO) A Geneva, Switzerland-based organization formed specifically to create a forum for negotiating and administering international trade agreements. On the Web at **www.weforum.org**.

CHAPTER SIX

The Money Makers: Corporations at Home and Abroad

PUBLIC COMPANY A corporation that offers ownership shares of the company for sale to public and private investors.

ANGEL INVESTOR An individual who provides startup money for a business enterprise. Unlike a venture capitalist, an angel investor does not typically participate in the operation of the business.

AUDIT COMMITTEE Members of a company's board of directors (BOD) who are responsible for the conduct of internal and external auditors.

AUDITOR An individual who inspects and verifies the accuracy of a company's operational and/or financial records. Public companies are required to use a public accounting firm for the conduct of an audit of their financial statements.

B2B Short for business-to-business and refers to companies that transact business primarily with other businesses rather than with retail customers.

B2C Short for business-to-consumer and refers to companies that transact business primarily with retail customers.

BIG FOUR The four largest U.S. public accounting firms: Deloitte, KPMG, PricewaterhouseCoopers, and Ernst & Young.

BIG THREE The three U.S. automobile manufacturers: General Motors, Ford, and Chrysler.

BOARD OF DIRECTORS (BOD) A group of individuals who are elected by a company's stockholders to oversee the conduct of business of a corporation. The duties of the board are usually dictated by the laws of the state in which the corporation is established. In most cases, some of their responsibilities include selecting the officers responsible for the daily operation of the company, overseeing periodic audits, and ensuring that the company operates in a manner that is consistent with the corporation's charter and by-laws.

CHAIRMAN OF THE BOARD The most senior position of the board of directors of a corporation. In addition to presiding over board meetings, in some companies the chairman may also have executive control of business operations.

CHIEF EXECUTIVE OFFICER (CEO) The senior officer of a corporation. The CEO is usually appointed by the board of directors, and charged with responsibility for overseeing the operation of the company. In some corporations, the Chairman of the Board also serves as the CEO. Compare to Chief Financial Officer (CFO); Chief Operating Officer (COO).

CHIEF FINANCIAL OFFICER (CFO) The officer of a corporation who is charged with managing the company's finances and complying with Securities & Exchange Commission (SEC) reporting requirements. The CFO is usually appointed by the board of directors. Compare to Chief Executive Officer (CEO); Chief Operating Officer (COO).

CHIEF OPERATING OFFICER (COO) The executive of a corporation who is responsible for day-to-day management of the company. Not all companies employ a COO. Compare to Chief Executive Officer (CEO); Chief Financial Officer (CFO).

CLOSELY HELD COMPANY A company that does not offer its stock for sale to the public at large. Also referred to as a privately owned company. Compare to Public Company; Publicly Held.

COMPTROLLER (CONTROLLER) A company's senior accountant.

CONGLOMERATE A corporation that owns business operations in unrelated industries.

CORPORATE OFFICERS The executives of a corporation charged with certain operational responsibilities. Typically appointed by the board of directors, the corporate officers usually include the Chief Executive Officer (CEO), Chief Financial Officer (CFO), President, and in some corporations the Chief Operating Officer.

CORPORATION A business entity formed by filing of Articles of Incorporation and meeting certain legal requirements. See Privately Held Corporation; Publicly Held Corporation.

DIVERSIFIED HOLDING COMPANY A company that owns a controlling interest in multiple companies. See Corporate Raider; Holding Company.

DOT COM An Internet-based company. Dot com companies typically conduct business only on the Internet rather than at a store-front location. Compare to brick and mortar.

DOW JONES & COMPANY, INC. Publisher of The Wall Street Journal, Barron's Magazine, Marketwatch, and the Far East Economic Review; provider of financial data for enterprises and the media; and the host of several investment Web sites. The company was founded in 1882 by Charles Dow, Edward Jones, and Charles Bergstresser. On the Web at **www.dowjones.com**. See Dow Jones Industrial Average (DJIA).

FEDERAL HOME LOAN MORTGAGE CORPORATION (FREDDIE MAC) A federally chartered organization that sells securities on the secondary market backed by mortgage notes it has purchased from the original lenders. Freddie Mac is a public company, traded on both the New York Stock Exchange and the Pacific Stock Exchange under the symbol FRE. On the Web at **www.freddiemac.com**.

FEDERAL NATIONAL MORTGAGE ASSOCIATION (FNMA or FANNIE MAE) A privately held corporation originally charted by Congress in 1933 to help ensure that banks have a continuous supply of money available for underwriting mortgage loans. Fannie Mae does not loan money for mortgages. Instead, it purchases existing mortgage notes from lenders, repackages them into portfolios, or mortgage-backed securities and sells them to investors on the secondary market. On the Web at **www.fanniemae.com**.

FINANCIAL INSTITUTION A company that uses its assets to invest in securities and debt instruments.

FORTUNE 500 COMPANY One of the 500 largest U.S. corporations, based on published financial data such as 10K reports filed with the Securities & Exchange Commission (SEC). The list of Fortune 500 companies is compiled by and published in Fortune magazine.

GOVERNMENT NATIONAL MORTGAGE ASSOCIATION (Ginnie Mae) A federally chartered corporation that guarantees timely payments on insured mortgage-backed securities (MBS), that provide investors of those instruments a greater degree of financial safety. On the Web at **www.ginniemae.gov**.

GOVERNMENT SPONSORED ENTERPRISE (GSE) A private enterprise corporation, chartered by the federal government to provide public financial services. The Federal Depository Insurance Corporation is an example of a GSE.

HOLDING COMPANY A corporation that owns enough shares in another company to influence the decisions of the board of directors (BOD). See Control Shares; Controlling Share.

INSIDER An individual who has access to confidential company information. See Insider Trade; Material Insider Information.

INVESTMENT COMPANY A company whose primary business is investing or trading in securities with money collected from individual investors. A mutual fund is an example of an investment company.

LISTED COMPANY A corporation whose stock trades on one of the seven U.S. stock exchanges. Each exchange establishes its own listing criteria, which may include financial standards requirements and a minimum number of shares traded. A company can be listed on more than one exchange, a practice referred to as dual listing.

MULTINATIONAL CORPORATION A company that has operations in more than one country.

NATIONAL QUOTATION BUREAU The 1902 originator of the paper-based quotation system for over-the-counter stocks and bonds known as the Pink Sheets and Yellow Sheets, respectively. On the Web at **www.pinksheets.com**.

PRESIDENT The most senior corporate executive after the Chairman of the Board. The functions of president and Chief Executive Officer (CEO) may be filled by the same person. See Corporate Governance.

PRIVATELY HELD COMPANY A business entity that does not offer the sale of its stock to the general public. Compare to Publicly Traded; Public Company.

PUBLIC COMPANY A corporation that offers ownership shares of the company for sale to public and private investors. Certain public companies are required to register with the Securities & Exchange Commission (SEC) and comply with stringent reporting requirements. Laws governing the conduct of public companies are intended to provide stockholders with accurate information on the financial condition of the company and are spelled out in the Securities Act of 1933, its subsequent revisions, and the Sarbanes-Oxley Act of 2002.

PUBLICLY TRADED COMPANY See Public Company.

REGULATED INVESTMENT COMPANY An investment company that is authorized to pass along expenses (capital gains) and earnings (dividends and interest) to its account holders, who are taxed as individuals. See Subchapter M.

SALLIE MAE See Student Loan Marketing Association.

STUDENT LOAN MARKETING ASSOCIATION (SALLIE MAE) A privately-owned corporation that provides student loans for undergraduate and graduate students and their families. Originally founded as a government-sponsored entity (GSE), Sallie Mae became a private company in 2004. On the Web at **www.salliemae.com**.

SUBSIDIARY A company in which the majority shareholder is another company. See Wholly Owned Subsidiary; Holding Company.

TARGET COMPANY or **TAKEOVER TARGET** The company that another company wants to acquire in a takeover. Also referred to as a Target. See Controlling Interest; Corporate Raider; Friendly Takeover; Hostile Takeover; Diversified Holding Company; Holding Company; Takeover; Two-Tier Tender Offer.

WHOLLY OWNED SUBSIDIARY A company whose shares are owned exclusively by a parent company and not offered to the public.

CHAPTER SEVEN

Investors—Big and Small

INSTITUTIONAL INVESTOR A business enterprise or organization whose primary function is to hold financial assets. Pension Funds, insurance companies, banks, mutual funds, and hedge funds are examples of institutional investors.

ARBITRAGEUR A trader who uses arbitrage strategies to take advantage of price disparities between the same security, currency, or commodity in two different markets.

BEAR A person who believes that the market is in a downtrend cycle and is more likely to continue going down than to go up. A bear interprets an upward price retracement as a temporary interruption in the overall downward trend. Compare to Bull. See Bear Correction; Bear Market; Bull Market; Correction; Market Cycle.

BOND HOLDER The owner of record of a bond. The bond certificate displays the bond holder's name (except for a bearer bond, which is not registered to a specific bond holder).

BUFFETT, WARREN Billionaire Chairman of the Board and Chief Executive Officer (CEO) of Berkshire Hathaway Corporation. Nicknamed the Oracle of Omaha, Buffett is generally viewed as a uniquely savvy investor and stock market guru. See Smart Money.

BULL A person who believes that the market is in an uptrend and is more likely to continue to go up than to go down. A bull interprets a downward price retracement as a temporary interruption in the overall uptrend. Compare to Bear. See Bull Correction; Bull Market; Correction; Market Cycle.

BUYER Technically anyone who purchases a security is a buyer, whether it is to initiate a long position or to buy to cover a short position. However, the term is usually used to refer to a trader who is long in the market and to a degree is a reflection of an investor's market sentiment. Compare to Seller; Short.

CHARTIST A person uses stock charts as an investment analysis tool. See Technical Analysis; Technician.

COMMERCIAL HEDGER A company that buys commodity futures contracts to lock in favorable pricing at a future date.

COMMODITY POOL OPERATOR An individual or business enterprise engaged in the solicitation and/or management of a pool of funds that are used to trade futures contracts. Commodity pool operators are regulated by the Commodity Futures Trading Commission (CFTC).

CONTRARIAN An investor whose perception of the market opposes the generally accepted view. A contrarian would likely buy when others are selling and visa versa.

CORPORATE RAIDER An investor who seeks to take control of a publicly traded company by acquiring a controlling interest of the company's stock and then replacing the board of directors and/or the Corporate Officers. See Control Stock; Diversified Holding Company; Holding Company; Hostile Takeover; Two-Tier Tender Offer.

DAYTRADER A person who buys and sells one or more securities multiple times within the same trading session. Daytraders seek to make money from small intraday price fluctuations. Also referred to as a Scalper. Compare to Investor; Position Trader; Swing Trader.

GRANTOR An individual who writes an option contract and assumes the obligation to buy or sell the underlying asset if the option holder chooses to exercise the option. Also called an Option Writer. See Covered Call, Covered Put.

HOLDER See Option holder.

IN-AND-OUT TRADER A person who trades on small moves in a stock. See Daytrader; Scalper.

INDIVIDUAL INVESTOR An investor who purchases relatively small lots of stocks for his or her own portfolio. Also called a small investor. Compare to Institutional Investor.

INSTITUTION or INSTITUTIONAL INVESTOR A business enterprise or organization whose primary function is to hold financial assets. Pension Funds, insurance companies, banks, mutual funds, and hedge funds are examples of institutional investors.

INVESTMENT CLUB A group of individual investors who pool their money and research to make investments. Investment clubs typically have written rules which spell out membership obligations, including contribution schedules, how investment decisions are made and the procedure for withdrawing from membership.

INVESTOR 1) A person who buys an asset with the expectation that its market value will increase and yield a profit when sold. 2) A person whose investment strategy focuses on the long-term, rather than speculation about short-term market movements. Compare to Daytrader; Scalper.

LONG A person who buys a security or futures contract seeking to sell it later at a profit. Compare to Short-Seller.

MAJORITY SHAREHOLDER A person or company that owns at least 51 percent of the outstanding shares of a private or publicly-traded corporation.

MOMENTUM INVESTOR An investor who makes buy-and-sell decisions at least in part on the basis of increases and declines in the trading momentum for a given security.

OPTION BUYER See Bond holder.

OPTION SELLER See Grantor.

OPTION WRITER See Grantor.

OPTION HOLDER An individual who has purchased a call option or a put option. Compare to Grantor.

OWNER OF RECORD The shareholder to whom a security is registered. Dividends are paid to the owner of record on the record date. Also referred to as Shareholder of Record.

PENSION BENEFIT GUARANTY CORPORATION (PBGC) A federally chartered corporation that insures private-sector defined benefits pension funds. On the Web at **www.pbgc.gov**.

A Closer Look at Pension Benefit Guaranty Corporation

The PBGC was created by the Employee Retirement Income Security Act of 1974. It currently pays benefits to about 683,000 retirees in 3,595 pension plans that have ended, either through a standard termination or under distress.

To qualify for a standard termination, the plan sponsor is required to show that it has sufficient assets to meet the current and future obligations. PBGC will then assume both the assets and the obligations of plans so that there are no interruptions in benefits for plan participants.

The obligations for distress terminations are assumed by PBGC and paid monthly up to a maximum allowable amount from premiums set by Congress and paid by the program sponsors, earnings from PBGC investments, assets from pension plans under the trusteeship of PBGC, and recoveries from former plan sponsors.

PENSION FUND A fund established by an employer to pay retirement benefits to employees. Pension Funds are major institutional investors. See Pension Benefit Guaranty Corporation (PBGC).

POSITION TRADER See Swing Trader.

PRINCIPAL An individual or entity that is a party to a transaction or business arrangement. Compare to Agent. See Broker, Broker Dealer.

ROBBER BARONS A reference to 19th century businessmen who increased their wealth and power by unethical means. Today, the term is used to refer to corporate raiders.

SCALPER A trader who buys and sells stocks or commodities frequently, attempting to profit from small price movements. See Daytrader, In-and-Out Trader.

SELLING SHAREHOLDERS Investors in a private company who sell their shares at the Initial Public Offering (IPO). Investors often interpret a significant volume of trades from selling shareholders as undermining confidence in the new issue.

SHAREHOLDER An individual or institutional investor possessing ownership interest in a company. Also known as a stockholder.

SHAREHOLDER OF RECORD See Owner of Record.

SHORT One who seeks to profit from the decline in the price of a security or futures contract.

SHORT-SELLER An investor who seeks to profit from the decline in the price of a security or futures contract. See Sell Short.

SMART MONEY A term that refers to investors with a track record of making smart investment decisions that return consistent profits. Warren Buffett would be considered an example of smart money.

SPECULATOR A person who makes risky investments, anticipating a major change in the future price of the asset. Some people differentiate between an investor and a speculator based on the intrinsic risk associated with the type of transactions each is prone to make.

STOCKHOLDER OF RECORD The person or institution whose name is on the records of the issuing corporation. Dividends are paid only to the stockholder of record. See Ex-Dividend.

STOCKJOBBER A term that generally applies to a person who earns his or her livelihood from buying and selling securities. Traders, stockbrokers, and investors are all considered stockjobbers.

SWING TRADER An investor who seeks to profit from price cycles that last anywhere from a day or two to several weeks. Compare to Daytrader; Scalper.

TECHNICAL ANALYST A person who uses price charts and mathematical computations to make investment decisions. Also known as a Technician.

TECHNICIAN See Technical Analyst.

TRADER An investor who seeks to profit from price fluctuations rather than a change in the intrinsic value of a security or derivative product. A trader typically holds a security for periods as short as a few minutes to several weeks. See Daytrader, Swing Trader.

VENTURE CAPITALIST An individual who supplies funding to a company. In exchange for the cash infusion, venture capitalists will often assume a seat on the board of directors and participate in the operation of the company.

CHAPTER EIGHT

The Industry Guard Dogs: Regulators, Enforcers, and Safety Nets

CENTRAL REGISTRATION DEPOSITORY (CRD) A Securities & Exchange Commission (SEC) database containing licensing and complaint information about brokers and some investment advisors and their representatives.

ACCOUNTING PRINCIPLES BOARD (APB) The former standards board for the accounting industry. It was succeeded by the Financial Accounting Standard Board (FASB) in 1973.

AMERICAN MUNICIPAL BOND ASSURANCE CORPORATION (AMBAC) An insurance provider serving issuers of municipal bonds. Insured bonds command the highest credit ratings from bond rating services such as Standard & Poor's, Moody's Investors Service, and Fitch because they carry the lowest default risk. On the Web at **www.amback.com**.

ARBITRATOR A person who serves as an impartial referee in an arbitration action.

CENTRAL REGISTRATION DEPOSITORY (CRD) A Securities & Exchange Commission (SEC) database containing licensing and complaint information about brokers and some investment advisors and their representatives.

CERTIFIED PUBLIC ACCOUNTANT (CPA) An individual who is certified by the American Institute of Certified Public Accountants (AICPA) to practice in the field of accounting. To earn the AICPA certification, a candidate must meet academic and work experience requirements and pass a written examination. By law, only a certified public accountant can conduct an audit of the financial statements of a public company.

COMMITTEE ON UNIFORM SECURITY IDENTIFICATION PROCEDURES (CUSIP) SERVICE BUREAU The group that establishes and administers the nine-character numbering system used to identify registered U.S. and Canadian stocks, municipal bonds, and U.S. government securities by issuer and type. The CUSIP Service Bureau is operated by Standard & Poor's. See CUSID. On the Web at **www.cusip.com**.

COMMODITY FUTURES TRADING COMMISSION (CFTC) A federal agency charged with overseeing and regulating trading in the futures and options markets. The agency was established in 1974. On the Web at **www.cftc.gov**.

COUNCIL OF ECONOMIC ADVISERS (CEA) A committee established by the Employment Act of 1946 with responsibility for providing the U.S. President with objective economic analysis and advice. On the Web at **www.whitehouse.gov/cea**.

EDGAR (Electronic Data Gathering Analysis and Retrieval) The Securities & Exchange Commission's database of corporate filings; not to be confused with EDGAR Online, which is a publicly traded company that provides value added data services based on EDGAR. On the Web at **www.sec.gov/edgar.shtml**.

EUROPEAN BANKING FEDERATION (FBE) An association representing the banking industry within the European Union. On the Web at **www.fbe.be**.

FEDERAL HOUSING ADMINISTRATION (FHA) A U.S. government agency that administers housing programs, including subsidized mortgages, rental assistance, and mortgage insurance. On the Web at **www.fha.gov**.

FEDERAL THRIFT REGULATOR An examiner with the Office of Thrift Supervision who is certified to oversee the safety and soundness of thrift institutions.

FEDERAL TRADE COMMISSION (FTC) The U.S. government agency responsible for regulating trade. The FTC's chief focus is to prevent fraud and deceptive business practices and to ensure fair competition. See Antitrust; Monopoly. On the Web at **www.ftc.gov**.

FINANCIAL ACCOUNTING STANDARDS BOARD (FASB) The self-regulatory body for the accounting industry. FASB is comprised of seven members from the accounting field. Their primary function is to develop and publish the Generally Accepted Accounting Principles (GAAP), which establishes standards for preparing and auditing corporate financial reports. See GAAP. On the Web at **www.fasb.org**.

INTERNAL REVENUE SERVICE (IRS) The U.S. government agency authorized to collect federal income taxes and enforce the tax laws embodied in the IRS Code. On the Web at **www.irs.gov**.

INTERNATIONAL ACCOUNTING STANDARDS BOARD (IASB) The self-regulatory body that establishes international accounting standards. Compare to Financial Standards Accounting Board (FASB).

INTERNATIONAL FEDERATION OF STOCK EXCHANGES (FIBV) The former name of the World Federation of Exchanges.

INTERNATIONAL ORGANIZATION FOR STANDARDS (ISO) An organization that facilitates fair trade by developing and disseminating internationally recognized standards. The ISO is comprised of one representative from the national standards organization of 156 countries. On the Web at **www.iso.org**.

MUNICIPAL SECURITIES RULEMAKING BOARD (MSRB) The organization that establishes the rules that regulate municipal bond and securities dealers. On the Web at **www.msrb.org**.

NASD DISPUTE RESOLUTION, INC. An arm of NASD that facilitates resolution of investor disputes with brokerage firms and exchanges. On the Web at **http://www.nasd.com/ArbitrationMediation/index.htm**.

NATIONAL ASSOCIATION OF SECURITIES DEALERS (NASD) A Self-Regulatory Organization (SRO) for the securities industry. In addition to licensing and oversight, NASD also provides mediation and arbitration services to resolve disputes between investors and brokerage firms, exchanges and industry professionals. See NASD Dispute Resolution, Inc. On the Web at **www.nasd.org**.

NATIONAL FUTURES ASSOCIATION (NFA) A self-regulatory organization for the futures industry. As such, the NFA develops trade practices, oversees and enforces compliance of NFA rules, and serves as the registration authority for industry participants. On the Web at **www.nfa.futures.org**.

NORTH AMERICAN SECURITIES ADMINISTRATORS ASSOCI-ATION (NASAA) An international investor protection organization comprised of the state securities agencies, provincial, and territorial securities administrators for the District of Columbia, Puerto Rico, the U.S. Virgin Islands, Canada, and Mexico. On the Web at **www.nasaa.org**.

NYSE REGULATION The internal self-regulatory organization (SRO) for the NYSE Group.

OFFICE OF COMPLIANCE INSPECTIONS AND EXAMINATIONS (OCIE) The department within the Securities & Exchange Commission (SEC) responsible for inspecting and examining brokers, dealers, self-regulatory organizations, clearinghouses, and other market participants.

PUBLIC ACCOUNTING FIRM A firm that is registered with the Public Accounting Oversight Board to provide accounting services to a public company. The Sarbanes-Oxley Act of 2002 included a provision prohibiting any company that is not registered with the board from preparing, furnishing, or participating in an audit of a public company.

PUBLIC COMPANY ACCOUNTING OVERSIGHT BOARD (PCAOB) A non-profit corporation that oversees the auditors who provide services to publicly-traded companies. The PCAOB was chartered by the Sarbanes-Oxley Act of 2002 in the wake of a series of securities accounting scandals, including Enron and WorldCom.

SECURITIES AND EXCHANGE COMMISSION (SEC) A federal agency charged with providing oversight and enforcement of the securities industry, including responsibility for registering, regulating and overseeing brokerage firms, clearinghouses, and self-regulatory organizations. On the Web at **www.sec.gov**.

SECURITIES INVESTOR PROTECTION CORPORATION (SIPC) A non-profit corporation that insures investment accounts held by member brokerage firms against fraud and insolvency. The insurance covers both cash and investment holdings and is capped at $500,000 ($100,000 in cash) per depositor. The SIPC is funded by member firms and does not insure deposits against investment losses or the purchase of worthless stocks. On the Web at **www.sipc.org**.

SECURITIES TRADERS ASSOCIATION (STA) A trade association for securities industry professionals. On the Web at **www.securitytraders.org**.

SELF-REGULATORY ORGANIZATION (SRO) An organization that is authorized to develop and enforce regulations for an industry. NASD, NYSE Regulation, Financial Accounting Standards Board (FASB), International Accounting Standards Board (IASB) and the National Futures Association (NFA) are all examples of self-regulatory organizations.

WORLD FEDERATION OF EXCHANGES An international trade organization for the securities and derivatives markets.

Market Forces

CHAPTER NINE

Economics for Investors: The Ups and Downs of the Business Cycle

ECONOMIC INDICATOR A statistical study designed to measure economic conditions and/or predict changes in the business cycle.

ACCOMMODATIVE MONETARY POLICY Central Bank policy that seeks to stimulate economic growth by loosening money supply. An accommodative monetary policy is typically characterized by a succession of decreases in the Federal funds rate which makes money easier (cheaper) for business to borrow. See Federal Open Market Committee (FOMC); Federal Reserve. Compare to Tight Monetary Policy.

AMERICAN CURRENCY QUOTATION A standard method of stating the value of foreign currency on a per unit basis compared to the U.S. Dollar. For example: $US per YEN. See American Quotation Terms; European Quotation Terms; Foreign Exchange.

A Closer Look at American Currency Quotations	
Exchange Rate	**Explanation**
Eur/USD 1.23	One Euro would purchase 1.23 U.S. Dollars ($1.23)
USD/AUD 1.35	One U.S. Dollar ($1) will purchase 1.23 Australian Dollars

AUSTRALIAN DOLLAR (AU $) The currency unit for Australia.

BANK NOTE Currency issued by a bank. In the United States only the Federal Reserve is authorized to issue bank notes.

BANK RATE The discounted interest rate at which a central bank makes loans to a national bank. See Federal Reserve.

BRICK AND MORTAR A term that refers to a physical location for businesses, such as an office, warehouse, or store front, where it conducts business face to face with its customers. Many brick and mortar companies now maintain an e-commerce operation.

BRITISH POUND STERLING (GBP or U.K.£) National currency of the United Kingdom. Sometimes called the British Pound. To date, the UK has not joined the 12 European countries that have adopted the EURO.

BUSINESS CYCLE The inevitable ups and down of economic activity, as measured by periods of economic growth and contraction. An economist uses key economic indicators to gauge where a local, regional, national, or international economy stands in the business cycle at any given time, including gross domestic product, inflation, unemployment, and productivity. As the central bank of the United States, the Federal Reserve uses monetary policy to stimulate growth during periods of contraction and to restrain the pace of growth during periods of expansion to prevent extremes in the cycles. See Depression; Federal Open Market Committee; Federal Reserve System; Inflation; Recession.

CALL LOAN A loan that can called due by the lender or paid off by the borrower at any time. Margin is an example of a call loan. See Call Loan Rate.

CALL LOAN RATE The interest rate charged by a lender for a call loan. A brokerage firm pays the call loan rate on money it borrows from a bank to loan to its account holders as margin. An investor pays the call loan rate when he or she borrows money from a brokerage firm to make margin-funded investments. Call loan rates typically run on par with short-term interest rates plus a percentage point or two.

CALL MONEY Cash that a bank has loaned to a broker for a call loan.

CANADIAN DOLLAR (CAN $ or CND) The currency denomination for Canada.

CAPITALISM An economic system in which the enterprises that produce and deliver goods and services are privately or publicly owned and operated on a for-profit basis. Capitalism is the cornerstone of the free market system in which competition and supply and demand determine the cost of products and the ultimate success of a business venture. The U.S. economy is a hybrid system, referred to as a mixed economy in that it marries the principles of capitalism with some government limits and ownership of some enterprises. Compare to Socialism. See Keynesian Economics; Laissez-Faire.

CHINESE YUAN (CNY or ¥) The currency unit of the Republic of China.

COINCIDENT INDICATOR Data that is used to evaluate current economic conditions. Compare to Lagging Indicator; Leading Indicator. See Business Cycle; Economic Indicator.

CULPEPER SWITCH A Federal Reserve computer facility that is used to transmit wire transfer messages over the Fedwire.

CURRENCY Denominated money issued by the central bank of any nation.

DEFLATION A broad-based decline in prices attributable to slowing demand and/or a tight money supply. Compare to Inflation. See Depression; Monetary Policy; Recession; Stagflation.

DEMAND DEPOSIT Funds on deposit with a bank that can be withdrawn without advance notice (on demand) or penalty. Compare to Time Deposit.

DENOMINATION The value designation of a unit of a coin or currency. U.S. currency is dollar denominated.

DEPRESSION An extended period of wide-spread, declining business activity, typically marked with wide-spread unemployment and deflation.

DEVALUATION A significant decline in the value of a unit of currency relative to a baseline such as gold or another currency unit. For example, if the foreign exchange rate for the Japanese Yen were to drop substantially relative to the U.S. Dollar (meaning that it takes more Yen to buy one U.S. Dollar), it could be said that the Yen has been devalued.

DIGITAL MONEY A method of payment that is executed electronically, such as over the Internet. PayPal and similar services are forms of digital money.

DISINFLATION A decline in the rate of inflation. Compare to Deflation. See Consumer Price Index (CPI); Personal Consumption Expenditures (PCE).

DOLLAR The currency unit of the United States, Canada, Australia, and more than twenty other countries. See Denomination.

DOUBLE DIP RECESSION A situation in which an economic recovery falters and the economy drops back into a recession. See Economic Growth; Economic Recovery.

E-COMMERCE Business transactions that take place electronically.

ECONOMIC CONTRACTION A period of time in which gross domestic product (GDP) declines. Also referred to as negative growth. Compare to Economic Expansion. See Business Cycle; Recession.

ECONOMIC CYCLE See Business Cycle.

ECONOMIC EXPANSION A period of time in which gross domestic product (GDP) increases. Compare to Economic Expansion. See Business Cycle.

ECONOMIC INDICATOR A statistical study designed to measure economic conditions and/or predict changes in the business cycle. Gross domestic product (GDP), consumer price index (CPI) and new home sales are three examples of the many economic indicators economists and investors follow for clues about current economic conditions and expectations for the future.

ECONOMIC RECOVERY A period of growth following an economic contraction. See Depression; Recession.

EFFICIENT MARKET THEORY An economic principle that states that the market price of a security or commodity reflects its underlying intrinsic value. In other words, efficient market theory presumes that the selling price of a stock, for example, is set by the balance between supply and demand, which in turn has been influenced by taking into account everything good and everything bad known about the company and its products.

EURO (€) The common currency adopted by participating European countries.

A Closer Look at Countries that Have Adopted the Euro			
Austria	Germany	Italy	Spain
Finland	Greece	Luxembourg	The
France	Ireland	Portugal	Netherlands

EUROCURRENCY Non-European currency on deposit in European banks.

EURODOLLAR U.S. currency held on deposit at any foreign bank. U.S. Dollars make their way to these financial institutions when they are used to pay for foreign good and services and when they are exchanged for foreign currency at a non-U.S. bank.

EUROPEAN CURRENCY UNIT (ECU) An accounting unit based on a representative basket of currency units from European Union member states. The adoption of the Euro made the ECU obsolete.

EX-FOOD AND ENERGY A designation used in conjunction with the consumer price index that indicates that the numbers cited exclude the highly volatile cost of food and energy.

FED FUNDS RATE See Federal Funds Rate.

FED SPEAK A colloquialism that refers to statements made by the members of the Federal Reserve Board of Governors, and in particular by the Chairman of the Federal Reserve, relating to the economy and monetary policy.

FEDERAL FUNDS RATE The rate at which funds are loaned between Federal Reserve depository institutions on an overnight basis. Often referred to as Fed funds rate.

FEDWIRE The Federal Reserve computer system that is used to transfer reserve account balances and U.S. government securities. See Culpeper Switch.

FIAT CURRENCY A monetary system in which the value of currency is established by declaration and is not backed by a fixed asset, such as gold. Today most of the world currencies are fiat currencies. Compare to Gold Standard.

FIXED CURRENCY A currency that is valued by a fixed relationship to another currency, such as the U.S. Dollar. Also referred to as a Pegged Currency. Compare to Floating Exchange Currency. See Foreign Exchange Market; Foreign Exchange Rate.

FOREIGN EXCHANGE The exchange of paper currency and other financial instruments from one nation's currency to another.

FOREIGN EXCHANGE RATE The value of one country's currency expressed in the denomination of another currency.

A Closer Look at Foreign Exchange Rates			
USD	**EURO**	**EXCHANGE RATE**	**EURO**
1	1.2699	.7875	.7879

USD	**EURO**	**EXCHANGE RATE**	**USD**
1.2699	1	1.2699	1.2699

FREE MARKET SYSTEM An economic system in which prices are established exclusively by supply and demand, without regulatory influence or control. Compare to Keynesian Economics; Socialism. See Laissez-Faire.

GLOBALIZATION A movement toward the creation of worldwide market for goods and services. See Common Market; G5; G7; G24; World Bank; World Trade Organization (WTO).

GOLD STANDARD An obsolete monetary system in which a unit of currency is fixed to the value of a set unit gold. A government operating under the gold standard promises to redeem its notes in an equivalent amount of gold. The gold standard has been replaced, world wide, by either fiat currency or fixed currency. See Floating Exchange Currency; Foreign Exchange Market; Foreign Exchange Rate.

GREAT DEPRESSION The name given to the greatest economic decline in American history that began in the 1920s and lasted until 1939. See Depression; Economic Contraction; Recession.

HARD CURRENCY See Major Currency.

HARD LANDING A rapid move from economic expansion to recession brought about by an overly restrictive monetary policy.

HONG KONG DOLLAR (HKD) The currency unit for Hong Kong.

INDIAN RUPEE (INR or Rs or Rp) The currency unit for India.

INFLATION An increase in prices for goods and services. Inflation is measured by a number of economic indicators. The consumer price index (CPI) is the most closely followed. A high rate of inflation can stifle consumer spending, slow the rate of production of goods and services, and eventually jam brakes on economic growth. The Federal Reserve uses monetary policy to control the rate of inflation. Compare to Deflation; Disinflation. See Personal Consumption Expenditures (PCE).

INTEREST-RATE SENSITIVE The tendency of a product, service, company, or investment to be easily affected by a change in interest rates. For example, demand for expensive items that consumers tend to purchase on credit often slow when interest rates rise, but they boom when interest rates decline. Likewise, the price of stocks, bonds and commodities often react to small interest rate changes.

ISO CURRENCY CODE A three-letter alphabetic code and three-digit numeric code that identify a unit of currency and its minor units, according to its denomination and country of issue. ISO currency codes are assigned by the International Organization for Standards (ISO).

JAPANESE YEN (JPY or ¥) The currency unit for Japan.

KEYNESIAN ECONOMICS An economic theory that holds that full employment and stable prices can be best achieved in a mixed economy that incorporates both capitalism and government controls. Compare to Laissez-Faire; Supply-side Economics.

LAGGING INDICATOR A sign of a change in the business cycle that can only be measured after the change has taken place. GDP and CPI are two examples of lagging indicators. Compare to Coincident Indicator; Leading Indicator.

A Closer Look at How Economists and Investors Use Economic Indicators

Leading Indicator	...to predict a change in the economic cycle.
Coincident Indicator	...to measure current economic conditions.
Lagging Indicator	...to confirm an economic trend.

LAISSEZ-FAIRE A belief that the economy should be free to operate free of governmental interference. Compare to Keynesian Economics. See Supply-Side Economics.

LEADING INDICATOR An economic indicator that can be used to predict a change in the business cycle. Compare to Coincident Indicator; Lagging Indicator. See Leading Indicator Index (LEI).

LOMBARD RATE The interest rate charged by the central bank of Germany for loans on a collateralized security.

LONDON INTERBANK BID RATE (LIBID) The current interest rate a London bank will pay to attract deposits from other banks.

LONDON INTERBANK OFFERED RATE (BBA LIBOR) The interest rate certain London banks are willing to pay to attract deposits of U.S. currency.

M1 MONEY SUPPLY The most liquid forms of monetary assets currently in circulation. M1 includes coins and currency, moneys on deposit in checking and credit union accounts, travelers' checks, and automatic transfer accounts.

M2 MONEY SUPPLY A portion of monetary assets currently in circulation, comprised of M1 money supply plus deposits in savings accounts, time savings accounts with a balance under $100,000 and deposits in retail money market accounts.

M3 MONEY SUPPLY Total monetary assets currently in circulation, including M2 money supply plus time savings deposits of $100,000 or more, institutional deposits and certain Eurodollar deposits. Effective March 23, 2006, the Federal Reserve ceased publication of the M3 money supply, citing that the information contained in it is already embodied in other reports.

MAJOR CURRENCY A currency that is sufficiently liquid to be readily convertible to the currency of other nations. Major currency is most often associated with politically stable, highly industrialized nations. The U.S. Dollar, British Pound, Euro, and Japanese Yen are major currencies. Also called Hard Currency.

MIXED ECONOMY An economic system in which the government imposes boundaries on capitalism to limit the concentration of power and achieve social balance. The U.S. economic system is a mixed economy. Compare to Laissez-Faire. See Keynesian Economics.

MONETARY POLICY Action taken by a central bank to stabilize a nation's economy. For example, by regulating money supply (printing more money or removing currency from circulation) and controlling the cost of money (raising and lowering interest rates), the central bank can stimulate a sagging economy or cool things off when it begins to grow at an undesirable rate.

MONEY MARKET ACCOUNT A savings account that sweeps unused cash into short-term debt instruments. See Sweep Account.

MONEY MARKET DEMAND ACCOUNT See Money Market Deposit Account.

MONEY MARKET DEPOSIT ACCOUNT A type of savings account in which the bank or brokerage firm invests funds held on deposit in short-term debt obligations. A money market deposit account often offers limited check-writing privileges and pays an interest rate that is typically higher than a regular savings account but lower than a certificate of deposit or other time deposit. Also referred to as a Money Market Demand Account or simply as a Money Market Account. Compare to Money Market Fund.

MONEY SUPPLY Monetary assets currently in circulation, taking into consideration coins, currency, funds on deposit in savings, checking accounts, money market, credit union and brokerage accounts, and some Eurodollar deposits. Money supply measurements are used by the Federal Reserve to develop monetary policy.

A Closer Look at Money Supply		
M1	**M2**	**M3**
Coins	M1 plus…	M2 plus…
Currency	Savings Accounts	Time Savings
Checking Accounts	Time Savings (< 100K)	Accounts (> $100K)
Credit Union Accounts	Retail Money Market Accounts	Institutional Deposits
Travelers Checks		Certain Eurodollar Deposits
Automated Transfer Accounts		

NATIONAL DEBT The total debt owed by the federal government.

NATIONALIZATION The process of bringing privately owned business or property under the control of government. Compare to Privatization.

PEAK The highest point in the economic cycle. The peak forms after a period of economic expansion and before the beginning of a period of economic contraction. Compare to Trough.

PEG A monetary policy that ties the value of one nation's currency to the value of another nation's currency. For example, at the time of this writing, the Chinese Yuan is pegged at 8.027 Yuan per U.S. Dollar (USD/CNY 8.027). See fixed Currency; Floating Exchange Currency.

PEGGED CURRENCY See Fixed Currency.

PETRODOLLARS Currency transferred from one country to another as payment for imported oil. Petrodollars are a major factor in the growing U.S. trade deficit.

POUND STERLING See British Pound Sterling.

PRIME RATE The lowest interest rate a bank charges for loaning money. The prime rate is reserved for a bank's most creditworthy customers, which typically are large, well-established, and financially stable companies.

PRIVATIZATION The process of transferring control of

government-owned commercial services to the private sector. Compare to Nationalization.

QUOTATION AMERICAN TERMS   A method of quoting the foreign exchange rate as U.S. Dollars per a unit of another currency. See American Currency Quotation.

QUOTATION EUROPEAN TERMS   A method of quoting the foreign exchange rate of a currency in terms of foreign currency per one U.S. Dollar. Compare to American Currency Quotation; Quotation American Terms.

RECESSION   A period of economic contraction, as measured by negative growth in Gross Domestic Product (GDP) lasting at least two consecutive quarters. Compare to Deflation; Depression; Stagflation.

A Closer Look at the Role of Recession in the Business Cycle

Every business cycle is comprised of two phases: an expansion phase and a contraction phase.

In the expansion phase, the economy begins to heat up as businesses hire more workers to meet the growing demand for goods and services. More workers with more money spawn even more consumer demand and another wave of business growth in the form of building expansion and equipment purchases and more hiring. GDP growth soars. Competition for workers, raw materials, transportation, and other finite resources puts upward pressure on prices, and soon inflation raises its ugly head. Consumers retreat taking demand with them. With a surplus of supply and dwindling demand, businesses tighten their collective belts, triggering the end of the economic expansion and the start of a recession.

The cooling off cycle follows a similar, but opposite, pattern until the downward momentum bottoms out and the recession ends with GDP entering a new growth cycle. What happens in between determines the severity of the impact on businesses, individuals, and investors.

In a mild recession, a slump in consumer demand reduces corporate earnings, causing a temporary pause in hiring and capital expenditures. An extended recession, on the other hand, can result in wide-spread job losses and a freeze on capital expenditures for months and sometimes years. After demand for big ticket items dries up, more unemployment follows, further sucking the air out of consumer demand for both domestic and imported products, posing a risk that a long, deep recession can affect foreign economies as well.

RESERVE RATIO See Reserve Requirement.

RESERVE REQUIREMENT Liquid assets a bank is required to hold in reserve. In the U.S., the reserve requirement is determined by the Federal Reserve and is expressed as a percentage referred to as the reserve ratio.

REVALUATION An official change in the basis for a county's currency valuation.

A Closer Look at Revaluation

Historically the Chinese government has pegged the Yuan to the U.S. Dollar. If it eventually bows to international pressure and makes an official change to allow the Yuan to float on the foreign exchange market, the action would be termed a revaluation.

ROBUST CURRENCY A currency that is resilient and capable of weathering shocks to the economic system.

SCRIP A privately issued credit or note such as an IOU that can be redeemed only by the issuer. Frequent flyer miles and the voucher a local video store offers for a free movie rental are examples of scrip.

SEASONALLY ADJUSTED Data that have been statistically adjusted to remove normal, recurring variations such as the effects of cold winter weather or back-to-school shopping. The accuracy of trend identification and other historical comparisons is improved through the use of seasonally adjusted data.

SOCIALISM An economic system in which goods and services are provided through a central system of cooperative and/or government ownership rather than through competition and a free market system.

SOFT CURRENCY A national currency that is not in sufficient demand to be readily convertible to the currency of other nations. Soft demand for a currency is often due to a county's political or economic instability or an unfavorable foreign exchange rate.

SOFT LANDING A reduction in the rate of economic expansion to a point where inflation can be restrained without the economy slipping into a recession. Compare to Hard Landing.

STAGFLATION An economic cycle marked by a sluggish economy, deflation, and a high unemployment rate.

STAGNATION An economic cycle marked by economic growth of less than 1 percent a year. See Economic Expansion; Gross Domestic Product.

STRONG DOLLAR POLICY A monetary policy that favors a strong foreign exchange rate for the U.S. Dollar (USD/AUD 1.35, which indicates that one U.S. Dollar will buy 1.35 Australian Dollars). A strong dollar makes imported goods more affordable for the American consumer, but makes U.S. exported goods more costly on the international market. Compare to Weak Dollar Policy.

SUPPLY AND DEMAND An economic theory stating that when supply exceeds demand, the market value (price) of a product will drop and when demand exceeds supply, its value will rise. In the financial markets, the relationship between supply and demand is said to be reflected in selling price of a security, derivative, or debt instrument. See Efficient Market Theory; Free Market System.

SUPPLY-SIDE ECONOMICS An economic theory that holds that creating a positive investment environment by reducing taxes on businesses and wealthy individuals will stimulate job creation and economic opportunity at all levels. Also known as trickle-down economics. Compare to Keynesian Economics.

SWISS FRANC (CH) The currency denomination for Switzerland.

TIGHT MONETARY POLICY Central bank policy that seeks to slow economic growth and ease inflation by loosening the money supply. A tight monetary policy is typically characterized by a succession of increases in the Federal funds rate which makes money more difficult (expensive) to borrow. Compare to Accommodative Monetary Policy. See Federal Open Market Committee; Federal Reserve.

TRADE DEFICIT The amount by which U.S. imports exceed U.S. exports. So International Trade Deficit; PetroDollars.

TRICKLE-DOWN ECONOMICS See Supply-Side Economics.

TROUGH The lowest point in the economic cycle. The trough forms after a period of contraction ends and before a period of expansion begins. Compare to Peak.

TURNAROUND A change for the better after a period of decline in an economic cycle or the financial performance of a company. Not to be confused with a reversal in stock prices. While a turnaround might trigger a trend reversal in the market or the stock price of an individual company, the two are separate and distinct evaluations.

UNEMPLOYMENT A measure of the number of workers who are currently seeking but unable to secure employment.

VELOCITY A measure of economic strength that estimates the number of times an individual dollar changes hands in a given period of time. It is calculated by dividing gross domestic products (GDP) by money supply. Velocity is one tool the Federal Reserve Open Market Committee uses to manage monetary policy.

WEAK DOLLAR POLICY A monetary policy that favors a low foreign exchange rate for the U.S. Dollar. A weak dollar can make U.S. exported good and services more competitive on the international market, but it also came make imported goods expensive for American consumers. Compare to Strong Dollar Policy.

CHAPTER TEN

Economic Indicators: Taking the Business Cycle Temperature

LEADING ECONOMIC INDICATORS (LEI) A composite index of ten underlying economic indicators that are used individually and together to predict a change in the economic cycle.

AUTO AND TRUCK SALES A sales report released by each U.S. automobile manufacturer during the first week of each month. The numbers in the report represent units sold and are adjusted for seasonal variations, allowing them to be examined on a month-over-month as well as a year-over-year basis. Because auto and truck sales are large ticket items and tend to be interest-rate sensitive, the numbers can provide insight into current consumer behavior and its potential impact on the economy in the out-months. See Seasonal Adjustment; Leading Indicator.

AVERAGE HOURLY EARNINGS A monthly report on the previous month's average hourly payroll earnings for production and non-supervisory non-farm workers. The data are part of the Employment Report that is released by the Bureau of Labor Statistics on the first Friday of each month. The report is available at a number of financial information Web sites and at **www.bls.gov**. See Average Workweek; Total Non-Form Payrolls; Unemployment Rate.

AVERAGE WORKWEEK A monthly report on the average number of hours worked by production or non-supervisory workers in non-farm jobs. The data are part of the Employment Report that is released by the Bureau of Labor on the first Friday of each month.

The report is available at a number of financial information Web sites and at **www.bls.gov**. See Average Hourly Earnings; Total Non-Farm Payrolls; Unemployment Rate.

BALANCE OF PAYMENTS (BOP) A quarterly report on international trade that tracks cash payments coming in and flowing out of the country. These cash flows are generated by imports, exports, and the transfer of financial assets. The Balance of Payments for the previous quarter is released by the Bureau of Economic Analysis around the second week of March, June, September, and December. See Current Account; Capital Account; Foreign Reserves; PetroDollars.

A Closer Look at Balance of Payments (BOP)

BOP is an indication of a country's economic health and stability because a positive net balance indicates strong investment from foreign sources. By contrast, a negative balance indicates that investors see more opportunity in foreign markets.

The report is divided into three sections:

- Dollar values for goods and services traded on the international market and unilateral payments in the form of foreign aid and grants.

- The estimated value of U.S.-owned assets abroad verses foreign-owned assets in the United States.

- Foreign Reserves of gold, foreign exchanges, Strategic Defense Reserves, and International Monetary Fund (IMF) reserves.

BEIGE BOOK A report published by the Federal Reserve that summarizes economic conditions based on statistical and economic data. The information used to generate the Beige Book is submitted by each of the 12 Federal Reserve Banks and is reported by district and business sector. Each Federal Reserve Bank president takes turns producing an overall summary that is included in the report, released eight times a year. The Beige Book is one of the most anticipated and scrutinized market indicators because it heralds a change in monetary policy. Available on the Web at **www.federalreserve.com**.

BUILDING PERMITS A monthly report on the number of residential building permits issued in the United States during the previous month. The report is divided into geographic regions and then by single and multi-family units. Investors typically interpret steady growth in building permit numbers as an indication that Americans have confidence in the economy and their own personal financial positions. Likewise, they watch the month-to-month and year-over-year trend for any indication of weakness that might suggest a spending contraction on the part of consumers. The building permits report is released by the Bureau of the Census in the middle of each month and is announced on various financial news and research Web sites. It is also available at the Census Bureau's Web site at **www.census.gov**. See Housing Starts.

CAPACITY UTILIZATION A monthly report that measures excess U.S. manufacturing capacity. Some economists believe that manufacturing output that exceeds 85 percent of industrial capacity creates inflationary pressures on the economy. Capacity utilization is a component of a joint report that also includes industrial production. The report is released by the Federal Reserve around the 15th of the month and is based on data collected for the prior month.

CHAIN DEFLATOR An economic indicator used to track prices of consumer products. Unlike the Consumer Price Index (CPI), the basket of goods surveyed to calculate the Chain Deflator changes periodically along with consumer buying habits. It can be highly volatile from month to month. Investors and economists look for signs of inflation by watching the trend on a quarterly basis. The Chain Deflator is a component of the Gross Domestic Product (GDP) report, which is in the last week of the month by the Bureau of Economic Analysis. It is reported on various financial news and research Web sites and is available at the BEA's Web site: **www.bea.gov**.

CONSUMER CONFIDENCE An economic indicator that gauges how consumers interpret the present economic environment and their expectations for the future. A decline in consumer expectations can be a leading indicator of slowing economic activity. The Consumer Confidence report is a product of the Conference Board and is based on a monthly survey of 5000 households. It is a timely economic report in that the data released on the last Tuesday of each month is based on the current month's survey.

CONSUMER CREDIT A monthly report showing rate of change in credit-based consumer spending. It reflects the annualized, seasonally adjusted rate of change for revolving (credit cards) and non-revolving (automobile loans and education) debt, excluding real estate-secured loans. The Consumer Credit report is of limited interest to investors because much of the information in it hits the markets from other sources before the data covering a period two months earlier are released by the Federal Reserve on the fifth business day of the month.

CONSUMER PRICE INDEX (CPI) An economic indicator that measures the rate of inflation by tracking the cost of a fixed market basket of goods and services for urban consumers. The Consumer Price Index is reported as a total number and as the core CPI, which excludes the highly volatile food and energy prices. CPI is used as the basis for benefit adjustments in government entitlement programs, such as Social Security, and for cost of living allowances (COLAS) for private-sector organizations. Unlike the Chain Deflator, the market basket does not change with consumer spending habits. It is released by the Bureau of Labor Statistics around the middle of each month. Compare to Core PPI; Personal Consumption Expenditures (PCE); Producer Price Index (PPI).

CONSUMER SENTIMENT See University of Michigan Survey of Consumers Index.

CORE CPI A subset of the total Consumer Price Index (CPI) that excludes the highly volatile food and energy prices. It is released by the Bureau of Labor Statistics around the middle of each month. Compare to Personal Consumption Expenditures (PCE); Core PPI; Producer Price Index (PPI).

CORE PPI A subset of the total Producer Price Index (PPI) that excludes the highly volatile food and energy prices. Preliminary PPI data and a final revision from the previous four months are released by the Bureau of Labor Statistics during the second week of each month. Compare to Consumer Price Index (CPI); Core CPI; Producer Price Index (PPI).

CURRENT POPULATION SURVEY (CPS) See Employment Report.

CURRENT ACCOUNT DEFICIT See Balance of Payments (BOP).

DURABLE GOODS Products that are expected to last more than three years.

DURABLE GOODS ORDERS A monthly economic report that measures the spending on durable products (items intended to last for three or more years) within the manufacturing and mining industries. The report breaks down the numbers by industry, making it possible to isolate and identify volatility associated with a single sector. Strength or weakness in orders for durable goods is thought to be a leading indicator for manufacturing demand and changes in the economic cycle. The previous month's data on Durable Goods Orders are released by the U.S. Census Bureau around the 26th of each month. The official name of the report is the Manufacturer's Shipments, Inventories and Orders (M3) and is available on the Web at **www.census.gov/indicator/www/m3**.

A Closer Look at Non-Durable Goods: What Are They?			
Alcoholic beverages	Drugs	Magazines	Petroleum and petroleum products
Apparel	Farm products	Newspapers	
	Flowers	Nursery stock	
Books	Footwear	Paper and paper products	Textiles and Textile products
Chemicals and chemical products	Groceries		
			Tobacco Products

EMPLOYMENT REPORT A comprehensive report on multiple measurements of the state of employment in the United States, including the total non-farm payrolls, unemployment rate, average hourly earnings, and average workweek. Data for the survey period ending on the 12th of the prior month are released by the Bureau of Labor Statistics on the first Friday of each month. Also referred to as the Employment Situation Report or simply as the Non-farm Payrolls Report, the employment report available at a number of financial information Web sites and at **www.bls.gov**.

A Closer Look at the Monthly Employment Report

This monthly report is based on two surveys that produce four primary measures of supply and demand forces within the labor market:

The Current Population Survey (CPS) polls approximately 60,000 households.

- Unemployment Rate: The percentage of individuals who are out of work, but seeking employment.

The Establishment Survey examines the payroll records of about 160,000 businesses and government agencies (a sampling that covers approximately one-third of all non-farm payroll workers).

- Non-farm Payrolls: The total number of new non-farm jobs added to the economy.
- Average Workweek: The average number of hours worked per week by production or non-supervisory workers in non-farm jobs.
- Average Earning: The average weekly earnings for production or non-supervisory workers in non-farm jobs.

Source: U.S. Bureau of Labor Statistics.

How Employment Contributes to Inflation

Supply and Demand Forces	Employment Report Indicator
Demand for employees increases	Longer Average Workweek
Supply of available workers decreases	Less Unemployment
Employers have to pay more to attract qualified workers	Higher Average Earnings

EMPLOYMENT SITUATION REPORT See Employment Report.

EXISTING HOME SALES A monthly report from the National Association of Realtors that tracks the sale of existing homes, used to gauge the demand in the housing market. Robust home sales mean economic growth and an optimistic consumer. The data for sales during the previous month are released around the 25th of each month. The data is available on the Web at **www.realtor.org**. Compare to New Home Sales.

EXPORT/IMPORT PRICES A monthly report that measures inflationary pressures created by foreign exchange rates and international demand for U.S. products. When the U.S. Dollar is strong against foreign currencies, foreign consumers are forced to spend more of their currency to purchase U.S. goods and services, thus stifling demand. By contrast, a weaker U.S. Dollar gives foreign markets more buying power for U.S. products, but makes imported goods more expensive for U.S. consumers. Import/export price data for the prior month are released by Bureau of Labor during the second week of each month and is available on the Web at **www.bls.gov**.

FACTORY ORDERS A monthly report that includes data on durable goods orders, non-durable goods (products expected to last less than three years), and factory inventories. Of the three components in this report, a change in the demand for durable goods would be of the most interest to economists and investors. The importance of the report, however, is minimal because by the time the report on Factory Orders hits the street, the market has already had two weeks to absorb roughly the same data from the separate Durable Good Orders report. The factory orders report is released by the U.S. Census Bureau within the first few days of each month and is available online at **www.census.gov/ftp/pub/indicator/www/m3/index.htm**.

GROSS DOMESTIC PRODUCT (GDP) The total dollar value of goods and services produced within a country. Economists regard increases and decreases in GDP as the best overall indication of whether an economy is expanding or contracting and at what rate. The Bureau of Economic Analysis releases the GDP figures the last week of each month. The data are available on the Web at **www.commerce.gov**.

A Closer Look at Gross Domestic Product (GDP)

Everyone from federal policy makers, corporate board rooms, and investors to investment professionals watches GDP numbers closely for indications of a change in the economic trend. An increase in GDP indicates a growing demand for goods and services, boding well for business and stock prices.

A Closer Look at Gross Domestic Product (GDP)

By contrast, a decline in GDP means that consumption of American products, either domestically or abroad, is slowing down. Several months of negative growth (decline) in GDP is generally regarded as confirmation of the start of a recession.

GDP Components

Food and Beverages	Medical Care	Special Indexes
Housing	Recreation	Food
Apparel	Education and Communication	Energy
Transportation	Other Goods and Services	

HOUSING STARTS A monthly report that tracks the start of construction on new residential housing units by geographic region. The number of housing starts is strongly influenced by interest rates and can be highly volatile because of weather and natural disasters, but is a reflection of economic strength. The report on housing starts for the previous month is released between the 16th and 20th of each month by the Census Bureau and is available on the Web at **www.census.gov**.

INDEX A method of measuring a segment of the economy by tracking changes in representative data. See Consumer Price Index; Employment Cost Index; Export Price Index; Import Price Index; Help Wanted Index; ISM Index; Leading Indicator Index; Producer Price Index; Consumer Sentiment Index.

INDUSTRIAL PRODUCTION A monthly report that tracks total output from the nation's factories, mines, and utilities. The Federal Reserve releases the industrial production report for the previous month around the 15th of each month. The data are available at a number of financial information Web sites and at **www.federalreserve.gov**.

INITIAL CLAIMS A weekly report on the number of first-time applications for unemployment compensation. The report, which is officially titled the Unemployment Insurance Weekly Claims Report, is released each Thursday morning by the Bureau of Labor Statistics. The data are available at a number of financial information Web sites and at **www.bls.gov**.

INTERNATIONAL TRADE DEFICIT A monthly report that tracks the amount by which U.S. imports exceed U.S. exports. Key factors influencing the trade deficit include the strength of the U.S. Dollar, which determines whether American-made products can compete on the international market, the off-shoring of U.S. manufacturing operations, and U.S. imports of foreign oil. Sustained trade deficits account for an outflow of U.S. Dollars to foreign markets. The report is issued by the U.S. Census Bureau. It is available at a number of financial information Web sites and at **www.census.gov**. See Eurodollar; Petrodollar.

ISM MANUFACTURING REPORT ON BUSINESS A monthly report based on a national survey of purchasing managers that tracks month-over-month changes in new orders, production, employment, supplier delivers and inventories for the manufacturing sector. The resulting Purchasing Manager's Index (PMI) establishes the neutral point at 50 percent. Anything above that number represents growth and anything below it represents a decline in the index. The report is released on the first day of the month and is based on data from the prior month, making it the first comprehensive manufacturing data available each month. The ISM report on manufacturing is available at a number of financial information Web sites and at **www.ism.ws**.

ISM NON-MANUFACTURING REPORT ON BUSINESS A monthly report based on a national survey of purchasing managers that tracks month-to-month changes in business activity in service industries. Like the PMI index, the ISM report on services establishes a neutral point at 50 percent. An index reading above that number represents growth and anything below it represents a decline. The report is released by the Institute for Supply Management on the third business day of each month and is based on data from the prior month. The data are available at a number of financial information Web sites and at **www.ism.ws**.

LEADING ECONOMIC INDICATORS (LEI) A composite index of 10 underlying economic indicators used individually or together to predict a change in the economic cycle. The report is released by the Conference Board on or around the 20th of each month. The index of leading indicators is available on various financial information Web sites and at **www.conference-board.org**. Also known as the Composite Index of Leading Indicators.

A Closer Look at the Composite Index of Leading Indications

- Average Workweek for Manufacturing Workers
- Unemployment Insurance Weekly Claims Report
- Factory Orders
- Vendor Performance (Speed of Delivery, New Merchandise from the ISM Index)
- Durable Goods (non-defense)
- Building Permits
- S&P 500
- M2 Money Supply
- 10-Year Treasury Bond minus Fed Funds Rate
- Consumer Sentiment

MANUFACTURERS' SHIPMENTS, INVENTORIES and ORDERS (M3) See Durable Goods Orders.

MICHIGAN SENTIMENT See University of Michigan Survey of Consumers.

NON-DURABLE GOODS Products that are expected to last less than three years.

PERSONAL CONSUMPTION EXPENDITURES (PCE) A component of the monthly Personal Income Report. The PCE measures inflation by tracking changes in prices. Unlike the Consumer Price Index, which uses a fixed basket of goods and services, the PCE changes along with consumer spending habits. The PCE is released by the Bureau of Economic Analysis near the first business day of each month for a period ending two months prior. Compare to Consumer Price Index. The PCE report is available at **http://www.economicindicators.gov**.

PERSONAL INCOME A monthly report that tracks income from all sources (wages, salaries, and investment income). The report is released by the Bureau of Economic Analysis around the first business day of each month for a period ending two months prior. The data on person income is available at **http://www.economicindicators.gov**. See Personal Consumption Expenditures (PCE).

PRODUCER PRICE INDEX (PPI) An economic indicator that tracks the rise and fall of prices at the wholesale level. It is reported as a total number and as the CORE PPI, which excludes the highly volatile food and energy prices. Preliminary PPI data and a final revision from previous four months are released by the Bureau of Labor Statistics during the second week of each month. Compare to Consumer Price Index (CPI); Core CPI.

PERSONAL SPENDING See Personal Consumption Expenditures.

RETAIL SALES A monthly report that measures consumer demand by tracking total non-service receipts from retail businesses. The retail sales data for the prior month are released by the U.S. Census Bureau around the 13th of each month. The data are available at various financial information Web sites and at **www.census.gov**.

TOTAL NON-FARM PAYROLLS A monthly report on the number of U.S. workers employed in non-farm jobs. The data are part of the Employment Report that is released by the Bureau of Labor Statistics on the first Friday of each month. The report is available at a number of financial information Web sites and at **www.bls.gov**. See Average Hourly Earnings; Average Workweek; Unemployment Rate.

TRADE BALANCE A monthly report that tracks U.S.-international trade in goods and services by product category and country. The report is released by the Census Bureau and the Bureau of Economic Analysis around the 10th day of each month and reflects the trade balance for the reporting period ending two months prior. The trade balance data are available at a variety of financial Web sites and at **www.census.gov**.

TREASURY BUDGET A U.S. Treasury Department report that tracks federal revenue and spending. Highly volatile month-to-month swings on both the income and outlay columns of this report make it useful for year-to-year comparisons. The data, the Monthly Treasury Statement, are released during the third week of each month and cover the Treasury budget as of the prior month. It is available at a number of financial Web sites and at **www.fms.treas.gov/mts/index.html**.

UNEMPLOYMENT RATE A monthly report on the number of workers currently seeking but unable to secure employment. The data are part of the Employment Report that is released by the Bureau of Labor Statistics on the first Friday of each month. The report is available at a number of financial information Web sites and at **www. bls.gov**. See Average Hourly Earnings; Average Workweek; Total Non-Form Payrolls.

UNIVERSITY OF MICHIGAN SURVEY OF CONSUMERS A monthly survey of 500 households to determine consumer sentiment about current economic conditions and financial expectations for the future. Like the Consumer Confidence report from the Conference Board, the market looks to indications of weakening consumer sentiment as a precursor to slowing consumer demand. A preliminary report is released by the University of Michigan on the second Friday of each month, followed by a revised report on the fourth Friday. Also referred to as the Consumer Sentiment Index or simply as Consumer Sentiment, the report is available at a variety of financial information Web sites and at **www.sca.isr.umich.edu**.

WHOLESALE INVENTORIES A monthly report issued by the U.S. Census Bureau that tracks changes in wholesale sales and inventory levels. Of the two numbers, the wholesale inventory number is the more significant because high inventory levels can reflect slowing demand and translate into decreased manufacturing production, which in turn can affect Gross Domestic Product (GDP). The significance of the report is reduced, however, because it covers a reporting period two months prior. The data are released around the 10th day of each month and is available at a variety of financial information Web sites and at **www.census.gov**.

Table 2 Economic Report Calendar

A Close Look at the Economic Report Calendar

| Common Name | Official Name | Release Schedule | | | Source Data |
		Cycle	Day/Date	Time (Eastern)	
Auto Sales	Auto Sales	Monthly	+/- 3rd	Varies	Newswires
Average Hourly Earnings	Average Hourly and Weekly Earnings	Monthly	1st Friday	8:30 AM	http://stats.bls.gov
Average Workweek	Average Weekly Hours Production	Monthly	1st Friday	8:30 AM	http://stats.bls.gov
Beige Book	Summary Commentary on Economic Conditions	Other	Every Six Weeks	2:00 PM	http://www.federalreserve.gov
Building Permits	Building Permits	Monthly	+/- 15th	8:30 AM	http://www.census.gov
Business Inventories	Total Business Sales	Monthly	+/- 15th	10:00 AM	http://www.census.gov
Capacity Utilization	Capacity Utilization	Monthly	+/- 15th	8:30 AM	http://www.federalreserve.gov
Chicago PMI	Chicago Business Barometer	Monthly	Last Business Day	10:00 AM	http://www.napm-chicago.org
Construction Spending	Construction Spending	Monthly	1st Business Day	10:00 AM	http://www.census.gov
Consumer Confidence	Conference Board Consumer Confidence Index	Monthly	Last Tuesday	10:00 AM	http://www.conference-board.org

A Close Look at the Economic Report Calendar

Consumer Credit	Consumer Credit	Monthly	5th Business Day	8:30 AM	http://www.federalreserve.gov
Core CPI	Consumer Price Index - Ex Food & Energy	Monthly	+/- 15th	8:30 AM	http://stats.bls.gov
Core CPI	Core CPI	Monthly	2nd Week	8:30 AM	http://stats.bls.gov
Corporate Profits	Corporate Profits	Quarterly	Last week of March, June, September and December	8:30 AM	http://www.bea.gov
CPI	Consumer Price Index	Monthly	+/- 15th Day	8:30 AM	http://stats.bls.gov
Balance of Payments (Current Account Deficit)	U.S. International Transactions (Balance Payments)	Quarterly	+/- 15th Day of March, June, September, and December	8:30 AM	http://www.bea.gov
Durable goods orders	Manufacturers'' Shipments, Inventories and Orders (M3 Survey Advance Report)	Monthly	Third Week	8:30 AM	http://www.census.gov
Employment Cost Index	Employment Cost Index	Monthly	Last week of January, April, July, October	8:30 AM	http://stats.bls.gov
Existing Home Sales	Existing Home Sales	Monthly	+/- 25th	8:30 AM	http://www.realtor.org
Export/Import Price Index	U.S. Import and Export Price Indexes	Monthly	2nd Week	8:30 AM	http://stats.bls.gov

A Close Look at the Economic Report Calendar

Factory Orders	Manufacturers' Shipments, Inventories and Orders (M3 Survey Regular Report)	Monthly	1st Week	8:30 AM	http://www.census.gov
Chain Deflator (GDP Deflator)	Implicit Price Deflator for GDP	Monthly	Last Week	8:30 AM	http://www.bea.gov
Gross Domestic Product	Gross Domestic Product	Monthly	Last Week	8:30 AM	http://www.bea.gov/bea/newsrel
Help Wanted Index	The Conference Board Help-Wanted Online Data Series	Monthly	+/- 27th	8:30 AM	http://www.conference-board.org
Housing Starts	New Residential Construction	Monthly	+/- 15th	8:30 AM	http://www.census.gov
Housing Vacancies	Housing Vacancies and Homeownership	Quarterly	Last week of January; April; July; October	10:00 AM	http://www.census.gov
Industrial Production	Industrial Production	Monthly	+/- 15th	8:30 AM	http://www.federalreserve.gov
Initial Claims	Unemployment Insurance Weekly Claims Report	Weekly	Every Thursday	8:30 AM	http://www.dol.gov
ISM Index	ISM Manufacturing Report on Business (Manufacturing ROB)	Monthly	1st Business Day	10:00 AM	http://www.ism.ws
ISM Services	ISM Non-Manufacturing Report on Business	Monthly	3rd Business Day	10:00 AM	http://www.ism.ws
Leading Indicators	Leading Economic Indicators (LEI)	Monthly	3rd Week	10:00 AM	http://www.conference-board.org

A Close Look at the Economic Report Calendar

Michigan Sentiment: Preliminary	Index of Consumer Sentiment (Also University of Michigan Survey of Consumers)	Monthly	2nd Friday	9:45 AM	http://www.sca.isr.umich.edu
Michigan Sentiment: Revised	Index of Consumer Sentiment (Also University of Michigan Survey of Consumers)	Monthly	4th Friday	9:45 AM	http://www.sca.isr.umich.edu
Money Supply	Money Stock Measures	Weekly	Every Thursday	Varies	http://www.federalreserve.gov
New Home Sales	New Residential Sales	Monthly	Last Week	10:00 AM	http://www.census.gov/const
Employment Report (Non-farm Payrolls) (Employment Situation Report)	Non-farm Employment	Monthly	1st Friday	8:30 AM	http://stats.bls.gov
NY Empire State	Empire State Manufacturing Survey	Monthly	3rd Monday	8:30 AM	http://www.ny.frb.org
Personal Income	Personal Income and Outlays	Monthly	1st Business Day	8:30 AM	http://www.economicindicators.gov
Personal Consumption Expenditures (PCE) (Personal Spending)	Personal Income and Outlays	Monthly	1st Business Day	8:30 AM	http://www.economicindicators.gov
Petroleum Inventories	Weekly Petroleum Status Report	Weekly	Wednesday	10:30 AM	http://www.eia.doe.gov
Philadelphia Fed	Leading Indexes for PA, NJ, and DE	Monthly	3rd Thursday	8:30 AM	http://www.phil.frb.org

A Close Look at the Economic Report Calendar

PPI	Producer Price Index	Monthly	2nd Week	8:30 AM	http://stats.bls.gov
Productivity - Preliminary	Productivity and Costs - Preliminary	Quarterly	1st Wk of 2nd Month of Quarter	8:30 AM	http://stats.bls.gov
Quarterly Services Survey	Quarterly Services Survey	Quarterly	+/- 15th of March, June, September, December	10:00 AM	http://www.census.gov
Retail Sales	Advance monthly retail sales	Monthly	+/- 13th	8:30 AM	http://www.census.gov
Retail Sales: Ex Auto	Advance monthly retail sales	Monthly	+/- 13th	8:30 AM	http://www.census.gov
Trade Balance	U.S. International Trade in Goods and Services	Monthly	+/- 10th	8:30 AM	http://www.census.gov
Treasury Budget	Monthly Treasury Statement	Monthly	3rd Week	Varies	http://fms.treas.gov
Truck Sales	Truck Sales	Monthly	+/- 3rd	Varies	Newswires
Unemployment Rate	Unemployment Rate	Monthly	1st Friday	8:30 AM	http://stats.bls.gov
Wholesale Inventories	Monthly Wholesale Inventories	Monthly	+/- 10th	10:00 AM	http://www.census.gov

The Long and Short of Trends, Cycles, and Crashes: Market Movement and the Indexes that Track Them

MARKET CYCLE The longer-term price movements in a broader market index, including one complete uptrend and one complete downtrend. A market cycle is measured from the lowest low or highest high for a given time and is deemed finished when the prices of the index approach the starting point.

BEAR MARKET An extended period of widespread decline in stock prices. On average, bear markets have lasted about 406 days.

BLACK FRIDAY 1) The day after Thanksgiving, the busiest shopping day of the year. Black Friday derives its name from the historic trend for U.S. retailers to operate at a loss (in the red) for the first eleven months of the year and begin to earn a profit (operate in the black) when the holiday shopping season begins on Black Friday. 2) The stock market crash of September 24, 1869. The crash was triggered by panic selling when President Grant released $4 million to drive down the price of gold after two financiers attempted to corner the market.

BLACK THURSDAY October 24, 1929, the day that marked the start of the stock market Crash of 1929. See Black Tuesday.

BLACK TUESDAY October 29, 1929, the day that marked the conclusion of the stock market Crash of 1929. See Black Thursday.

BROAD-BASED INDEX An index comprised of a sufficiently diverse group of securities to reflect the movement of the market as a whole. The Dow Jones Industrial Average (DJIA), Wilshire 5000, and S&P 500 are three examples of broad-based indexes used by investors to measure overall market performance.

BROADER MARKET A term that refers to the movement of the market as a whole, rather than a specific industry or sector. Broad-based indexes and various technical analysis tools evaluate the performance of the broader market.

BUBBLE A market condition in which stock prices rise quickly to levels that cannot be justified through financial or business analysis. A bubble can occur within an individual industry, sector, or the broader market. See Correction; Efficient Market Theory; Fundamental Analysis; Price to Earnings Ratio (P/E or PE).

A Closer Look at Market Bubbles

Efficient Market Theory suggests that over time every bubble will eventually lose air and prices will decline to a level that reflects the underlying value of the company or companies, in the case of a bubble in broader market.

The difficulty with bubbles is what former Federal Reserve Chairman, Alan Greenspan, called "irrational exuberance," when he referred to the Tech bubble of the late 1990s. Whether it's a bubble in the stock market or real estate market or any other market, prices rise because investors are buying the market all the way up. Sooner or later the last investors to join the party are in for a real surprise when the balloon loses its air and efficiency returns to the market.

Whether the ensuing decline is gradual, like a left-over party balloon or a sudden pop from a pin prick will determine how traumatic the move will be for individual investors, the market, and economy as a whole.

BULL MARKET An extended period of broad-based increases in market prices.

CORRECTION A temporary interruption in a market trend in which prices lose some of their gains (bull market) or regain some of their lost ground (bear market). Generally speaking, technicians expect prices in a typical correction to retrace approximately 10 percent of the distance from the beginning of the most recent move.

CRASH OF 1929 The stock market crash which started on September 24, 1929, and lasted for four consecutive trading days. During that period investors lost $25 billion, and the marked dropped by roughly 30 percent. Economic policies implemented after the Crash that were designed to prevent a recurrence are widely attributed with creating the conditions that led to the Great Depression. See Black Tuesday; Black Thursday, Black Friday; Crash of 1987.

CRASH OF 1987 October 19, 1987, the day on which the Dow Jones Industrial Average dropped 22.6 percent. Also known as Black Monday, the Crash of 1987 was the largest one day drop in stock prices in U.S. history. See Black Friday; Crash of 1929; Stock Market Crash.

CYCLICAL MARKET A short-term market trend prompted by seasonal or cyclical business conditions. Compare to Primary Market Trend; Secondary Market Trend; Secular Market Trend.

DEAD CAT BOUNCE A brief, abrupt rise (bounce) in the price of a security or index that occurs after a steep drop. While a dead cat bounce is caused by a small contingent of buyers and profit-taking from short-sellers, the term reflects overall investor lethargy that keeps the rally from gaining momentum. See Catch a Falling Knife.

THE DOW See Dow Jones Industrial Average.

DOW JONES INDUSTRIAL AVERAGE (DJIA) A price-weighted index made up of 30 Blue Chip stocks that are either within or closely aligned with the industrial sector. The Dow Jones Industrial Average is one of the best known and closely followed of the broad-based indexes. Often referred to as The Dow. Compare to S&P 500; Wilshire 5000. See Broader Market.

FLIGHT TO QUALITY A market trend in which investors and fund managers adjust their portfolio holdings during periods of economic uncertainty. It can reflect a movement from investments associated with geopolitical risk or a switch from speculative domestic holdings to Blue Chip stocks or investment grade debt instruments, for example.

HEAVY MARKET A market that is marked by falling or stagnant prices due to a shortage of buyers. A heavy market can be an indication of investor uncertainty.

INDEX A composite measure of 1) a segment of the economy or the economy as a whole 2) the performance of an industry, sector, or the broader market. See Dow Jones Industrial Average; S&P 500; NASDAQ 100; Russell 3000; Wilshire 5000.

A Closer Look at Global Indexes		
Index	**Symbol**	**Country**
BEL 20	BEL20	Belgium
CAC 40	CAC40	France
DAX	GDAXI	Germany
Dow Jones Industrial Average (DJIA)	INDU	United States
DJEuro	Stoxx50	Germany
FTSE 100	UKX100	United Kingdom
NASDAQ 100	IXNDX	United States
NASDAQ Composite	IXIC	United States
NIKKEI 225	NIK/O	Japan
S&P 500	SPX	United States
S&P/TSX Composite	TSX	Canada
Shanghai Composite	000001.SS	China

JANUARY EFFECT A seasonal rally in the broader market created in part by heavy buying among institutional investors.

MARKET BIAS A term that is used to reflect whether the majority of investors view the broader market as being in an uptrend (a bullish bias) or in a downtrend (a bearish bias). Technicians measure market bias with breadth-of-market indicators. Also referred to as market sentiment.

MARKET CYCLE The longer-term price movements in a broader market index, including one complete uptrend and one complete downtrend. A market cycle is measured from the lowest low or highest high for a given time and is deemed finished when the prices of the index approach the starting point. See Market Trend.

Figure 1 Market Cycle

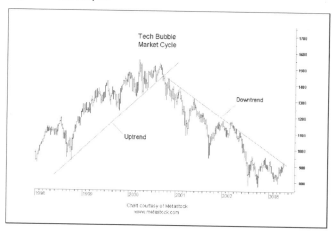

Chart courtesy of Metastock
www.metastock.com

MARKET TREND The overall direction of trading in the broader market on either a short-, mid-, or long-term basis. A trend that moves generally higher is called an uptrend, and one that moves generally lower is called a downtrend. Trends can be short- or long-term. Short term trends cycle within the broader trend, sometimes moving with it and sometimes against it. For example, a long-term bull market is typically comprised of a series of shorter-term uptrends and downtrends. See Cyclical Market; Primary Market Trend; Secondary Market Trend; Secular Market.

NASDAQ 100 An index made up of the 100 largest non-financial NASDAQ-listed companies. Compare to Dow Jones Industrial Average; S&P 500; Russell 3000; Wilshire 5000.

NOISE Short-term price movements that do not affect mid- to long-term trends.

PRIMARY MARKET TREND An extended period within a market cycle in which prices continue to make higher highs (bull market) or lower lows (bear market) before peaking out and reversing and establishing a trend in the opposite direction. A primary trend can last up to two years and consists of a series of secondary market trends. Compare to Secular Market. See Cyclical Market; Market Cycle.

PROFIT TAKING A brief rally created when a large number of investors closes some or all of their profitable positions to capture the gains after an upward move in prices. After the profit-taking is complete, the stock or index will typically correct slightly and then resume its previous trend. See Correction; Paper Profit.

RALLY A trend in a security or the broader market marked by higher highs and higher lows. A rally generally indicates investor confidence.

RELIEF RALLY A sharp upward spike in prices following a period of investor uncertainty.

REVERSAL See Trend Reversal.

RUSSELL 2000 An index made up of the 2,000 smallest companies in the Russell 3000. Compare to Dow Jones Industrial Average; NASDAQ 100; S&P 500; Wilshire 5000.

RUSSELL 3000 An index made up of the 3,000 largest U.S. stocks. Compare to NASDAQ 100; S&P 500; Wilshire 5000.

S&P 500 A weighted index of 500 of the widely-held mid-cap and large-cap stocks. The movement of the S&P 500 is generally regarded as accurately reflecting the performance of the market as a whole. See Broader Market; NASDAQ 100; Russell 3000; Wilshire 5000.

SANTA CLAUS RALLY A seasonal rise in stock prices that sometimes occurs between Christmas and New Year.

A Closer Look at the Santa Claus Rally

Theories behind the Santa Claus Rally vary, but most attribute the short-term price gains associated with it to increased market participation from individual investors. One factor that supports that theory is that many professional investors take vacation during the week between Christmas and New Years, leaving the market in the hands of individual investors, the vast majority of whom shun short-selling in favor of buying long.

SECONDARY MARKET TREND A short-term change in the direction in which prices move within a primary market trend. See Bear Rally; Correction; Market Cycle; Trend.

SECULAR MARKET A market cycle that lasts between five and 20 years. A secular market consists of a series of shorter primary market trends. Compare to Cyclical Market.

SELL OFF Heavy selling of an individual security, sector, or the broader market at rapidly declining prices.

SENSITIVE MARKET A market condition characterized by exaggerated price reactions to both positive and negative news.

SHAKEOUT Panic selling by nervous investors in response to negative news or market uncertainty.

SHORT COVERING A short-term rise in the trading price of a security or futures contract due to short-sellers buying their way out of their positions.

SHORT SQUEEZE A situation that occurs when short-sellers, trapped in a rising market, begin to buy their way out of their losing positions, fueling upward price momentum and further panic-buying for the short-sellers still in the market. Professional traders will sometimes try to take advantage of a short squeeze by buying into the upward price pressure and selling short when the momentum begins to weaken. They will then ride the price back to a correction point, take profits, and re-enter the market as buyers. Compare to Bull Squeeze.

SIDEWAYS MARKET A market condition characterized by trading that takes place within a relatively flat trading range. Sideways trading is typically a sign of investor uncertainty.

SLUMP A modest decline in the price of a security or the broader market.

SOFT MARKET A market in which there are more sellers than buyers. Also called a heavy market because without buyers the market fails to generate upward momentum.

SQUEEZE A situation that occurs when an investor is trapped in a losing position. For example, a trader who is long when prices are rapidly declining might feel pressure (squeeze) to capitulate and take the loss rather than risk greater losses while waiting for a reversal. See Short Squeeze.

STOCK MARKET CRASH Wide-spread, panic-selling that results in a sudden and extreme drop in stock prices on the broader market. See Crash of 1929; Crash of 1987; Black Tuesday; Black Thursday; Black Friday.

TREND The overall direction of trading on either a short-, mid-, or long-term basis. A trend that moves generally higher is called an uptrend, and one that moves generally lower is called a downtrend. Major trends are typically comprised of a series of short-term trends that move with and sometimes in opposition to the long-term trend. Technicians watch both long-term and short-term trend for individual securities, sectors, and the broader market. See Market Trend; Trend line.

TREND REVERSAL A change in the direction of trading that exceeds a normal correction point. Often referred to simply as a reversal. See Retracement.

WILSHIRE 5000 An index representing virtually every listed U.S. company, making it the broadest measure of performance for the U.S. stock market.

STOP-RUNNING A practice among professional traders of pushing the price of a stock up (or down) through a resistance (or support) level where they believe investors have placed stop orders. When the stop orders are hit, they trigger market orders and/or limit orders, which cause a spike (or drop) in the price at which point the professionals reverse their positions and ride the stock in the opposite direction. See Stop Out.

Asset Classes

CHAPTER TWELVE

Stocks: Owning a Piece of Something Big

EQUITIES Financial instruments representing ownership interest in a corporation.

AMERICAN DEPOSITARY RECEIPT (ADR) A U.S. security that is backed by shares of non-U.S. stock held on deposit at a U.S. bank. Federal law prohibits trading non-U.S. stock on a U.S. stock exchange. By depositing the non-U.S. stock in an American bank and using those shares as assets to back an American depositary receipt, American investors are able to buy and sell non-U.S. stock without dealing directly with a foreign stock exchange.

AMERICAN DEPOSITARY SHARE (ADS) A share of a security that is backed by shares of non-U.S. securities held on deposit at a U.S. bank. See American Depositary Receipt (ADR).

ASSET CLASS A category of investment such as stocks, bonds, funds, options, futures.

AUTHORIZED CAPITAL STOCK The maximum number of shares of stock that a corporation is authorized to sell, as stipulated in its articles of incorporation.

BACKDOOR LISTING The practice of an unlisted company securing an exchange listing by merging with a company that is already listed on the exchange. Companies sometimes seek a backdoor listing when they have tried and failed to meet exchange listing requirements.

BASKET A group of stocks or products traded or tracked as one unit. See Basket Order; Consumer Price Index (CPI); Equity Linked Note; European Currency Unit (ECU); Exchange Traded Fund (ETF); Folio; HOLDRS; Personal Consumption Expenditures (PCE).

BENEFICIAL OWNERSHIP Owning or having control over voting shares of a security. An individual or company holding a beneficial ownership of more than 5 percent of a publicly traded company is required to disclose the fact to the Securities & Exchange Commission (SEC) by filing a Schedule 13D. Schedule 13D filings can be accessed on the SEC's EDGAR database.

BULLETIN BOARD STOCK The stock of a publicly owned company that is traded on the Over-The-Counter Bulletin Board system (OTCBB). Although bulletin board stocks are not required to meet minimum financial requirements or a threshold of trading volume, they are required to file financial reports with the Securities & Exchange Commission (SEC) or other Self Regulatory Organizations (SRO). A bulletin board stock can be identified by the ".OB" suffix on its stock symbol. For example: ONEV.OB is the symbol for One Voice Technologies, Inc., which is traded on the OTC market.

CLASS A SHARES Common stock that is typically assigned more voting rights than Class B Shares. The voting rights for each class of stock are spelled out in the company's prospectus. Compare to B Shares; Preferred Shares; Restricted Shares.

CLASS B SHARES Common stock that is typically assigned fewer voting rights than Class A Shares. The voting rights for each class of stock are spelled out in the company's prospectus. Compare to B Shares; Preferred Shares; Restricted Shares.

COLLATERALIZED SECURITY A security that is backed by a specific asset or a pool of assets. See Collateralized Bond Obligation.

COMMON SHARES A class of securities that represents an ownership interest in a company and entitles a shareholder to vote on certain matters pertaining to the operation of the company as well as to participate in the distribution of dividends. Compare to Preferred Shares; Restricted Shares.

COMMON STOCK A security that represents an ownership

interest in a company that typically includes eligibility to participate in dividend distributions and confers voting rights on certain matters pertaining to the operation of the company, such as mergers and acquisitions or a change to the company's by-laws. Compare to Preferred Stock.

CONVERSION PRICE The price per share basis for calculating how many shares of stock the holder of a convertible security will receive at the time a conversion option is exercised. The conversion price included is stipulated in the bond indenture or the prospectus, depending on the nature of the security. See Convertible Bond; Convertible Debenture; Convertible Preferred Stock.

CONVERSION RATIO A stipulation in a company's prospectus that spells out how many shares of common stock a holder of convertible preferred stock will receive upon exercising the conversion provision.

CONVERTIBLE PREFERRED STOCK Preferred stock that can be traded for common stock according to the time-table and conversion ratio spelled out in the company's prospectus.

CREATION UNIT A large block of shares of an Exchange Traded Fund or other Unit Investment Trust (UIT), which are sold to institutional investors.

CYCLICAL STOCK A security issued by a company whose profits are sensitive to economic trends. A cyclical stock will tend to move up during periods of economic growth and decline during periods of economic contraction. Automobiles, housing, and oil are examples of cyclical stocks. Compare to Non-Cyclical Stock.

CUSIP NUMBER A nine-character numbering system that identifies registered U.S. and Canadian stocks, municipal bonds, and U.S. government securities by issuer and type. It is administered by the Committee on Uniform Securities Identification Procedures.

DEPOSITARY RECEIPT A security that is backed by shares of stock held on deposit at a U.S bank. See HOLDRS; Holding Company Depositary Receipts; American Depositary Receipt (ADR).

DIAMONDS The name for an Exchange Traded Fund (ETF) that mirrors the Dow Jones Industrial Average.

DUAL LISTED A security that is traded on more than one exchange is said to be dual listed. See Listed stock; Unlisted Stock.

EQUITIES Financial instruments representing ownership interest in a corporation. See Equity; Stock.

EQUITY 1) Ownership interest in a company. 2) Another word for stock.

EQUITY UNIT INVESTMENT TRUST An investment company formed for the sole purpose of establishing a professionally managed portfolio of equities that trades like a security on a stock exchange. The holdings within the portfolio are fixed at the time the UIT is established and do not vary except in rare circumstances. Compare to Fixed Income Unit Investment Trust. See Unit Investment Trust (UIT).

EXCHANGE TRADED FUND (ETF) An index-based fund that can be bought and sold like shares of stock. Exchange traded funds are comprised of a representative basket of the underlying securities.

A Closer Look at Exchange Traded Funds (ETFs)

ETFs are registered with the Securities & Exchange Commission (SEC) as a unique form of open end company or Unit Investment Trust (UIT). The first ETF was introduced at the American Stock Exchange in 1993. The SPDR (pronounced: spider), as it was called, tracks the S&P 500 Index Composite Price Index. Today there are almost 200 ETFs that track indexes for stocks, bonds, and industries.

Some ETFs, like the SPDR, purchase all of the securities in the underlying index. Alternatively, the fund may purchase a representative sample of stocks. In either case, the fund typically packages the holding into large blocks of shares, called a creation unit, which they sell to institutional investors. The owner of a creation unit has the options to sell it back to the fund or divide it into smaller units, which are then sold as individual shares on the secondary market through a stock exchange.

FOLIO A personalized basket of investments that is traded as one issue, giving investors the ease of investing in a mutual fund without the tax penalties associated with them. Folios can be selected from a list and customized to suit the investor or designed from scratch. In either case, brokerage firms offering folios will charge a fee to set up the account in which the folio will be held.

GOLD STOCK A publicly traded company engaged in gold exploration, mining, or production. Not to be confused with owning or trading in the futures price of the physical commodity. See Gold Fund.

GROWTH STOCK A security issued by a company with earnings that are growing at a faster rate than other companies in the same industry or the market as a whole. Growth stocks typically use their earnings to finance company expansion or product development in lieu of paying dividends to their shareholders. Compare Income Stock. See Growth Fund.

HOLDING COMPANY DEPOSITARY RECEIPTS (HOLDRs) A security comprised of a basket of individual shares of stock that are held on deposit at a U.S. bank and can be bought or sold in a single transaction. Unlike the similar Exchange Traded Fund, HOLDRs represent beneficial ownership in the underlying securities, meaning that investors who own them possess voting rights and can participate in dividend distributions. HOLDRs are traded only on the American Stock Exchange. See Depositary Receipt.

HOLDRS See Holding Company Depositary Receipts.

INCOME STOCK A security issued by a company that uses its earnings to pay dividends to its shareholders rather than to fund expansion or product development. Income stocks are typically mature companies with a history of steady earnings.

ISSUE Another word for a security.

LARGE-CAP STOCK Securities issued by very large companies with a market capitalization of at least $5 billion. Compare to Mega Cap Stock; Micro Cap Stock; Mid-Cap Stock; Small-Cap Stock.

LISTED STOCK A security traded on the New York Stock Exchange, the American Stock Exchange, NASDAQ, or one of the regional stock exchanges. Compare to Unlisted Stock. See Unlisted Trade.

MEGA-CAP STOCK A security with a market capitalization of $200 billion or more. Compare to Large-Cap Stock; Micro-Cap Stock; Mid-Cap Stock; Small-Cap Stock.

MICRO-CAP STOCK A security with a market capitalization of less than $300 million. Compare to Large-Cap Stock; Mega-Cap Stock; Mid-Cap Stock; Small-Cap Stock.

MID CAP STOCK A company with a market capitalization of more than $2 billion and less than $10 billion. Compare to Large-Cap Stock; Mega-Cap Stock; Micro-Cap Stock; Small-Cap Stock.

MORTGAGE-BACKED SECURITY A financial instrument that is secured by a pool of mortgage notes. See Government National Mortgage Association (Ginnie Mae).

NON-CYCLICAL STOCK Stock in a company whose earnings are relatively immune to economic upturns and down turns. Makers of non-durable goods such as paper, cleaning, and office supplies are examples of non-cyclical stocks. Compare to Cyclical Stock.

PENNY STOCK A security that trades for less than one dollar per share. Penny stocks do not meet listing requirements for U.S. stock exchanges and are traded on the over-the-counter (OTC) market. See Listed Company; OTCBB; Pink Sheets.

PREFERRED SHARES One of several classes of securities, representing an ownership interest in a corporation. Preferred stock derives its name from the fact that they hold a higher priority than common shares in both the payment of dividends and claims against the assets of the company in the case of a bankruptcy.

PROXY A written document in which a shareholder authorizes someone else, typically another shareholder or the company's management, to vote his or her shares at a shareholder meeting. See Proxy Fight; Proxy Statement.

QUALIFYING SHARE A share of common stock that a candidate for a company's Board of Directions (BOD) is required to own. The term does not reflect a difference in the properties of a qualifying share compared to common shares held by other shareholders. Instead, it refers to the requirement that a member of the board must hold a vested interest in the operation of the enterprise in the form of company stock.

QUID PRO QUO A Latin phrase that vows a favor for a favor, a reciprocal agreement between two parties to exchange tangible or intangible objects of similar value. Quid pro quo agreements can be ethical and legal or not, depending on whether the actions involved constitute a breach of fiduciary trust or the rules and legislation enacted to ensure fairness and prevent fraud.

REAL ESTATE INVESTMENT TRUST (REIT) A business entity that uses its assets to purchase and manage real estate holdings. A REIT can be either a publicly traded company or privately held.

REDEMPTION The process of selling back shares of preferred stock or mutual fund shares to the issuer. See Redemption Fee.

RESTRICTED SHARES A class of securities with certain restrictions that make them less valuable on the open market. Restricted shares are typically offered to employees of the issuing company and may limit or exclude the shareholder's voting rights and/or dividend participation.

REVERSE STOCK SPLIT A consolidation of outstanding shares taken by a company to reduce the number of shares on the market. For example, in a one for two (1:2) reverse split, a company or investor who owns 200 shares of a company's stock at $20 before a reverse split will own 100 shares at $40 after the reverse split. Compare to Stock Split.

SECONDARY OFFERING The offer to sell a large block of shareholder-owned stock to the public. Secondary offerings are typically made by an institutional investor and do not increase the total number of outstanding shares. The company whose stock is being offered does not receive proceeds from a secondary offering. Compare to Initial Public Offering (IPO); Subsequent Distribution.

SECURITY Any investment instrument that is secured by an ownership interest (equity), debt obligation (note), or contractual right to buy or sell (option) a financial instrument or commodity. See Bond; Derivative; Stock.

SHAREHOLDER MEETING A gathering of company officers, board of directors (BOD), and shareholders. An annual shareholder meeting is held after the close of each fiscal year when the company's performance over the past year is reviewed, the shareholders elect the board of directors, and vote on matters affecting the company's operation. The board of directors can also call special shareholder meetings to discuss business that cannot be deferred until the next annual meeting. See Proxy Statement.

A Closer Look at the Annual Shareholders' Meetings

Shareholders have an opportunity annually to question the company's key decision makers face to face about the company's operation. History is rife with stories of contentious shareholders banding together to demand changes they believe will improve the company's stock performance and their own profitability. It is also the venue in which shareholders in attendance have an opportunity to vote their shares on the election of the board of directors and force changes that can't be accomplished otherwise.

Before the annual meeting, all shareholders are mailed a proxy statement summarizing matters that will be discussed and presented for a vote at the meeting.

SMALL-CAP STOCK A security with a market capitalization of more than $300 million and less than $2 billion. Compare to Large-Cap Stock; Mega-Cap Stock; Micro-Cap Stock; Mid-Cap Stock.

STANDARD & POOR'S DEPOSITARY RECEIPT (SPDR) Like other depositary receipts, SPDRs are securities that are backed by shares of stock held on deposit at a U.S. Bank. The shares that secure a SPDR mirror those on which S&P 500 is based and represent a beneficial ownership in each company.

STOCK CERTIFICATE A printed document certifying ownership interest in a company. See Street Name.

STREET NAME Stocks that are held in the name of the brokerage firm instead of the name of the investor are said to be held in the "street name," typically the case with most shares traded on a stock exchange, as it makes the subsequent sale of the shares faster and easier. Buyers wishing to take delivery of a stock certificate can do so, but it will cost roughly $25 and will delay the process of reselling the shares at a later date.

TECH STOCK A company engaged in a technology-related business. Software, computer hardware, and biotechnology are examples of tech stocks.

THINLY TRADED STOCK A security with historically low volume and a wide spread between the bid and ask prices.

TRACKING STOCK A special type of security issued by a company for tracking performance of a segment of its business. For example, mature companies, mainly conglomerates, might issue a tracking stock for a rapidly growing division.

UNLISTED STOCK A security that is not traded on an exchange. Over-the-counter stocks are unlisted stocks. Compare to Listed Stock. See Listed Company; Unlisted Trade.

UPSTAIRS MARKET A security transaction in which the sale of shares of a listed stock is negotiated and executed "upstairs" within the offices of a brokerage firm rather than going through an exchange.

VOTING RIGHTS A privilege assigned to certain stock issues that gives the shareholder a voice in certain corporate decisions, such as electing the board of directors (BOD) and voting on a merger, acquisition, or spin off. Voting rights are spelled out in the company prospectus. See Class A Shares; Class B Shares; Common Shares; Prospectus; Restricted Shares; Voting Stock.

VOTING STOCK A class of stock that endows the shareholder with a right to vote on certain company issues.

WARRANT A certificate issued by a corporation conveying the right of the holder to buy a specified number of shares of stock at a specified price. The time in which the option can be exercised may be limited or it may be granted in perpetuity. Warrants can be bought and sold on U.S. stock exchanges.

CHAPTER THIRTEEN

Funds:
Letting a Professional
Make the Decisions

MUTUAL FUND An investment company that pools investor funds to purchase financial instruments.

12b-1 FEE An ongoing marketing and distribution fee charged by certain mutual funds.

12b-1 MUTUAL FUND A fund that charges an ongoing marketing and distribution fee based on the value of the assets held in the fund. See 12b-1 Fee.

ACCOUNT FEE A maintenance fee charged by some mutual funds over and above the annual management fees and distribution fees.

ACCUMULATION PLAN An arrangement with a mutual fund in which an investor acquires additional shares in the fund on a regular and periodic basis. An accumulation plan can make it possible to expand a holding in a particular mutual fund over time and avoid a large one-time cash outlay.

ASSET ALLOCATION FUND A fund that attempts to achieve diversification by dividing its holdings between a broad range of investments. The prospectus for every fund will disclose the specifics of its investment policy, but in general, an asset allocation fund is likely to hold assets in a range of stocks, bonds, U.S. government securities, precious metals, and cash instruments.

AVERAGE MATURITY The average length of maturity for all fixed-rate debt instruments held in a portfolio. A bond fund or mutual fund with a short average maturity is more sensitive to current interest rate fluctuations than one with longer average maturity.

AVERAGE PRICE See Net Asset Value.

BACK-END LOAD A fee charged by a fund when the investment is sold. Compare to Contingent Deferred Sales Load (CDSL); Front-End Load; Level Load; No Load.

BALANCED FUND A fund that buys a combination of stocks and bonds to achieve a balance between growth (higher risk) and income (lower risk) investments.

BOND FUND A mutual fund that invests primarily in a combination of corporate bonds, municipal bonds, and U.S. government securities.

BREAKPOINT The cumulative amount invested in a mutual fund that qualifies an investor for a discount in sales fees. Also called Rights of Accumulation (ROA). See Load.

CAPITAL APPRECIATION FUND A mutual fund that seeks a maximum rate of return by investing in high-growth securities. Compare to Balanced Fund.

CLASS A SHARES Mutual fund shares that carry a front-end load. Sometimes referred to simply as A Shares. See Load. Compare to Class B Shares; Class C Shares.

CLASS B SHARES Mutual fund shares that carry a back-end load. Sometimes referred to simply as B Shares. Compare to Class A Shares; Class C Shares.

CLASS C SHARES Mutual fund shares that are charged a back-end load if they are sold within one year and higher annual fees for the life of the investment than Class A shares, typically in the form of ongoing marketing and distribution fees. Sometimes referred to simply as C Shares. See Front-End Load; 12b-1 Fee.

CLOSED-END FUND A fund that issues a fixed number of shares in an initial public offering (IPO) which are then traded like a security on the stock market. The price of a closed-end fund is determined by market demand and net asset value (NEV). Contrary to common belief, a closed-end fund is not a type of mutual fund which the Securities & Exchange Commission (SEC) defines as an open-end company. See Open-End Fund.

COMMODITY POOL A company formed to manage a pool of commodity futures assets. See Commodity Pool Operator; Pool.

CONTINGENT DEFERRED SALES LOAD (CDSL) A back-end load that is calculated and charged by a mutual fund on the basis of how long the fund is owned before redemption. The CDSL reduction schedule is published in the fund's prospectus, but generally speaking, the CDSL is eliminated completely if the fund is held long enough. Compare to Front-End Load. See 12b-1 Fee.

DISCLOSURE DOCUMENT A document that explains the fee structure, potential risks, and the style of trading for a fund. The Securities and Trade Commission requires that all funds provide disclosure documents to prospective investors. See 12-b Fees; Commission; Load; Management Fee; A Shares; B Shares; C Shares.

DISTRIBUTION FEE See 12b-1 Fee.

DIVERSIFIED FUND A mutual fund that manages market risk by holding securities in a variety of business sectors. Compare to Focused Fund.

EMERGING MARKET FUND A mutual fund that primarily holds investments in developing nations or in companies that derive a major portion of their earnings from the sale of goods and services to those countries.

EQUITY FUND A mutual fund that invests in stocks.

EXCHANGE FEE A fee charge by some mutual funds when a shareholder transfers from one fund to another within the same family of funds.

FAMILY OF FUNDS A mutual fund company offering an assortment of funds, each designed to meet a specific investment objective.

FOCUSED FUND A mutual fund that holds large positions in fewer than 30 stocks or in fewer than three sectors. Compare to a Diversified Fund.

FRONT-END LOAD A fee charged when an investor purchases Class A Shares in a mutual fund. Compare to Back-End Load; Level Load; No Load.

FUND An investment company that pools investor funds to purchase financial instruments. See Mutual Fund; Bond Fund; Equity Fund.

GLOBAL FUND A mutual fund that invests in U.S. companies as well as those located in other parts of the world. Compare to International Fund.

GOLD FUND A mutual fund that invests in gold stocks and, in some instances, in the metal itself.

GREEN FUND A mutual fund that limits its holdings to environmentally friendly companies.

GROWTH AND INCOME FUND A mutual fund that balances risk by investing in both growth stock and income stocks.

GROWTH FUND A mutual fund that invests in stocks that are in the growth stage of their business cycle. Growth stocks are generally viewed as entailing more risk to principal than income stocks.

HEDGE FUND A fund that is allowed to employ aggressive investment strategies, such as short selling, options, and program trading, which are prohibited in mutual funds. Hedge funds typically require a minimum investment of several hundred thousand dollars, limiting participation to high-net worth individual investors and institutions. See Private Investment Fund.

HIGH WATER MARK The highest level an investor's money has attained within a hedge fund. Certain funds stipulate that when an investor's assets fall below the high water mark, the fund manager cannot collect performance fees until the assets have been raised again to a level above the previous high water mark.

INCOME FUND A mutual fund that buys income-bearing investments, such as bonds or dividend-bearing stocks.

INDEX FUND A mutual fund that holds a portfolio of stocks that closely matches a broad-based index like the S&P 500 or the NASDAQ 100. An index fund employs a passive investment management strategy. Compare to Managed Fund.

INSTITUTIONAL FUND A highly diversified mutual fund designed for high net worth investors, such as pension funds. Institutional funds have a higher than normal minimum investment.

INTERNATIONAL FUND A mutual fund that invests in stocks and bonds only from non-U.S. companies.

LARGE-CAP FUND A mutual fund that invests in securities issued by very large companies with a market capitalization, typically in the range of at least $5 billion. Compare to Mega-Cap Fund; Micro-Cap Fund; Mid-Cap Fund; Small-Cap Fund.

LEVEL LOAD An annual fee associated with Class C Shares of a mutual fund.

LOAD A sales fee charged at the time of purchase for certain classes of mutual fund shares. Sales fees can be characterized by when they are paid, Front-End Load, Back-end Load, or Level-Load. Compare to No Load.

Table 3

A Closer Look at Mutual Fund Loads	
Front-End Load	A sales fee charged at the time of purchase.
Back-End Load	A sales fee that is deferred until redemption.
Level Load	A sales fee that is charged annually for as long as Class C Mutual Fund Shares are held.
Load Spread Option	A sales fee that is broken up into a series of payments, rather than being paid in one lump sum.

LOAD SPREAD OPTION An alternative to paying the sales fees for a mutual fund in one lump sum. Selecting the load spread option allows an investor who makes periodic contributions to a mutual fund account to spread the load payments across a series of smaller payments. Also called Spread Load Contractual Plan.

MANAGED FUND A mutual fund that employs a fund manager who makes investment decisions. Compare to Index Fund; Passive Investment Strategy.

MANAGEMENT FEE Fees that are deducted from the assets of a mutual fund to pay the fund manager and cover certain other administrative costs.

MICRO CAP FUND A mutual fund that invests in securities with a market capitalization usually of less than $300 million. Micro-cap stocks are typically low-priced, thinly traded stocks. Compare to Large-Cap Fund; Mega-Cap Fund; Mid-Cap Fund; Small-Cap Fund.

MID-CAP FUND A mutual fund that invests in securities with a market capitalization typically in the range of more than $2 billion and less than $10 billion. Compare to Large-Cap Fund; Mega-Cap Fund; Micro-Cap Fund; Small-Cap Fund.

MONEY MARKET FUND A mutual fund that invests in short-term debt instruments, such as Treasury Bills and CDs. Because money market funds are extremely liquid, financial institutions use them as a place to park unused money temporarily. See Sweep Account.

MUTUAL FUND An investment company, legally known as an open-end company, meaning that the fund assets are equally divided among and owned by the investors in the fund and that the fund can issue and redeem shares of the fund at any time. The profit, loss, and expenses of a mutual fund are equally shared across all of its investors. Compare to a Closed-End Fund.

MUTUAL FUND CUSTODIAN A firm that holds the securities and other financial instruments owned by a mutual fund.

NET ASSET VALUE (NAV) The value of a mutual fund or other investment company, calculated by subtracting its total liabilities from its total assets. See Net Asset Value Per Share (NAVPS).

NET ASSET VALUE PER SHARE (NAVPS) The value of a single share of a mutual fund. Calculated by subtracting the fund's total LIABILITIES from its total ASSETS and dividing the result by the OUTSTANDING SHARES. Also known as Average Price.

A Closer Look at Calculating Net Asset Value Per Share

Market Value of Fund Assets - Total liability ÷ Total number of shares

NO LOAD FUND A fund that does not charge a fee to buy or sell the investment. Compare to Back-End Load; Front-End Load; Level Load.

OPEN-END COMPANY See Mutual Fund.

OPEN-END FUND Another name for a mutual fund. An open-end fund is free to add new shares as demand increases and remove shares as demand decreases. The market value of an open-end fund is determined by dividing the total value of the fund by the number of shares and adding any sales fees charged at the time of the purchase. Compare to Closed-End Fund.

POOL Collective assets that are combined to fund investments, investment clubs, commodity pools, and pooled income funds.

POOLED INCOME FUND A fund of donated investments operated by a charitable organization. The fund obtains its assets through charitable contributions of securities from individual investors. The donations are combined to form a pool of investments that are managed by the fund with the annual net pro rata earnings being shared by the donors throughout their lifetimes. Upon a donor's death, his or her share of the earnings passes to the charitable organization.

PRIVATE INVESTMENT FUND A fund comprised of a pool of assets from a limited number of investors, typically those with a very high net worth. See Hedge Fund.

PURCHASE FEE A fee charged by some mutual funds at the time the shares are purchased. Unlike the Front-end Fund charged by some mutual funds, the purchase fee is used to cover operating costs and is not paid to the broker.

REDEMPTION FUND See Sinking Fund.

RIGHTS OF ACCUMULATION (ROA) A provision offered by some mutual funds that grants a reduction in the sales fee when an investor increases his or her holdings beyond a specified threshold. Also called Breakpoint.

SALES CHARGE See Sales Fee.

SALES FEE See Back-End Load; Front-End Load; Load.

SECTOR FUND A mutual fund that limits its portfolio holdings to securities within a specific sector within an industry.

SMALL-CAP FUND A mutual fund that invests in companies with a market capitalization typically of more than $300 and less than $2 billion. Compare to Large-Cap Fund; Mega-Cap Fund; Micro-Cap Fund; Mid-Cap Fund.

SOCIALLY CONSCIOUS MUTUAL FUND Any one of a number of mutual funds that excludes investments in companies whose products or business practices might be considered morally or ethically troubling.

SPREAD-LOAD CONTRACTUAL PLAN See Load Spread Option.

STATEMENT OF ADDITIONAL INFORMATION (SAI) An addendum to the prospectus for a mutual fund that provides useful information about the fund's operation over and above what the Securities & Exchange Commission requires.

STYLE BOX A classification system used by Morning Star to assist investors with asset allocation decisions. The style box assigns a relative rank to mutual funds based on market capitalization, as well as value and growth characteristics for the fund.

TRAILER FEE A commission paid to an investment advisor by a mutual fund. Some investors believe that trailer fees can create a conflict of interest by motivating the advisor to recommend a fund on the basis of his personal gain rather than what is most appropriate for the investor.

UNIT INVESTMENT TRUST (UIT) An investment company formed for the sole purpose of establishing a professionally managed investment portfolio that trades like a security on a stock exchange. The holdings within the portfolio are fixed at the time the UIT is established and do not vary except in rare circumstances.

Bonds:
Loaning Corporations
and Governments Money

BOND A debt obligation issued by a corporation or government that includes a promise to repay the principal and interest at a fixed rate.

ACCRUAL BOND See Zero Coupon Bond.

ARBITRAGE BOND A bond issued by a municipality to take advantage of a disparity in interest rates between two different debt instruments. For example, a municipality issues an arbitrage bond at a lower interest rate and for a shorter term than one of its own existing debt securities. It then might use the assets raised by the arbitrage issue to buy Treasury securities that are paying a higher interest rate than its own issue. Prior to maturity of its own higher-rate issue, the municipality will sell the Treasury securities and pay off the debt on the arbitrage bond, profiting from the difference.

ASSET-BACKED SECURITY A debt instrument that is secured by a pool of assets, such the accounts receivable of credit card companies or other lending institutions.

BABY BOND A bond with a par value of less than $1,000.

BEARER BOND A bond that is not registered to the owner. A bearer bond is payable by the issuer to whomever presents it for redemption.

BOND A debt obligation issued by a corporation or government that includes a promise to repay the principal and interest at a fixed rate.

BOND ANTICIPATION NOTE (BAN) A small, short term bond that is expected to be paid off with the subsequent issue of a larger bond.

BOND INDENTURE The contract between a bond issuer and bond holder that documents the terms of the debt obligation, including the interest rate, maturity date, conversion rights, and the terms under which a bond issuer can retire the debt early. See Callable Bond.

BOND RATING A rating system used by investment research firms such as Fitch Ratings, Moody's Investors Service, and Standard & Poor's to reflect an opinion on the creditworthiness of a company issuing a debt instrument. Each rating service has developed its own variation on a letter-based designation system, but in general they follow a similar pattern in which AAA denotes the least risk of default on the debt and a rating of C or lower denotes the highest. See Investment Grade; Junk Bond.

A Closer Look at Bond Ratings

Bond ratings are an opinion of creditworthiness of the issuer. In general, they are divided into two broad categories: Investment grade and speculative, often referred to as a junk bond.

As with any investment, there is a trade-off between yield and safety when investing in debt instruments. As the risk goes up, so does the interest rate attached to the bond. Following is a high-level summary of bond ratings from Standard & Poor's and Moody's Investor Services.

Investment Grade		Speculative/Junk	
Standard & Poor's*	Moody's Ratings**	Standard & Poor's*	Moody's Ratings**
AAA	Aaa	BB	Ba
AA	Aa	B	B
A	A	C	Caa
BBB	Baa		Ca
			C

* Source: Standard & Poor's, www.standardandpoors.com
** Source: Moody's Investor Service, www.moodys.com

CALLABLE See Callable Bond.

CALLABLE BOND A debt instrument that is issued with a stipulation that allows the issuer to buy it back at a stated time and stated price.

CALLED BOND A bond that has been called back by the issuer. See Callable Bond.

CERTIFICATE OF DEPOSIT (CD) An interest-bearing, time-obligated debt instrument issued by a bank or savings and loan. CDs typically earn a higher interest rate than regular savings accounts in exchange for the depositor's willingness to tie the funds up for the stipulated period of time. CDs are issued for periods ranging from three months to several years. A CD can be redeemed at any time, but an early withdrawal penalty will apply if it is redeemed prior to the maturity date.

COLLATERALIZED BOND OBLIGATION (CBO) An investment grade debt instrument that is backed by a portfolio of high-yield, risky bonds. Bonds backing a CBO can range in quality but typically hold a bond rating below BBB, classifying the underlying assets as junk bonds. Taken individually, the holdings in the portfolio are rated high risk, but depth and diversification of the mix of assets mitigates sufficient risk to raise the bond rating of a CBO to investment grade.

CONVERTIBLE BOND A debt instrument issued with a provision allowing the bond holder to swap it for another asset, typically shares of common stock. The terms of the conversion are spelled out in the bond certificate and/or the bond indenture. Compare to Convertible Preferred Stock; Convertible Debenture.

CONVERTIBLE DEBENTURE An unsecured debt instrument that carries a provision giving the creditor the right to exchange the debt for shares of stock according to the terms of the agreement. See Debenture; Indenture; Subordinate Debenture.

CORPORATE BOND A debt instrument issued by a corporation for the purpose of raising cash. Compare to Municipal Bond; Muni.

COUPON A slip of paper attached to coupon bond that the bond holder submits to the issuer to redeem a periodic interest payment.

COUPON BOND A debt instrument that is issued with coupons attached that can be redeemed at stated intervals (usually semi-annually) for the interest due. Compare to Zero Coupon Bond.

DEBENTURE An unsecured debt instrument issued by a corporation and backed only by the creditworthiness of the issuer. The terms of the debt are spelled out in a contract called an indenture. Because of the increased the risk associated with an unsecured debt, it typically pays a higher interest rate than one secured by collateral. See Convertible Debenture; Subordinate Debenture.

DEBT INSTRUMENT A written pledge to repay a debt. In the financial markets, debt instruments like government and corporate bonds are bought and sold in the form of securities.

EQUITY LINKED NOTE A security that is backed by a debt instrument that does not pay a fixed interest rate. Instead, the return on investment for an equity linked note is tied to the performance of a single security, a basket of securities, or a broader market index. Some Equity Linked Notes have a minimum redemption value that protects the principal.

EURO CD See Euro Certificate of Deposit.

EURO CERTIFICATE OF DEPOSIT (EURO CD) An interest bearing, time-obligated debt instrument issued by a non-U.S. bank. To compensate for their lower liquidity and increase their attractiveness to investors, Euro CDs typically earn a higher yield than CDs issued by U.S. banks.

EUROBOND A bond that is denominated in one country's currency and sold to investors in a country that uses a different currency. Eurobonds from multinational corporations and foreign governments are typically sold by international banking syndicates.

FINANCIAL INSTRUMENT A document having monetary worth.

FIXED INCOME INVESTMENT Financial instrument that yields a steady, predictable income from the payment of interest at a fixed rate.

FIXED INCOME UNIT INVESTMENT TRUST An investment

company formed for the sole purpose of establishing a professionally managed portfolio comprised primarily of municipal and/or corporate bonds and other fixed income investments.

GENERAL MORTGAGE BOND   A bond that uses a blanket mortgage on some or all of its property as collateral to secure the debt. The mortgage securing a general mortgage bond may be secondary to a more senior note, increasing investment risk.

GENERAL OBLIGATION BOND A municipal bond that is backed by the good faith and credit of a taxing authority. In the case of default, investors holding general obligation bonds can force a tax levy to enforce payment.

I BOND A U.S. Savings Bond issued in both electronic and paper form. An"I" bond is an accrual bond and is issued at face value, meaning that a $50 bond costs $50, and earns a fixed rate of return for up to 30 years.

INCOME BOND A bond that ties the company's obligation to pay interest to its own earnings.

INTEREST BEARING INVESTMENT   Any financial instrument that earns interest, such as a bond, certificate of deposi, or money market fund. Compare to Derivatives; Futures; Options; Stocks.

INVESTMENT GRADE DEBT INSTRUMENT   A bond rating assigned to debt instrument carrying a BBB or better rating by Fitch Ratings, Moody's Investors Service, or Standard & Poor's. Investment grade debt instruments are generally approved for purchase by banks.

JUNIOR NOTE A promissory note that holds secondary priority for repayment in case of bankruptcy. Compare to Senior Note.

JUNK BOND   A high-risk debt instrument. The term is used as a catch-all classification for any bond with a rating below BBB. Compare to Investment Grade.

LONG-BOND A bond with a maturity date of 10 years or longer. The 30-year Treasury Bond is the longest bond issued by the U.S. government and typically pays the highest yield because the investor's money is tied up for a longer term and thus exposed to increased risk from fluctuating interest rates.

LONG COUPON 1) Another term for long bond. 2) An interest payment covering a longer period than the other coupons on a bond. Long coupons are typically associated with the first interest installment.

MARKET INDEX DEPOSIT (MID) A certificate of deposit that pays a return based on the performance of a broader market index, such as the S&P 500, rather than a fixed interest rate. Also referred to as Market Linked Certificate of Deposit.

MARKET LINKED CERTIFICATE OF DEPOSIT See Market Index Deposit (MID).

MATURITY DATE The date at which a debt, such as a bond, money market fund, or certificate of deposit becomes due and payable.

MUNI A nickname for a municipal bond.

MUNICIPAL BOND A bond issued by a state or local government. Municipal bonds are exempt from federal taxation and may be exempt from state and local taxes, as well. Also called a Muni. See Double Exemption.

PAPER A term used to refer to short-term debt instruments.

PAR The face value of a bond. See Above Par.

REDEMPTION The repayment of a bond's principal by the issuer. See Redemption Fee.

REGISTERED BOND A bond that is registered to a specific bond holder. Compare to Bearer Bond.

REVENUE BOND A municipal bond that is issued to fund a specific revenue-producing project. A revenue bond is backed by the income generated by the project, which will theoretically retire the debt when the project has paid for itself. Football stadiums are often funded with revenue bonds.

SELF-LIQUIDATING BOND Another term for revenue bond. Also called Self-Supporting Debt.

SELF-SUPPORTING DEBT See Revenue Bond.

SERIAL BONDS Bonds that are issued on the same date but with staggered maturity dates. Serial bonds are used to fund projects associated with periodic, predictable expenses.

SERIES E SAVINGS BOND A U.S. Savings bond that was issued at a 75 percent discount to the face value. Series E bonds were replaced by Series EE bonds on June 30, 1980.

SERIES EE SAVINGS BOND A U.S. Savings Bond that is issued in both electronic and paper form. The paper bond is purchased at a 50 percent discount to the face value, whereas the electronic bond is purchased at face value. Both issues are accrual bonds.

SPECIAL ASSESSMENT BOND A municipal bond issued to fund a specific development project. Investors holding special assessment bonds are paid interest from a special tax levied on the beneficiaries of the project.

A Closer Look at Special Assessment Bonds

A classic example of a special assessment bond is the installation of a sewage system in a rural area, previously serviced by individual septic systems. Homes and businesses benefiting from the new system pay a special tax levy that covers all or part of the cost of the installation plus the interest that is returned to the investors who purchased the special assessment bonds that funded the project.

SPECULATIVE DEBT INSTRUMENT A bond or other note from an issuer with a bond rating lower than BBB. A speculative debt instruments is seen as entailing notable risk to the investment principal. Compare to Investment Grade Debt Instrument. See Fitch Rating; Junk Bond; Moody's Investors Service; Standard & Poor's.

TIME DEPOSIT Funds held in a certificate of deposit or savings account for a fixed period of time and at a fixed interest rate. Time deposits typically pay a higher interest rate than demand deposits, but penalties apply if the funds are withdrawn before the maturity date.

U.S. GOVERNMENT SECURITIES Debt obligations of the U.S. Government that are traded on the securities market. They include Treasury notes, TREASURY bonds, Treasury bills, and Treasury Inflation-Protected Securities (TIPS), all of which can be purchased through a bank, brokerage firm, or directly from the Treasury Department at **www.treasury.gov**.

U.S. SAVINGS BONDS An accrual bond issued by the U.S. Treasury Department. Certain savings bonds are issued at a discount to the face value; others are issued at face value. On each, interest accrues monthly and compounds semi-annually. U.S. Savings Bonds can be purchased through a bank or directly from the Treasury Department at **www.treasury.gov**. See Series EE Savings Bonds.

Table 4

A Closer Look at Series EE Savings Bonds and I Bonds
Series EE Paper Bonds*
Sold at a 50 percent discount to face value *You pay $25 for a $50 bond*
Denominations Available
$25
$50
$75
*$30,000 maximum purchase in one calendar year.
Both Series EE and "I" bonds are accrual bonds, meaning that the interest is paid at redemption rather than in periodic installments. The interest compounds semi-annually.
There is a one-year holding period before either can be redeemed and both Series EE and "I" bonds held less than five years are subject to a three-month interest penalty.

A Closer Look at Series EE Savings Bonds and I Bonds

Series EE Interest Rates

(Paper and Electronic) Determined by the date of purchase:

- Series EE bonds purchased between May 1997 and April 30, 2005 earn the current interest rate for up to 30 years.

- Bonds purchased after that date earn a fixed rate of return for up to 30 years. The interest rate for new issues of Series EE bonds is adjusted each May and November and remains in effect for all Series EE bonds issued until the next adjustment date.

I Bond Interest Rates

Pays a composite interest rate for up to 30 years, based on:

A fixed rate for the life of the bond and

An inflation rate that is adjusted each May and November.

U.S. TREASURY BILLS Short-term U.S. government securities. T-Bills, as they are sometimes called, are sold at a discount to their face value and have maturity dates that range from a few days to six months. They can be purchased through a brokerage firm or directly from the Treasury Department at **www.treasury.gov**.

U.S. TREASURY BOND Long-term debt instruments issued by the U.S. government. Treasury bonds earn interest at six-month intervals and can have a maturity date as long as thirty years out. They can be purchased through a brokerage firm or directly from the Treasury Department at **www.treasury.gov**. See Long Bond.

U.S. TREASURY INFLATION-PROTECTED SECURITIES (TIPS) A U.S. government security whose principal rises with inflation and declines with deflation, as measured by the Consumer Price Index (CPI). They can be purchased through a brokerage firm or directly from the Treasury Department at **www.treasury.gov**.

U.S. TREASURY NOTE A U.S. government security with a maturity date of two, three, five, or ten years. Treasury notes earn interest every six months. They can be purchased through a brokerage firm or directly from the Treasury Department at **www.treasury.gov**.

UNLIMITED TAX BOND A municipal bond that is backed by a pledge to raise taxes as high as is necessary to repay the debt.

YIELD The net interest rate on a bond.

ZERO COUPON BOND A debt obligation that accrues interest that is payable only at the maturity date of the bond. U.S. Saving Bonds are zero coupon. Compare to Coupon Bond. See Accrual Bond.

CHAPTER FIFTEEN

Options and Futures: Taking Bigger Chances

DERIVATIVE A contract based investment, such as futures and options, that derive their value from the underlying asset represented in the contract.

Options

AMERICAN OPTION An option contract that can be exercised anytime during the life of the contract. Compare to European Option. See Exercise.

CALL OPTION An option contract that conveys the right, but not the obligation, for the option holder to buy a specified number of shares of a security or a futures contract at a specified price, and within a specified period of time. Options traders purchase call options when they believe the price of a security is going to increase because it allows them to lock in their purchase price at the lower, current level. If the price goes down instead of up, the trader's loss is limited to the cost of the option contract. Often referred to simply as a Call. Compare to Put Option. See Expiration Date.

COVERED See Covered Call; Covered Put.

COVERED CALL A contract for a call option that is written by an investor who holds a position in the underlying asset for the purpose of locking in the cost of delivering the shares if the option holder chooses to exercise the option. Compare to Covered Put. See Naked Option. See Grantor.

A Closer Look at Covered Calls and Covered Puts

One might reasonably ask why an investor who holds either a long or a short position in a security or other financial product would choose to write a covered call or covered option. The answer is simple. It's one relatively sure way to make money from an investment.

Normally, if you're holding a long position and the price goes up, you make money. The same is true if you're short and the price goes down. But not if the market moves against you—unless you've used your position to write a covered call or covered put.

That's because the buyer (option holder) pays the grantor (the investor who writes the option) a premium for the privilege of retaining the right to buy or sell the underlying security if it turns into a profitable opportunity and the right to walk away from the investment if it doesn't. So whether the option holder chooses to exercises the option or allows it to expire worthless, you've made a profit from the premium.

A grantor's single biggest risk in writing an options contract is that he or she accepts a contractual obligation to deliver the underlying assets if the option holder chooses to exercise the option. By buying (or selling short) the underlying assets before writing the option contract, however, the grantor covers the risk by locking in the price of the assets – hence the name, covered put or covered call.

COVERED PUT A contract for a put option that is written by an investor who holds a position in the underlying asset for the purpose of locking in the cost of delivering the shares if the option holder chooses to exercise the option. Compare to Covered Call. See Naked Option. See Grantor.

DERIVATIVE A contract-based investment. Futures and options contracts derive value from the underlying asset represented in the contract. See Call Option; Commodity; Contract Unit; Put Option.

DOUBLE WITCHING WEEK The week beginning on Monday prior to the Saturday expiration of any two classes of option contracts. The week leading up to options expirations can be particularly volatile because option holders scramble to exercise their options prior to the closing bell on Friday afternoon. Options not exercised by that time will expire worthless resulting in a loss for the option holder. See Max Pain; Triple Witching Week; Options Calendar; Quadruple Witching Week.

EUROPEAN OPTION An option contract that can only be exercised at expiration. Compare to American Option.

EXERCISE Action taken by an option holder for the purpose of taking advantage of a contractual right to buy or sell the underlying security, commodity, or financial instrument. Specifically, an investor holding a call option will buy the underlying asset, and an investor holding a put option will sell it. Options not exercised by the expiration day expire worthless and result in a loss for the option holder.

EXPIRATION DATE The last day on which the holder of an option contract can exercise the right to buy or sell an option contract's underlying asset to take a profit on the position. Option contracts that are not exercised expire worthless. See Double Witching Week; Maximum Pain; Options Calendar; Quadruple Witching Week; Triple Witching Week.

EXPIRATION MONTH 1) The month in which a call option or put option will expire worthless unless the option holder exercises the option to buy or sell the underlying asset. 2) Another way to refer to the spot month of a futures contract for a commodity or financial instrument.

IN THE MONEY An option contract that has earned a paper profit. For a call option, in the money means that the underlying security is trading below the strike price. For a put option, the term indicates that the security is trading above it. Compare to Out of the Money.

INDEX OPTION An option contract that is written on an index, such as the S&P 500 and the Dow Jones Industrial Average (DJIA).

LONG-TERM EQUITY ANTICIPATION SECURITY (LEAP) An option contract with an expiration date that is more than nine months out.

NAKED OPTION A put or call that is written by an investor who does not own a position in the underlying asset that locks in the cost of delivering the shares if the option holder elects to exercise the option. Trading naked options can be a highly risky business because if the option holder chooses to exercise his or her contractual right to buy or sell the underlying assets at the specified price, the grantor will be forced to acquire them on the open market and at the prevailing price. Compare to Covered Call; Covered Put.

OPTION CONTRACT A contractual agreement that conveys to the buyer the right, but not the obligation, to buy (call option) or sell (put option) the underlying asset at a specified price and within a specified time. See Expiration Date.

OPTIONS DISCLOSURE DOCUMENT See Risk Disclosure Statement.

OPTIONS EXPIRATION CALENDAR A calendar of option expiration dates. The options calendar is published on a number of financial information Web sites. See Double Witching Week, Triple Witching Week; Quadruple Witching Week.

OPTIONS PRICE REPORTING AUTHORITY (OPRA) Provides option pricing quotations and last sale data from participating exchanges. OPRA data are transmitted to data vendors who disseminate it to market participants.

OUT OF THE MONEY An option contract that has not yet earned a paper profit. For a call option, out of the money means that the underlying asset is trading above the strike price. For a put option, the term indicates that it is trading below it. Compare to In the Money.

PUT OPTION (PUT) An option contract that conveys the right, but not the obligation, for the option holder to sell short a specified number of shares of a security or a futures contract at a specified price, within a specified period of time. Option traders will buy a put option when they believe the price of a security is going to decline because it locks in the selling price for the underlying assets at the higher, current level, guaranteeing a profit if the price goes down prior to the expiration date. If the price goes up instead of down, the trader's loss is limited to the cost of the option contract. Often referred to simply as a "Put." Compare to call option. See Expiration Date.

QUADRUPLE WITCHING WEEK The week beginning on Monday prior to the Saturday expiration of any four classes of option contracts. The week leading up to options expirations can be particularly volatile because as option holders scramble to exercise their option to buy or sell the underlying assets prior the closing bell on Friday afternoon. Options not exercised by that time will expire worthless, resulting in a loss for the option holder. See Double Witching Week; Options Calendar; Triple Witching Week.

ROLL DOWN To replace an option contract with one of the same class (put or call), the same expiration date, and a lower strike price. Compare to Roll Forward; Roll Up.

ROLL FORWARD To replace an option contract with one of the same class (put or call), a later expiration date, and the same strike price. Compare to Roll Down; Roll Up.

ROLL UP To replace an option contract with one of the same class (put or call), the same expiration date, and a higher strike price. Compare to Roll Down; Roll Forward.

STRIKE PRICE The price at which an option holder can exercise the right to buy or sell the underlying asset in the option contract. Also referred to as the Exercise Price. See Call Option; In the Money; Put Option.

TIME VALUE In options trading, time value is the amount an options buyer is willing to pay above the intrinsic value of the underlying asset.

TRIPLE WITCHING WEEK The week beginning on Monday prior to the Saturday expiration of any three classes of option contracts. The week leading up to options expirations can be particularly volatile as option holders scramble to exercise their option to buy or sell the underlying assets prior the closing bell on Friday afternoon. Options not exercised by that time will expire worthless, resulting in a loss for the option holder. See Double Witching Week; Options Calendar; Quadruple Witching Week.

UNDERLYING ASSET The specific security, financial instrument or commodity represented in a derivative. An option holder secures the right to buy or sell the underlying assets when purchasing an option contract. Likewise a futures trader buys and sells contracts promising to take or make delivery of the underlying asset at a future date.

Futures

AGGREGATION An accounting of all futures positions owned or controlled by one investor or a group of investors. Aggregation is used to determine applicable reporting requirements. Positions that exceed a certain level must be reported to the Commodity Futures Trading Commission (CFTC). See Commitment of Traders Report; Open Interest; Reportable Positions; Speculative Position Limits.

ALUMINUM An industrial metal traded on the futures market. A contract unit for aluminum equals 44,000 tons. Contract prices for aluminum move in minimum increments of $.0005, or $.05 per pound, which means that a $.01 move in the price equals $440 per contract. In general, the maximum daily price fluctuation is capped at $.20 per pound from the previous day's close.

BACKWARDATION See Inverted Market; Contango.

BASIS The price difference between the spot price and the futures price of the same commodity.

CASH MARKET See Spot Market.

CASH SETTLEMENT A process in which a futures or option contract is settled with an exchange of money rather than the delivery of the physical commodity. Financial instruments use a cash settlement process.

COMMITMENT OF TRADERS REPORT (COT) A Commodity Futures Trading Commission (CFTC) report that examines the open interest for market where 20 or more traders hold reportable positions. The COT is released each Friday at 3:30 p.m. (Eastern time) for reportable positions held as of the close of the trading session on Tuesday of the same week. See Aggregation; Open Interest.

COMMODITY A widely-used tangible product like oil, precious and industrial metals, and agricultural goods that are traded on the cash market or a futures exchange.

CONTANGO A market condition in which a futures or option contract is trading progressively higher for each forward-looking contract month. Compare to Backwardation; Inverted Market.

CONTRACT The vehicle for transacting futures and options trades. Each contract for a commodity or option is standardized by the exchange on which it is traded. See Derivatives.

A Closer Look at Standardized Futures Contracts

	Contract Unit	Minimum Price Movement (Tick)	Maximum Daily Price Fluctuation (above or below previous day's close)
Aluminum: NYMEX trading symbol AL	44,000 tons	$.0005 per pound or $.05 per contract	$.20 per pound or $8,800 per contract
Copper: COMEX trading symbol HG	25,000 pounds	$.0005 per pound or $.05 per contract	$.20 per pound or $5,000 per contract
Gold: NYMEX trading symbol GC	100 troy ounces	$.10 per troy ounce or $10 per contract	$75 per troy ounce or $7,500 per contract
Palladium: NYMEX trading symbol PA	100 troy ounces	$.05 per troy ounce or $5 per contract	None
Platinum: NYMEX trading symbol PL	50 troy ounces	$.10 per troy ounce or $5 per contract	$50 per troy ounce or $2,500 per contract
Silver: COMEX trading symbol SI	5,000 troy ounces	$.005 per troy ounce or $25 per contract	$1.50 per ounce or $7,500 per contract

CONTRACT MONTH 1) The month in which a futures contract begins to trade on the cash market. Futures traders who fail to offset their long or short positions prior to the expiration date face the prospect of having to take or make a delivery of the commodity or financial instrument. 2) The month in which an option contract will expire worthless if the option holder fails to exercise the option to buy or sell the underlying asset. See Default.

CONTRACT UNIT The quantity of the underlying asset represented by a derivatives contract. For example, a gold contract unit represents 100 ounces of the metal. Also called a Trading Unit.

COPPER (Trading symbol HG) An industrial metal traded as a commodity on both the spot and the futures markets. On COMEX, a contract unit of copper equals 25,000 pounds. Contract prices for copper move in minimum increments of $.0005, or $.05, per pound which means that a $.01 move in the price equals $250 per contract. There are exceptions, but the exchange will call a halt to trading if the price on copper fluctuates more than $.20 per pound ($5,000 per contract) above or below from the previous day's closes. See Minimum Price Movement.

CORNER The illegal practice of attempting to acquire sufficient holdings in a commodity to control its price.

DEFAULT The failure to perform according to the terms of a derivatives contract to meet a margin call or take delivery on the spot market.

DELIVERY The seller of a contract of a physical commodity or financial instrument conveys the physical product to the buyer. The majority of futures contracts are bought and sold with an intention of liquidating the position before it becomes necessary to deliver or take delivery of the underlying asset.

DELIVERY MONTH See Contract Month.

DISCOUNT A reference to the relationship between the futures price for a commodity in two different months. Example: "May pork bellies are trading at a discount to April," means that the May contract for the commodity is selling for less than the April contract.

EXOTIC CURRENCY Currency that is seldom traded on the foreign exchange market and consequently has little liquidity. See Hard Currency; Soft Currency.

FLOATING EXCHANGE CURRENCY A monetary system in

which the value of currency is determined by supply and demand. The U.S. Dollar, Pound Sterling, Euro, and Japanese Yen are examples of floating exchange currencies. Compare to Fixed Currency. See Foreign Exchange Market; Foreign Exchange Rate.

FOREIGN EXCHANGE MARKET The spot, options, and futures market for world currencies. See Foreign Exchange Rate.

FORWARD CONTRACT A cash contract to purchase and take delivery of a physical commodity. Forward contracts are written and exercised off the exchange. Compare to Futures Contract.

FULLY DISCLOSED ACCOUNT An account carried by a Futures Commission Merchant (FCM) in the name of the account-holder, rather than the name of an FCM. Compare to Omnibus Account.

FUTURES A market in which exchange-traded contracts commit buyers and sellers to the actual exchange of physical commodities or financial instruments at a future date and at an agreed-upon price. Businesses that use commodities in the manufacture or production of their products often use the futures market as a hedge against future adverse price changes. Most futures traders, however, employ futures contracts for speculative investing. In either case, a contract that is resold prior to the contract month averts an obligation to take or make a delivery of the underlying asset. The futures market is regulated and overseen by the Commodity Futures Trading Commission (CFTC). See Derivative.

FUTURES CONTRACT A written contract to buy or sell a physical commodity or financial instrument at a future date and at an agreed upon price. With the exception of price, all other terms of a futures contract are standardized for each product by the exchange on which they are traded. See Delivery; Derivative; Futures; Futures Exchange.

GAS AT THE PUMP FUTURES A futures contract on the retail price of gasoline. Gas at the Pump Futures contracts are traded on the CBOE Futures Exchange (CFE).

GOLD (Trading Symbol GC) A precious metal traded on the spot and futures market. On NYMEX a contract unit of gold equals 100 troy ounces. One tick in the price of gold is $.10 per troy ounce, or $10 per contract. There are exceptions, but in general, the exchange will call a halt to trading if the price of gold fluctuates more than $75 per troy ounce ($7,500 per contract) above or below the previous day's closing price. Maximum daily price fluctuations are lifted during the final 20 minutes of the trading day. See Minimum Price Movement.

INDEX FUTURES An investment in which buyers and sellers agree to pay or receive payment in the future for the cash value of an underlying stock index. See Derivative; Futures Contract; Cash Settlement.

INITIAL MARGIN The minimum account balance required before an investor will be approved to buy or sell a futures contract. Compare to Maintenance Margin. See Margin.

INVERTED MARKET A condition in the futures market in which the con-tract for the current month is trading at a higher price than for a future month. Also known as Backwardation. Compare to Contango. See Futures; Derivatives; Options.

LIMIT MOVE On the futures markets, the maximum price fluctuation for a given contract. A limit move is measured against the previous day's close and typically triggers a trading halt. See Locked Limit Down; Locked Limit Up.

A Closer Look at Limit Moves and Trading Halts

Maximum price fluctuations and trading halt triggers vary by the individual commodity or financial instrument and by exchange. Some halts are triggered when trading is sustained at a certain level for a specified period of time. Others are triggered when the best bid or offer falls outside the range of a maximum price fluctuation. Likewise, the duration of the halt can range from a few minutes to all trading day. Regardless of the trigger, the rationale behind a trading halt is always the same: To give traders a cooling off period, after which normal trading can resume with order prevailing over emotion.

On occasion, trading re-opens limit down or limit up and another trading halt ensues. More than a few futures traders have found themselves trapped in a losing position during a series of locked limit trading sessions. When trading eventually resumed, the lucky ones still had enough money left to buy a cup of coffee.

LOCKED LIMIT DOWN A phrase used to indicate that the highest current bid on a futures contract is below the maximum price fluctuation level. See Limit Move.

LOCKED LIMIT UP A phase used to indicate that the lowest ask for a futures contract is above the maximum price fluctuation level. See Limit Move.

MAINTENANCE MARGIN The minimum account value an investor is required to maintain to continue holding one or more futures contracts. The dollar value for maintenance margin varies by the specific commodity or financial instrument. An account that falls below the combined maintenance margin for all positions in the account will receive a margin call and be subject to full or partial liquidation. Compare to Initial Margin. See Margin.

MARGIN In futures and options trading, funds borrowed and used as a performance bond assuring that the investor will comply with the terms of any derivatives contracts bought or sold in the account. See Call Loan; Call Loan Rate; Call Money; Initial Margin; Margin Account; Margin Call; Maintenance Margin; Remargining.

MAXIMUM PRICE FLUCTUATION The largest amount a futures contract can move in a single trading session before triggering a trading halt. Maximum price fluctuation varies by individual commodity or financial instrument and is measured from the previous day's close. Maximum price fluctuations typically do not apply to the nearby delivery month. Also referred to as a limit move. See Circuit Breaker.

MINIMUM PRICE MOVEMENT The smallest price change increment for a futures contract. Also referred to as a tick, the minimum price movement for a given contract is set by the exchange and is standardized by the underlying product. For example, a tick in gold futures represents $.10 per troy ounce or $10 per contract, whereas a tick on silver futures represents $.005 per troy ounce or $25 per contract.

NEARBY DELIVERY MONTH The calendar month that is closest to the expiration date of a derivative. See Spot Month.

NOTICE DAY The day on which a clearinghouse announces a pending delivery of a futures contract.

OMNIBUS ACCOUNT An account carried by a Futures Commission Merchant (FCM) that combines the transactions of two or more individuals and is held in the name of another FCM. Compare to Fully Disclosed Account.

OPEN INTEREST The total number of futures and options contracts that have not expired or have not been exercised. The Commodity Futures Trading Commission (CFTC) uses open interest data to generate its weekly Commitment of Traders Report (COT).

PALLADIUM (Trading Symbol PA) One of the six metals that comprise the platinum group of metals. Because of palladium's unique catalytic properties, the bulk of the demand for it comes from the automotive industry. It is also used in electronic applications, dental alloys, and jewelry. On the NYMEX, the Palladium contract unit is 100 troy ounces. Palladium contracts move in $.05 minimum increments, or $5 per contract. Unlike gold, silver, copper, and aluminum, there are no limits on the daily price fluctuations for palladium.

PLATINUM (Trading Symbol PL) The most well-known of a group of six metals that bears its name and the rarest of the three primary precious metals (gold, silver and platinum). Jewelry and bullion accounts for the bulk of its demand, but all six metals in the platinum group possess conductive and catalytic properties that make them suitable for specialized applications in the automotive, chemical, petroleum, and computer industries. On the NYMEX, a platinum contract unit equals 50 troy ounces. Platinum contracts move in minimum increments of $.10 per troy ounce, or $5 per contract. Except for the contract month, which has no maximum price fluctuation, the exchange will call a trading halt on platinum if the price fluctuates more $50 per ounce ($2,500 per contract) above or below the previous day's close.

PRECIOUS METALS Rare metals, including gold, silver, platinum, and palladium that are traded on the spot and futures markets.

PYRAMIDING Using paper profits as margin to buy (or sell short) additional futures contracts in the same commodity. See Initial Margin; Maintenance Margin.

REPORTABLE POSITIONS The number of open positions in the futures market over and above the threshold that requires an accounting of long and short positions to the Commodity Futures Trading Commission (CFTC). See Commitment of Traders Report.

SILVER (Trading symbol SI) A precious metal traded on the spot and futures markets. On COMEX, a futures contract for silver equals 5000 troy ounces. Contract prices for silver move in minimum increments of $.005 per troy ounce, or $25 per contract. With some exceptions, the exchange will call a halt to trading on silver if the price fluctuates more than $1.50 ($7,500 per contract) above or below the previous day's close.

SINGLE STOCK FUTURES (SSF) A futures contract in which the underlying asset is a single security rather than the more typical index, Exchange Traded Fund (ETF) or basket of 100. See OneChicago LLC.

SPOT MARKET The market on which a commodity is purchased for immediate delivery. Also called the cash market. Compare to Futures Market.

SPOT MONTH See Nearby Delivery Month.

SPOT PRICE The cash price for immediate delivery of a commodity. Also called the Cash Price. Compare to Futures. See Spot Market.

VARIABLE LIMIT An exception to the maximum price movement limitations that some exchanges evoke under certain circumstances such as periods of high volatility.

WAREHOUSE REPORT A statement guaranteeing the existence of a physical commodity and verifying its availability and quality. The warehouse report is commonly used to transfer ownership.

CHAPTER SIXTEEN

Initial Public Offerings:
The Darling of the 90s

IPO The process by which a company's stock is offered for sale to the investing public for the first time. Also referred to as a New Issue.

ALL HANDS MEETING One of several pre-IPO planning meetings among the company's management, underwriter, outside accountants, and counsel for both the underwriter and the company. See Initial Public Offering; Registration Statement.

ALL OR NONE An Initial Public Offering agreement that can be cancelled by the lead underwriter if all of the shares are not subscribed. See Subscription.

ALLOCATION The number of shares to be offered to the public by the underwriter in an IPO. The underwriter assigns shares to clients, often on the basis of previous trading volume. See Initial Public Offering; Best Effort; Subscription.

BEAUTY CONTEST Executives from a company that is beginning the Initial Public Offering (IPO) process invite prospective underwriters from investment banks to tour the company. The company has two objectives going into a beauty contest: to invite interest from the underwriters by making a good impression and to identify the underwriter it believes will do the best job with the IPO.

BEST EFFORT An underwriting agreement in which the investment bank commits to making a best effort to sell Initial Public Offering (IPO) shares. Best effort agreements typically contain a provision that gives the underwriter the right to cancel the IPO if their best effort falls short of expectations. Compare to Bought Deal. See All or None.

BOOK RUNNING MANAGER The underwriter who has ultimate control and responsibility for an initial public offering. Also referred to as the Lead Underwriter. See Co-Underwriter.

BOUGHT DEAL A firm commitment by an underwriter to buy all of the shares a company will offer at an Initial Public Offering (IPO). Compare to Best Effort; All or None.

BREAK ISSUE See Broken IPO.

BROKEN IPO An Initial Public Offering (IPO) in which the security sells below the IPO price after it begins trading on the secondary market. Also referred to as a Break Issue. See Stabilization.

COMPARABLES A study of similar publicly traded companies performed by an investment bank for the purpose of establishing the offering price of an Initial Public Offering.

COMPLETION The declaration of a completed Initial Public Offering. Com-pletion typically takes place several days after the commencement of trading on the security.

CO-UNDERWRITER Any one of several secondary underwriters involved in an Initial Public Offering (IPO). Also referred to as the Co-Manager. Compare to Lead Underwriter.

DAY TO DAY (DTD) An Initial Public Offering (IPO) without a scheduled release date on the IPO calendar. A day-to-day designation typically means that some portion of the offered shares has not yet been subscribed and will probably be delayed.

DIRECT PUBLIC OFFERING (DPO) An Initial Public Offering (IPO) in which a company bypasses the underwriter and sells its shares directly to the public.

FINAL NEGOTIATIONS A process by which the company and the under-writers settle on an offering price and offering size for an Initial Public Offering (IPO).

FINAL PROSPECTUS The official document that includes a formal offer to sell a security, describes the enterprise, its management and details about the product offering such as voting rights assigned to the security, and discloses the financial state of the company and risks associated with the enterprise. Compare to Red Herring Prospectus.

FIRM COMMITMENT See Bought Deal.

FIRST DAY CLOSE The closing price for an Initial Public Offering (IPO) on the first day it trades on an exchange.

FORM S-1 A Securities & Exchange Commission (SEC) filing in which a private company declares its intention to sell its stock to the public. See Initial Public Offering (IPO).

GREEN SHOE A provision in an Initial Public Offering (IPO) underwriting agreement in which the company agrees to sell additional shares to the underwriter at the offering price for a stipulated period of time.

GROSS SPREAD The underwriter's profit in an Initial Public Offering (IPO). The gross spread is the difference between the offering price and the dollar amount the underwriter agrees to pay the issuing company.

GUN-JUMPING The intentional solicitation of interest in an initial public offer (IPO) prior to filing a registration statement. It is illegal and can result in substantial penalties.

HOT ISSUE An Initial Public Offering (IPO) in which demand exceeds supply. They are typically from high-profile companies.

INDICATION OF INTEREST A measure of investor demand for an Initial Public Offering (IPO). Indication of interest is one of several factors the underwriter will use to establish the offering price for the IPO.

INITIAL PUBLIC OFFERING (IPO) A process by which a company's stock is offered for sale to the investing public for the first time. Also referred to as a New Issue.

A Closer Look at an Initial Public Offering

The process of "going public" is long and complex one, but one that can be boiled down to four broadly-grouped stages, each of which is comprised of dozens of individual steps.

1) The company declares its intention to sell its stock to the public and gets the regulatory ball rolling by filing form S1 with the Securities & Exchange Commission (SEC).

2) The company signs an agreement with an investment banker who becomes the lead underwriters for the IPO. In other words, the issuing company agrees to sell a block of its stock to an underwriter (who may head up a group of underwriters referred to as a syndicate).

3) The Securities & Exchange Commission issues registration approval for the issue.

4) The underwriter offers the stock for sale on a stock exchange (the secondary market) where individual and professional investors begin buying and selling it.

IPO HALT A circuit breaker process to suspend trading temporarily on an Initial Public Offering (IPO) to prevent gaming. See Trading Halt.

LOCK UP PERIOD A period of time following an Initial Public Offering (IPO) in which company insiders are prohibited from selling their shares. The lock up period is established by contractual agreement between the company and the underwriters.

NEW ISSUE See Initial Public Offering.

OFFERING PRICE The price at which the underwriter of an Initial Public Offering offers to sell the new issue to the public.

OFFERING RANGE The upper and lower price estimates at which a company expects the underwriter to set the offering price. The offering range is included in the prospectus, but is not binding, as demand will ultimately determine the final offering price.

OFFERING SIZE The number of shares to be issued in an Initial Public Offering (IPO).

ORDER BOOK A list of investors who have subscribed to purchase shares of an initial public offering (IPO).

OVERSUBSCRIBED A situation in which demand for subscriptions for an Initial Public Offering (IPO) exceeds the offering size. An oversubscribed IPO will typically trade above the offering price when it begins trading on a stock exchange.

PENALTY BID A fee charged by some brokerage firms when a client sells Initial Public Offering (IPO) shares immediately after purchasing them. The penalty bid is the obligation of the client's broker and is intended to discourage them from making shares available to investors whose only interest is to make a quick profit on the IPO.

PRE-IPO PROSPECTUS See Red Herring Prospectus.

PRELIMINARY PROSPECTUS See Red Herring Prospectus.

PRIMARY MARKET A market in which the buyer acquires an asset directly from the original owner. In the stock market, shares sold by a company to an underwriter in an Initial Public Offering (IPO) are exchanged on the primary market. Compare to Secondary Market.

PROCEEDS The cash raised from an Initial Public Offering. The company's prospectus will disclose how it intends to use the proceeds.

QUIET FILING The filing of a registration statement with certain facts about the Initial Public Offering (IPO) intentionally omitted. A company might choose a quiet filing if management wants to get the process moving but hasn't resolved certain issues. See Form S-1.

QUOTE-ONLY PERIOD A period of time prior to trading on an Initial Public Offering (IPO) in which NASDAQ accepts buy and sell orders for the IPO. Orders can be canceled during the quote-only period.

RED HERRING PROSPECTUS A preliminary prospectus distributed prior to an Initial Public Offering (IPO) used to solicit interest in the company's securities. Also referred to as a Pre-IPO Prospectus. Compare to Final Prospectus.

ROADSHOW A series of meetings with investors, analysts, and investment firms conducted by a company's the executive staff (typically the CEO and CFO) prior to an Initial Public Offering.

STABILIZATION A commitment from the lead underwriter that the under-writing syndicate will continue to support the stock price after the Initial Public Offering (IPO) to keep it from dropping below the offering price.

SUBSCRIBE To commit to purchase shares issued at an Initial Public Offering (IPO). See Subscription; Subscription Period.

SUBSCRIPTION A commitment to purchase shares issued at an Initial Public Offering (IPO). See Oversubscribed; Subscribed.

SUBSCRIPTION PERIOD The period of time in which investors can commit to purchase shares of a security to be issued at an Initial Public Offering (IPO). See Initial Public Offering (IPO), Subsequent Distribution. See Oversubscribed; Subscribe.

Analysis Strategies: Identifying a Good Investment When You See It

CHAPTER SEVENTEEN

Fundamental Analysis: Cheap or Undervalued?

FUNDAMENTAL ANALYSIS The evaluation of a security's market value that takes into consideration the company's operations and financial performance.

ACQUISITION See Takeover.

ANALYST CALL See Conference Call.

ANALYST CONSENSUS A mean average of analysts' opinions of a company's estimated future financial performance or stock price. See Buy Side Analyst; Sell Side Analyst.

ANALYST COVERAGE Having one or more analysts actively tracking and publishing opinions on a company and its stock. Some investors believe that a company with analyst coverage benefits from more investment activity than a company without analyst coverage. See Initiate Coverage; Suspend Coverage.

ANTI-DILUTION PROVISION A provision in a corporate charter that gives shareholders a right to purchase additional shares of common stock if their percentage of company ownership is reduced through an increase of outstanding shares. See Diluted Earnings Per Share; Subsequent Distribution.

ANTI-TAKEOVER MEASURE Any action a corporation takes to discourage or prevent a hostile takeover, such as staggering terms for the board of directors and diluting the value of shares. See Poison Pill; Takeover.

ARTICLES OF INCORPORATION A document establishing a corporation and including information such as the name of the corporation, its purpose, the number and type of shares of stock the corporation will issue, the names and addresses of the initial board of directors and founders, and the company's street address. Sometimes referred to as a Charter. See Corporate By-laws.

AUDIT The inspection and verification of an organization's records and/or procedures. An audit can be internal or external. The external audit of the financial statement of a public company is required to be performed by a public accounting firm.

BANKRUPTCY An individual, business, or corporate declaration of insolvency under the provisions of the U.S. Bankruptcy Code. The various chapters within the bankruptcy code spell out the protections afforded to qualifying debtors. Federal courts have sole jurisdiction over bankruptcy proceedings. As with other bankruptcy filings, a corporation can choose to liquidate its assets and use the proceeds to pay its creditors or to reorganize and continue to do business. In some instances under a reorganization, some of the corporation's debt may be forgiven. The reorganization will be overseen by a court trustee until the company emerges from bankruptcy.

A Closer Look at Bankruptcy	
What Does it Mean?	**Who Can File?**
Chapter 7 The total liquidation of assets	Business or Individual
Chapter 9 Reorganization: assets retained, debts adjusted and paid down over time	Municipal *(cities, towns, villages, counties, taxing districts, municipal utilities, and school districts)*
Chapter 11 Reorganization: assets retained, debts adjusted and paid down over time	Business or Individual
Chapter 12 Debt Adjustment: assets retained, debts adjusted and paid down over time	Family Farmers and Family Fishermen

A Closer Look at Bankruptcy	
What Does it Mean?	**Who Can File?**
Chapter 13 Debt Adjustment *(Petitioner can keep home and other assets and pay down all or part of his or her debt over time)*	Individual
Chapter 15 Facilitates ancillary cases where the filing has taken place in another country	Business

BEAR HUG An offer to buy a company at a price that is so attractive that the board of directors (BOD) cannot refuse it without breaching its fiduciary responsibility to the shareholders.

BELLWETHER STOCK A security that is widely accepted as being representative of the market as a whole or an industry. At one time, the market watched AT&T, IBM, and General Motors. Today Microsoft, GE, and Intel are examples.

BLENDED PRICE A calculation of the weighted-average price per share in a two-tier tender offer.

BLUE CHIP STOCK A security issued by a company that is generally regarded as financially sound, stable, and with a dependable earnings and dividend track record.

BOTTOM FISHING A stock selection strategy that focuses on cheap stocks.

A Closer Look at Bottom Fishing
Fishermen know the bottom of a lake or ocean is inhabited by second- and third-rate fish and a few choice catches. The same could be said about stocks. When it comes to bottom fishing for quality stocks, the difference between investing and speculating is skilled fundamental analysis revealing whether a stock is undervalued or just cheap.

CHARTER See Articles of Incorporation.

CONFERENCE CALL A teleconference or live Web-hosted meeting among a company's executives, analysts, and investors. The exact format of a conference call can vary from company to company but generally includes a prepared statement by either the Chief Executive Officer and/or the Chief Financial Officer announcing the company's operating performance for the fiscal quarter, followed by a question and answer period. Also referred to as an Analyst Call.

CONTROL STOCK Sufficient shares owned by one shareholder or a company to hold a controlling interest in a company. See Holding Company; Corporate Raider; Diversified Holding Company; Holding Company; Takeover; Two-Tier Tender Offer.

CONTROLLING INTEREST The ownership of a sufficient number of shares of stock in a company to influence the actions of the board of directors (BOD). See Control Stock; Corporate Raider; Diversified Holding Company; Holding Company; Takeover; Two-Tier Tender Offer.

CORPORATE BY-LAWS Rules of operation for a corporate entity. Corporate by-laws assign responsibilities to the corporate officers, establish procedures for conducting board meetings, and spell out how, when, and where shareholders will vote on corporate business. See Articles of Incorporation; Corporate Governance.

CORPORATE GOVERNANCE The policies and procedures that govern the way a corporation conducts business, including the fiduciary responsibility of the board of directors (BOD) and corporate officers to act in the best interest of the shareholders. See Corporate By-Laws.

DOWNGRADE A lowering in an analyst recommendation for a security based on a change in the analyst's estimates for the company's earnings and/or stock performance. Compare to Upgrade. See Analyst; Buy Side Analyst; Sell Side Analyst.

DUE DILIGENCE (DD) A discovery and analysis of the risks associated with an investment. Conducting due diligence includes gaining an understanding of a company's financial condition, whether company insiders are buying or selling the stock they own in the company, current products and those that are under development, the company's competitors, and the factors that increase or decrease risk within the sector.

EARNINGS ANNOUNCEMENT The public announcement of a company's financial performance for the most recent fiscal quarter. The earnings announcement is typically accomplished with a press release issued by the company and followed by a conference call between company executives and analysts shortly afterwards.

EARNINGS CALENDAR A schedule of company earnings announcements. Earnings calendars are listed on a number of Web sites such as www.**finance.yahoo.com**, and **www.marketwatch.com**.

EX-DIVIDEND The period of time after a company declares a dividend and the time it is paid to shareholders. See Ex-Dividend Shares; Owner of Record; Record Date.

EX-DIVIDEND SHARES Stock that is bought during the ex-dividend period. Ex-dividend shares do not participate in the most recently declared dividend distribution, which are paid only to the owner of record on the record date.

FALLEN ANGEL A financially sound company whose stock is trading below its Initial Public Offering (IPO) price.

FIDUCIARY 1) A person or institution with a special relationship of financial trust or responsibility that obligates the fiduciary to fulfill certain duties in the best interest of others. 2) A special relationship of financial trust or responsibility. See Articles of Incorporation; Corporate By-Laws; Corporate Governance; Discretionary Account; Managed Account; Prudent Man Rule.

FLOAT The total number of shares of stock for a given company that are available to the trading public. Float is calculated by subtracting restricted shares from outstanding shares.

FORM 10K The audited annual financial report that publicly traded companies are required to file with the Securities & Exchange Commission (SEC) within 90 days of the close of the company's fiscal year. The 10K is the most comprehensive of the SEC-required filings and includes detailed information about the company's financial performance for the previous year. See EDGAR.

FORM 10Q An audited quarterly financial statement that publicly traded companies are required to file with the Securities & Exchange

Commission (SEC) within 45 days of each fiscal quarter. Compare to Form 10K. See EDGAR.

FORM 8Q A Securities & Exchange Commission (SEC) filing that reports material changes in a publicly traded company's operations. Compare to Form 10K; Form 10Q. See EDGAR.

FORM S4 A Securities & Exchange Commission (SEC) filing stating that a company wants to issue additional shares of its stock. See Subsequent Distribution. Compare to Form S1.

FRIENDLY TAKEOVER A corporate acquisition in which the board of directors (BOD) of the target company invites or welcomes the advances of the acquiring company.

FUNDAMENTAL ANALYSIS The evaluation of a security's market value that takes into consideration the company's operations and financial performance.

HOSTILE TAKEOVER A corporate acquisition in which the board of directors (BOD) of the target company resists the advances of the acquiring company.

ILLIQUID ASSETS Property and other holdings that cannot be readily converted to cash. Also referred to as Capital Assets. Compare to Liquid Assets.

INCENTIVE STOCK OPTION (ISO) An employer-sponsored stock option plan in which the tax burden from the option grant falls on the employee rather than the company. Unlike a non-qualified stock option in which the employer is taxed when the option is granted or exercised, with an ISO the employee is taxed on the capital gain (or loss) at the time the security is sold.

INDUSTRY A classification of business operations based on the type of goods or service produced: Industrial Mining and Minerals, Auto Manufacturers, Conglomerates. Investors often analyze a company's stock price and financial performance by comparing it to individual companies within the industry or the industry as a whole. Compare to Sector.

INITIATE COVERAGE To begin analyst coverage of a particular company and its stock. Some investors believe the number of analysts tracking and offering estimates on a security can correlate to increased investor interest in the stock. Compare to Suspend Coverage.

INTRINSIC VALUE The value of the underlying assets of an investment. Compare to Market Value. See Book Value; Options.

JUSTIFIED PRICE See Market Value.

LAST FISCAL YEAR A reference to the time for which earnings or other financial performance of a company is being measured. Compare Most Recent Quarter (MRQ); Trailing 12 Months (TTM); Year-over-year (YOY).

LEVERAGED BUYOUT The use of borrowed capital to purchase another company. A leveraged buyout allows the purchasing company to avoid tying up its own cash assets for the acquisition, typically by using stock in the target company as collateral to secure the loan.

LONG-TERM DEBT Debt obligations (loans, leases, bonds, debentures) with a due date at least 12 months out or longer. Compare to Short-Term Debt.

MARKET VALUE The price at which an asset can be bought or sold on the open market.

MATERIAL INFORMATION Any information about a company or its products that is likely to change the perceived value of a security when it is disclosed to the public. Bankruptcy filings, a change in the board of directors (BOD), corporate officers or public accounting firm, changes in the company's fiscal year, and revisions to financial statements are all examples of material information. See Insider Trading; Material Insider Information; Rule FD.

MERGER The union of two companies by acquisition or consolidation of assets.

MERGERS AND ACQUISITIONS A department or division of a financial services company that facilitates corporate mergers and takeovers. See Merger; Acquisition.

NON-QUALIFIED STOCK OPTION An employer-sponsored stock option plan that is relatively easy to set up and administer but that lacks the tax advantages of an incentive stock option plan. Also referred to as a Non-Statutory Stock Option.

NON-STATUTORY STOCK OPTION See Non-Qualified Stock Option.

OUTPERFORM An analyst rating reflecting an opinion that the price of a security will rise faster than the market as a whole, as measured by a broader market index.

OUTSTANDING SHARES The total number of investor-owned shares of a particular security, including both restricted shares and those that are available for purchase by the public. Shares that have been repurchased by the company are not included when calculating outstanding shares.

OVERVALUED A security whose price is expected to decline because it is trading above a price that can be justified by its current or estimated earnings, as measured by its price to earnings ratio. Compare to Undervalued.

PEER-PERFORM An analyst opinion that the price of a security will increase or decrease at roughly the same rate as the market as a whole, as measured by a broad-based index.

POISON PILL An anti-takeover provision employed by some corporations that allows shareholders of a target company to acquire additional shares of stock at a greatly discounted price, effectively slashing the value of the company. See Anti-Takeover Measure; Hostile Takeover.

PRICE The last price at which a security, options contract, or commodity trades during the trading session. Price is a component in a number of technical and fundamental analysis strategies. See Close; Last.

PROXY FIGHT A competition between a target company in a takeover bid and the acquiring company, in which both sides vie for control over the target's proxy statements. The objective behind a proxy fight is that ultimately one side will cast a majority share of the votes when shareholders decide on an offer to buy the company. See Friendly Takeover; Hostile Takeover.

Q1 (2,3,4) The abbreviation designating a specific quarterly reporting period within a company's fiscal year. See Fiscal Quarter.

RECORD DATE A snapshot date used to determine which shareholders qualify for dividend distributions. An investor must hold shares of stock on the record date to participate. See Ex-Dividend; Ex-Dividend Share.

RELATIVE VALUE The attractiveness of one investment in comparison to another.

SECTOR A subcategory of business within an industry.

SHARES AUTHORIZED The number of shares approved for issue, as authorized by the company's charter or a vote by its shareholders.

SHARES OUTSTANDING See Outstanding Shares.

SHORT INTEREST The percentage of shares held in short positions for a given security, calculated by dividing the number of shares held short by the number of outstanding shares. See Short Interest Ratio.

SLEEPER A stock that is trading well below its intrinsic value but that has not attracted widespread investor attention.

SPECIAL DIVIDEND A distribution of company profits to shareholders that is made either in addition to or at a higher rate than its regular dividend distributions.

SPIN OFF The process of establishing a subsidiary or division of a company as a separate entity by issuing shares of stock in the new company to shareholders in the parent company.

STOCK BUYBACK A strategy employed by companies in which they re-purchase their stock on the open market. A stock buyback can insert upward price pressure on a security because it reduces the supply of available shares. See Outstanding Shares.

STOCK RATING A designation by an analyst reflecting an opinion on the outlook for company earnings or stock performance.

STOCK SPLIT A measure taken by a company to increase in the number of its outstanding shares without altering its market capitalization or the ownership stake for each shareholder. A stock split is accomplished by dividing each share by a set ratio. In a two for one (2:1) split, for example each share is split into two shares. Therefore, an investor who owns 100 shares of a security that is trading at $80 before the split will own 200 shares of the same security after the split, with each one priced at $40. A company will typically announce a stock split whenever its stock price rises to a level that discourages investor interest. Compare to Reverse Stock Split.

SUBORDINATE DEBENTURE An unsecured debt instrument that is payable only after more senior debt has been satisfied. Because of the increased risk associated with a subordinate debenture, it typically earns a higher interest rate than either a senior note or a secured debt. See Debenture.

SUBSEQUENT DISTRIBUTION A company's offer to sell additional shares of its stock at some point after an Initial Public Offering (IPO). A subsequent distribution increases the number of outstanding shares. Compare to Secondary Offering. See Anti-Dilution Provision; Dilution.

SUSPEND COVERAGE To end analyst coverage on a particular security. Some investors believe the number of analysts tracking and offering estimates on a security can correlate to increased trading activity in the stock and that suspended coverage can cause the opposite effect. Compare to Initiate Coverage.

TAKEOVER The purchase of one company by another company. In the case of a publicly traded company a takeover is accomplished by acquiring a controlling interest in the target company. Also referred to as an Acquisition. See Bear Hug; Corporate Raider; Friendly Takeover; Hostile Takeover.

A Closer Look at a Takeover

A takeover can be either friendly or unfriendly. In the case of a friendly takeover, the boards of directors (BOD) of both companies agree on a selling price and cooperate in an orderly transfer of ownership. In a hostile takeover, the acquiring company purchases shares on the open market. Once a controlling interest has been secured, the acquirer is free to replace the opposing board of directors with one of its choice, completing the takeover process.

TAKE PRIVATE A move in which a company or a group of investors purchases all outstanding shares of a company's stock, returning it to a privately held company. A corporation sometimes takes the company private to eliminate the expense of regulatory compliance, or they change the enterprise in a way that makes it unattractive to investors.

TARGET PRICE An opinion of an analyst or investor about the future price of a security. Analysts typically offer target price opinions for the next 12 months.

TWO-TIER TENDER OFFER A strategy to acquire all of the outstanding shares of a company by offering to purchase a controlling interest in a company at one price and subsequently reducing the price per share offer for the balance. See Blended Price; Friendly Takeover; Hostile Takeover; Tender Offer.

ULTRA VIRES ACTIVITIES Corporate activities that are at odds with its charter. Ultra vires activities can expose the corporation to liability if shareholders believe the activities have adversely affected the company and its stock performance.

UNDERPERFORM An analyst rating for a security reflecting an opinion that its price will lag behind the market as a whole.

UNDERVALUED A SECURITY whose price is expected to rise because it is trading below a level that can be justified by its current or estimated earnings, as measured by its price to earnings ratio (P/E). See Bottom Fishing; Value Investing.

UNFRIENDLY TAKEOVER See Hostile Takeover.

UPGRADE An increase in an analyst recommendation for a security based on a change in the estimates for earnings and/or stock performance.

VALUE INVESTING A stock selection strategy in which an investor looks for undervalued securities. Compare to Technical Analysis. See Bottom Fishing; Price to Earnings Ratio (P/E).

WHISPER NUMBER An unpublished opinion within the investment community about a company's forthcoming earnings. Whisper numbers can mirror or contrast substantially with published analyst estimates.

Decoding Financial Statements: Seeing Beyond the Numbers

QUALITY OF EARNINGS A term used to distinguish between earnings associated with the company's primary operations versus those generated from financing and investing. See Core Earnings; S&P Core Earnings; Cash Flow Statement.

ACCOUNTS PAYABLE Monies owed by a company for the purchase of goods or services. Accounts payable are a component of current liabilities. Compare to Current Assets.

ACCOUNTS RECEIVABLE Monies due to a company for the sale of goods or services. Accounts receivable is a component of current assets. Compare to Accounts Payable.

ACCRUAL BASIS ACCOUNTING A method of accounting in which income and expense are recognized on the general ledger at the time they become owed, rather than when they are actually received, as is the case with cash basis accounting.

AFTER-TAX PROFIT See Net Income.

AMORTIZATION The reduction of debt through a series of payments over a set period of time. Amortization is carried as an expense on a company's books.

ANNUAL REPORT A comprehensive audited report on the financial condition of a public company that is provided to shareholders once a year. The annual report also includes such items as a summary of business activities for the past 12 months and disclosure of risk factors, pending legal proceedings, management changes, and forward looking statements. A report called the 10-K is a more detailed, electronic version of the annual report that is filed with the Securities & Exchange Commission (SEC).

ASSET Anything a company owns that has cash or economic value, such as real estate, equipment, prepaid expenses, accounts receivable, inventory, and goodwill.

BALANCE SHEET A snapshot statement of a company or organization's financial condition listing assets, liabilities, and net worth at the time of the report.

BOOKS A term commonly used to refer to a company's accounting records. See General Ledger.

BREAKUP VALUE A valuation for a company that considers the combined market capitalization of each of the firm's divisions that operate as separate publicly traded entities.

CAPEX See Capital Expense.

CAPITAL Assets that can be used to generate income.

CAPITAL ASSET An Asset that cannot be readily converted to cash. Also referred to as Illiquid Assets. Compare to Liquid Assets.

CAPITAL EXPENDITURE (CAPEX) An expense related to the purchase or improvement of business property, buildings, or equipment. Investors and economists watch capital expenditure rates for businesses as an indication of an economic expansion.

CAPITAL GOODS Raw material, property and equipment that is used to generate revenue.

CASH FLOW (CF) A measure of a company's financial condition calculated by subtracting cash outlays from cash receipts. Cash flow can be generated from operating activities, investments and financing. See Cash Flow Statement.

A Closer Look at Ways to Evaluate Cash Flow	
Cash Flow from Operations	Flow generated from the company's primary business operations. Does not include income or expenses related to investments or financing.
Cash Flow from Finance	Flow generated from obtaining bank loans and issuing debt instruments, such as bonds and debentures.
Cash Flow from Investments	Flow generated from various investments, such as rental income, interest received, and dividend distributions.
Cash Flow Return on Investments (CFRI)	Flow generated from investments, expressed as a percent of the capital invested.
Discounted Cash Flow (DCF)	An estimate of future cash flow on an investment after subtracting expenses, including the time value of money.
Cash Flow After Taxes (CFAT)	Flow from all sources calculated after subtracting the amounts paid in taxes.
Cash Flow Per Share (CFPS)	Net cash flow divided by outstanding shares.

CASH FLOW STATEMENT One of four reports that comprise a company's financial statement. The cash flow statement accounts for the company's inflow and outflows of cash during the reporting period, breaking it down by operating activities, investing activities, and financing activities. Investors pay particular attention to how much of the cash flow is generated by operations versus non-operations sources, like investments and the accumulation of debt.

CONSOLIDATED BALANCE SHEET A snapshot statement of the financial condition of a company and all of its subsidiaries, listing assets, liabilities, and net worth at the time of the report.

COST OF GOODS SOLD (COGS) The expense of raw materials and production costs to create a finished product. The cost of goods sold is a line item on a company's Income Statement.

A Closer Look at the Cost of Goods Sold	
+ Opening Inventory	+ $225,000
+ Materials/Products purchased	+ $350,000
- Ending Inventory	- $200,000
Cost of Goods Sold	= $375,000

COST OF SALES See Cost of Goods Sold.

CREDIT A journal entry recording an increase in assets. With cash basis accounting, credits are recorded when income is received. With accrual basis accounting, credits are recorded and recognized when income is earned. Compare to Debit.

CURRENT ASSETS Cash and other assets the company expects to convert to cash within one year, including accounts receivable and inventory. Current Assets is a line item on the balance sheet.

CURRENT LIABILITIES Debts and other obligations a company expects to pay off within one year. A line item on the balance sheet.

DEBIT A journal entry recording a subtraction from assets. With cash basis accounting, debits are recorded when a debt or other obligation is paid. With accrual basis accounting, debits are recorded and recognized when a debt or other obligation becomes owed. Compare to Credit.

DEBT OBLIGATIONS Loans, bonds, leases, and other debt instruments owed by a corporation. Debt obligations are carried on a company's books as a liability.

DEPOSITS PAID Funds paid out by a company as a demonstration of its intent to complete a transaction. Deposits paid are a component of Current Assets.

DEPRECIATION A non-cash expense that accounts for the decreased value of an asset due to wear and tear or age. Depreciation is a line item on a company's Income Statement.

DIVIDEND A periodic distribution of a portion of a company's earnings to its shareholders. Firms that pay dividends are typically mature companies that are no longer growing at a rate that provides incentives to investors in the form of significant increases in the price of their stock. Instead, they try to make the stock more attractive to investors through the payment of dividends. See Growth Stock, Income stock, Record Date; Ex-Dividend.

EARNINGS See Earnings Per Share (EPS); EBIDTA; Net Profit.

EQUITY The amount of money that would be left over if an asset were converted to cash and all liabilities against it paid. See Shareholder Equity.

EXPENSE An accounting transaction in which either a cash or non-cash asset is reduced. Rent, payroll, taxes, and amortization are all examples of an expense. Expense is the opposite of income.

FINANCIAL STATEMENT Audited documents that disclose a company's financial condition. There are four separate reports included in a company's financial statement: Balance Sheet, Income Statement, Statement of Retained Earnings, and Cash Flow Statement.

FINANCING ACTIVITIES A corporation's income and expense from activities such as selling stock and bonds, borrowing, paying off a bank loan. See Cash Flow Statement.

FISCAL QUARTER One of four three-month accounting periods that comprise a fiscal year for government, businesses, and other organizations. Publicly-traded companies are required to file a Form 10-Q disclosing their financial condition to the Securities & Exchange Commission within 45 days of the close of each fiscal quarter.

FISCAL YEAR (FY) A 12-month accounting period for government, businesses, and other organizations. The fiscal year is divided into four three-month fiscal quarters and may or may not coincide with calendar year. The fiscal year for the U.S. government runs from October 1 to September 30. Publicly traded companies are required to file their Form 10-K disclosing their financial condition to the Securities & Exchange Commission within 90 days of the close of their fiscal year. Common usage: FY06 represents a company's 2006 fiscal year. See Annual Report; Fiscal Quarter.

FIXED CHARGES Expenses that do not vary in relationship to the volume of business conducted.

FUNDED DEBT A company's debt obligations, such as bank loans, bonds, and debentures with a maturity date of more than one year.

GENERAL LEDGER The official accounting record for a company or organization in which the debit and credit balances are recorded for each account. Sometimes referred to as simply the company's books.

GENERAL PROPERTY TAX A tax on real estate and personal property.

GENERALLY ACCEPTED ACCOUNTING PRINCIPLES (GAAP) A set of standards that spells out how a company should keep its financial records, procedures for how audits are conducted, and the way financial statements are prepared. Each country has its own GAAP. The Financial Accounting Standards Board (FASB) establishes the generally accepted accounting principles that apply to U.S. corporations.

GROSS EARNINGS A calculation of a company's revenue from business operations before deducting associated expenses.

GROSS PROFIT A calculation of a company's revenue before subtracting the Cost of Goods Sold.

GROSS SALES Total sales revenue before deducting cash discounts, returns and freight.

INCOME An accounting transaction that increases a company's assets. Revenue received from the sale of goods and services, dividends, interest and rent are all examples of income. Income is the opposite of expense, which decreases a company's assets. See Net Income.

INCOME STATEMENT One of four reports that comprise a company's Financial Statement. The Income Statement is a declaration of revenue for the reporting period, expenses associated with earning it. The income statement is also where the company reports its earnings per share (EPS) and diluted earnings per share. Also known as a Profit and Loss Statement.

INTEREST A fee paid to a lender for the privilege of borrowing money. Interest is calculated by multiplying the principal by the quoted rate (percentage). See Interest Rate.

INVENTORY An accounting of stock on hand, including raw materials needed to produce finished products.

INVESTING ACTIVITIES A company's revenue and expenses from activities associated with investments, such as the purchase or sale of property and financial assets. See Cash Flow Statement.

JOURNAL ENTRY A record of a debit or credit transaction entered into a company or organization's accounting books.

LEDGER An accounting record of debits and credits by account.

LIABILITY See Current Liabilities.

LIQUID ASSETS Property and other holdings that can be readily converted to cash. Compare to Illiquid. See Capital.

LIQUIDITY The ease at which an asset can be converted to cash. See Liquid Assets; Quick Ratio.

NET INCOME A company's profit after deducting all expenses and taxes. Net profit is used to calculate a number of profitability and performance indicators. Also referred to as after tax profit, bottom line, net, or net profit.

NET SALES Revenue from the sales of goods and services after deducting cash discounts, returns, and freight from gross sales.

NET WORTH A measure of the intrinsic value of a company, measured by subtracting total liabilities from total assets. See Balance Statement; Shareholders' Equity.

NON-CASH EXPENSE An expense on an Income Statement that does not involve an actual cash transaction. Depreciation and amortization are examples of a non-cash expense.

OPERATING ACTIVITIES Revenue and expenses from activities that are directly related to a company's core business. See Cash Flow Statement; Core Earnings.

OPERATING INCOME Revenue generated from the company's primary business (making circuit boards or developing medical devices). See Core Earnings.

PREPAID EXPENSES Funds paid out by a company as prepayment for goods or services. Prepaid expenses are a component of Current Assets.

PRO FORMA A Financial Statement or an estimate of earnings that is based on an assumption of future events. [From the Latin pro forma, which translates literally as for form, but is used to indicate that something will be carried out in a particular manner.] Pro forma financial reports are sometimes used to present a picture of a company's financial condition if a merger or other major company restructuring were to take place and can vary greatly from numbers reported using generally accepted accounting procedures (GAAP).

PROFIT AND LOSS STATEMENT (P&L) See Income Statement.

QUALITY OF EARNINGS A term used to distinguish between earnings associated with the company's primary operations versus those generated from financing and investing. See Core Earnings; S&P Core Earnings; Cash Flow Statement.

REVENUE Income from sales of goods and services, dividends, interest and rent.

SALES, GENERAL & ADMINISTRATION (SG&A) An expense item on the Income Statement accounting for the cost of selling and marketing the company's products and for paying salaries, commissions, rent and other administrative costs.

SHAREHOLDERS' EQUITY A calculation of the amount of money that would be left over if all of the assets of the company were liquidated and all of the liabilities paid off. Also called the net worth or capital worth of a company. See Return on Equity.

SHORT-TERM DEBT A Debt obligation (loans, leases, bonds, debentures) that comes due within the 12 months. Compare to Long-Term Debt.

STATEMENT OF RETAIN EARNINGS One of four reports that comprise a company's Financial Statement. See Balance Sheet; Cash Flow Statement; Income Statement.

STOCKHOLDERS' EQUITY See Shareholders' Equity.

TOTAL CASH The sum of all of the cash a company has on its books, including petty cash and funds on deposit in a bank. Total Cash is a component of Current Assets.

TOTAL CURRENT ASSETS The sum of a company's total cash, accounts receivable, inventory, deposits paid, and prepaid expenses. Compare to Total Current Liabilities. Also See Current Ratio.

TOTAL CURRENT LIABILITIES The sum of a company's accounts payable, accrued salaries payable, payroll taxes payable, long-term debt, and other accrued liabilities.

CHAPTER NINETEEN

Equity Valuations:
It's All Relative

BASIC EARNINGS PER SHARE (EPS) A measure of a company's performance calculated by dividing its net earnings by its total number of outstanding shares.

ACID TEST RATIO A measure of a company's liquidity and by extension its ability to meet its current obligations. Acid test ratio is calculated by dividing the company's total liquid assets by total liabilities. Also referred to as Quick Ratio.

AVERAGE SHAREHOLDERS' EQUITY A five-month mean average of a company's Shareholders' Equity. See Return on Equity.

AVERAGE TOTAL ASSETS A five-month mean average of a company's total assets. See Return on Assets.

BASIC EARNINGS PER SHARE (EPS) A measure of a company's per-formance calculated by dividing its net earnings by its total number of outstanding shares. Also referred to as simply Earnings Per Share or EPS. Compare to diluted earnings per share; EBITDA.

BOND RATIO A method of measuring a company's indebtedness due to bond issues. Bond ratio is calculated by dividing the total bonds by the total market capitalization. The resulting percentage is the bond ratio. A lower bond ratio would represent a company that is less leveraged than one with a higher bond ratio.

BOOK TO BILL RATIO A ratio of the dollar value of a company's new orders booked to the amount it has shipped and billed. A ratio of

1 means that the company can fill and ship orders as quickly as they arrive. A ratio greater than 1 means that it has more orders than it can readily fill and a ratio less than 1 means that it has excess capacity to fill orders. The book-to-bill ratio is also tracked on an industry-basis and is widely used as an indication of the state of the semiconductor industry.

BOOK VALUE PER SHARE An accounting term that measures the intrinsic value of a single share of a company's stock. Book value is calculated by totaling the company's assets, subtracting all debts, liabilities, and the liquidation price of preferred stock, then dividing the result by the number of outstanding shares of common stock.

CASH ON CASH EQUIVALENT A valuation measure often used evaluate the performance of real estate investment trusts (REITs). Cash on cash equivalent calculates the return on cash invested and is calculated by dividing annual net profit by capital invested.

CORE EARNINGS A company's earnings from its core business operations. Calculated by totaling the revenue from its primary business (developing software) and subtracting expenses related to those operations. See Net Earnings; S&P Core Earnings.

A Closer Look at Core Earnings

Companies derive income from a number of sources not directly tied to their primary product or service. For example, a software development firm might lease a parcel of idle real estate, generating revenue unrelated to its core business. An examination of a company's core earnings can show an investor how successful the company has been at conducting its business as well as how it has performed in comparison to its competitors.

A Closer Look at S&P Core Earnings

Item	Included	Excluded
Adjustments for the reversal of prior years charges and provisions		X
Charges associated with goodwill impairment		X

A Closer Look at S&P Core Earnings		
Item	**Included**	**Excluded**
Charges for restructuring ongoing operations	X	
Charges for writing down, depreciating or amortizing operating assets	X	
Expenses for research and development purchases	X	
Expenses related to mergers and acquisitions	X	
Expenses related to Stock Option Grants	X	
Gains and losses generated from the sale of assets		X
Pension Costs	Limited to certain interest income	
Pension Gains		X
Revenue or expenses from insurance settlements or settling litigation		X
Unrealized gains and losses from hedging activities	X	

CURRENT EARNINGS PER SHARE (CURRENT EPS) An estimate of a company's basic earnings per share for the current year.

CURRENT RATIO A measure of a company's financial strength, calculated by dividing its total current assets by its total current liabilities.

DEBT TO EQUITY RATIO A measure of a company's relative financial strength, as measured by its degree of indebtedness. The debt to equity ratio is calculated by dividing the company's total long-term debt by shareholders' equity. The higher the resulting ratio, the lower the company's borrowing capacity and the greater the risk that the company might have difficulty meeting its obligations during a downturn in business.

DILUTED EARNINGS PER SHARE A measurement used to evaluate the quality of a company's earnings per share. Diluted earnings are calculated by adding convertible securities to outstanding shares and dividing that number into the company's net earnings. It is intended to convey a worst case scenario if every investor and employee with warrants, convertible debentures, and stock options exercised the option to convert them to outstanding shares. Compare to Basic Earnings Per Share.

DILUTION Anything that decreases a shareholder's proportional share of equity in a company, such as the issue of warrants and convertible debentures or an increase in the float through a subsequent distribution. See Diluted Earnings Per Share.

DIVESTITURE The sale or disposal of an asset. When a company sells off a division or subsidiary, it is said to have divested itself of the asset.

EARNINGS BEFORE INTEREST, TAXES, DEPRECIATION, AND AMORTIZATION (EBITDA) A useful measure of performance for a com-pany with large non-cash expenses like depreciation or amortization. Often used as an indication of the company's ability to meet their current debt obligations and acquire additional funding to finance growth. Calculated as: Revenue minus Expenses (excluding tax, interest, depreciation, and amortization).

A Closer Look at Earnings					
	Interest	Taxes	Depreciation	Amortization	Exploration Expense
NET	Included	Included	Included	Included	Included
EBITDA	Excluded	Excluded	Excluded	Excluded	Included
EBITD	Excluded	Excluded	Excluded	Included	Included
EBIT	Excluded	Excluded	Included	Included	Included
EBT	Included	Excluded	Included	Included	Included
EBI	Excluded	Included	Included	Included	Included
EBITDAX	Excluded	Excluded	Excluded	Excluded	Excluded

EARNINGS PER SHARE (EPS) Net profit for the trailing 12 months divided by outstanding shares. Compare to EBITDA.

EARNINGS SURPRISE An earnings announcement that varies substantially above or below analyst estimates or a company forecast.

EARNINGS WARNING A statement released by a company that it expects its next earnings announcement to fall below previous projections. See Earnings Surprise.

ENTERPRISE VALUE (EV) A measure of a company's market value from the standpoint of a takeover or acquisition. Unlike market capitalization, enterprise value takes into account the company's current debt. EV is calculated by adding together market capitalization and debt, which together equal the total outlay for the acquisition, and then subtracting the total cash and cash equivalents, which offset some of the acquisition costs.

ENTERPRISE VALUE TO EBITDA (EV/EBITDA) A measure of the intrinsic value of a security, calculated by dividing the company's takeover value by its Earnings Before Interest, Depreciation, Taxes, and Amortization (EBIDTA) for the trailing 12 months (TTM).

ENTERPRISE VALUE TO REVENUE A measure of a company's perfor-mance, calculated by dividing its takeover value by its revenue for the trailing 12 months (TTM).

RETURN ON EQUITY A measure of management effectiveness, calculated by dividing net income by average shareholders' equity.

FORWARD P/E An estimate of a company's price to earnings ratio (P/E) for the next 12 months.

FREE CASH FLOW (FCF) A measure of a company's financial strength, as measured by the amount of money it has left after paying its bills. Calculated by subtracting capital expenditures and dividends from cash flow from operations. A company can have a negative free cash flow if it is reinvesting its excess cash, so it bears examining whether a low (or negative) free cash flow number is caused by growth or an underlying financial weakness. See Cash Flow; Cash Flow Statement.

FULLY DILUTED EARNINGS See Diluted Earnings Per Share.

GROSS PROFIT MARGIN A measure of a company's profitability that is expressed as a percentage of gross profit. It is calculated by dividing gross profit by revenue.

LEVERAGE The amount of debt used by a business (or an investor) to control a large financial position with a relatively small amount of capital. Businesses often use bank loans, bonds, and other debt instruments to increase their ability to expand or develop new products. Investors use margin debt as leverage to take a larger position than would be possible with cash funding. Highly leveraged companies (and investors) face increased risk from unforeseen events.

MARKET CAPITALIZATION The value of a company in terms of its stock price. Capitalization is computed by multiplying the price of the stock by the number of outstanding shares.

MARKET SHARE The percentage of total revenue or unit sales for an industry or sector captured by one company.

MOST RECENT QUARTER (MRQ) A reference to the time for which earnings or other financial performance of a company is being measured. Compare to Last Fiscal Year (LFY); Trailing 12 Months (TTM); Year-over-year (YOY).

NET BOOK VALUE The value of an asset as it is carried on the company's books. Net book value is calculated by subtracting accumulated depreciation from the original cost of the asset.

NET PROFIT MARGIN A measure of a company's profitability calculated by dividing net income by net sales.

OPERATING MARGIN A measure of a company's profitability, calculated by dividing operating income by revenue.

PAYOUT RATIO A measure of what portion of company's earnings are returned to investors in the form of dividends. It is calculated by dividing the company's annual dividend payment by its net income. The trend of a company's payout ratio over several years is more meaningful that the ratio for a single year.

PRICE TO BOOK RATIO (P/B) A measure used to identify value stock investment opportunities. A company's price to book ratio is calculated by dividing its total market capitalization by its book value. Taken alone, the price to book ratio may or may not be meaningful. Compared with its competitors or the average for the industry or sector, the price to book ratio can identify a company that is undervalued and which might present an investment opportunity. Alternatively, P/B can be calculated on a per share basis, although the resulting ratio will be the same as for the company as a whole.

PRICE TO CASH FLOW RATIO A measure of a company's projected profitability, calculated by dividing price per share by cash flow per share (or market capitalization by cash flow). Like the price to earnings ratio (P/E), comparing a company's price to cash flow ratio to other companies within its sector can show how a company performs relative to its competitors. A lower ratio represents an expectation of greater profitability. See Cash Flow Statement.

PRICE TO EARNINGS RATIO (P/E) A measure of a company's relative market value, calculated by dividing the price per share by net earnings. A lower P/E when compared to other companies in the same industry can indicate that the security may be currently undervalued in the market. See Value Investing.

PRICE TO SALES RATIO A measure of a company's performance, calculated by dividing price per share by sales per share for the trailing 12 months (TTM). The price to sales ratio is particularly useful when evaluating a company with no earnings, especially when compared to other companies within the same industry. It can also be calculated on an enterprise basis by dividing market capitalization by revenue. See Value Investing.

PRIMARY EARNINGS PER SHARE An obsolete method of reporting earnings that is no longer recognized by accounting standards. It was replaced by basic earnings per share and diluted earnings per share.

PROFIT MARGIN See Gross Profit Margin; Net Profit Margin.

QUARTERLY EARNINGS GROWTH A measure of the rate at which a company's net earnings have increased during the previous fiscal quarter. While any increase in earnings might be viewed as positive for a company, on a quarterly basis investors are primarily concerned with whether the company reports earnings growth that matches what the company and analysts have forecast for the quarter.

QUARTERLY REVENUE GROWTH A measure of the rate at which a company's income has increased during the previous fiscal quarter. While any increase in revenue might be viewed as positive for a company, on a quarterly basis investors are primarily concerned with whether the company reports revenue growth that matches what the company and analysts have forecast for the quarter.

RETURN ON ASSETS (ROA) A measure of a management effectiveness, calculated by dividing after-tax income by average total assets.

RETURN ON EQUITY (ROE) A measure of a company's profitability, calculated by dividing net income by the shareholders' equity. Taken by itself, ROE may not be as useful as when it is compared to the ROE of other companies within the same industry.

REVENUE PER SHARE A calculation of the revenue for the trailing 12-months (TTM) divided by outstanding shares.

SALES PER SHARE A measure of a company's marketing efficiency, calculated by dividing revenue by outstanding shares.

SALES TO CASH FLOW RATIO A measure of a company's marketing efficiency, calculated by dividing sales per share by cash flow per share.

SHORT INTEREST RATIO A measure of how many days it would take for shares held in short positions for a given security to be liquidated. The short interest ratio is calculated by dividing the short interest by the security's average trading volume. A high short interest ratio can insert downward pressure on the price of the security because it indicates a negative bias in the market. When the ratio rises to an extreme level, however, it can indicate that the security is reaching an oversold condition.

TRAILING P/E A company's price to earnings ratio for the trailing 12 months (TTM).

TRAILING 12 MONTHS (TTM) A reference to the time for which earnings or other financial performance for a company is being measured, referring to the previous 12-month period. Compare to Last Fiscal Year (LFY); Most Recent Quarter (MRQ); Year-over-year (YOY).

YEAR-OVER-YEAR (YOY) A comparison of a company's current earnings or other financial performance with the same data for the previous year. Compare Last Fiscal Year (LFY); Most Recent Quarter (MRQ); Trailing 12 Months (TTM).

CHAPTER TWENTY

Bond Valuations:
All Debt is Not Created Equal

BOND PREMIUM The amount above face value (PAR) that a bond will bring on the open market. The bond premium is usually expressed as a percent and is calculated by dividing the bond's face value by its market value. See Bond Discount.

A RATING A bond rating assigned to an investment grade debt instrument. An A rating reflects an opinion that the issuer has the current capacity to meet its debt obligations and faces slightly higher solvency risk from changes in business, financial, or economic conditions than an AA-rated instrument. Bond investors rely on bond ratings from organizations like Standard & Poor's, Moody's Investors Service, and Fitch Ratings to evaluate the default risk associated with both corporate bonds and municipal bonds. Compare to AA Rating; AAA Rating; BBB Rating; Junk Bond.

AA RATING A bond rating assigned to an investment grade debt instrument. An AA rating reflects an opinion that the issuer has the current capacity to meet its debt obligations and faces slightly higher solvency risk from changes in business, financial, or economic conditions than an AAA-rated instrument. Bond investors rely on bond ratings from organizations like Standard & Poor's, Moody's Investors Service, and Fitch Ratings to evaluate the default risk associated with both corporate bonds and municipal bonds. Compare to A Rating; AAA Rating; BBB Rating; Junk Bond.

AAA RATING A bond rating assigned to an investment grade debt instrument. AAA is the highest possible rating and reflects an opinion that the issuer has the current capacity to meet its debt obligations and has an extremely low solvency risk from changes in business, financial, or economic conditions. Bond investors rely on bond ratings from organizations like Standard & Poor's, Moody's Investors Service, and Fitch Ratings to evaluate the default risk associated with both corporate bonds and municipal bonds. Compare to A Rating; AA Rating; BBB Rating; Junk Bond.

ABOVE PAR A condition in which a bond trades above its face value. A bond typically trades above par when demand for it increases because it has a yield that is higher than current interest rates.

AD VALOREM TAX A tax that is based on the assessed value of real or personal property. Real estate taxes and sales tax are examples of ad valorem taxes. Municipal bonds are sometimes retired by the assessment of ad valorem taxes. Compare to Fixed Rate Tax.

AFTER-TAX BASIS A measure of return on investment for taxable bonds that calculates the cost basis by subtracting the taxes paid from the bond's yield.

ASSIGNMENT FORM A form that is to transfer ownership of a bond from one bond holder to another. The assignment form is typically printed on the back of the certificate. See Bond Power.

B RATING A bond rating assigned to a moderately speculative debt instrument. A B rating reflects an opinion that the issuer has the current capacity to meet its debt obligations but faces more solvency risk than a BB-rated issue and less than a B-rated issue if business, financial, or economic conditions change measurably. Bond investors rely on bond ratings from organizations like Standard & Poor's, Moody's Investors Service, and Fitch Ratings to evaluate the default risk associated with both corporate bonds and municipal bonds. Compare to AAA Rating, BB Rating, B Rating; Junk Bond.

BACKDOOR BORROWING The government practice of issuing debt instruments without voter approval, often to get around legislatively enacted debt restrictions.

BB RATING A bond rating assigned to a somewhat speculative debt instrument. A BB rating reflects an opinion that the issuer has the current capacity to meet its debt obligations but faces more solvency risk than an A-rated issue and less than a BBB-rated issue if business, financial, or economic conditions change measurably. Bond investors rely on bond ratings from organizations like Standard & Poor's, Moody's Investors Service, and Fitch Ratings to evaluate the default risk associated with both corporate bonds and municipal bonds. Compare to AAA Rating, BBB Rating, B Rating; Junk Bond.

BBB RATING A bond rating assigned to an investment grade debt instrument. A BBB rating reflects an opinion that the issuer has the current capacity to meet its debt obligations but faces more solvency risk than an A-rated issue and less than a BB-rated issue if business, financial, or economic conditions change measurably. Bond investors rely on bond ratings from organizations like Standard & Poor's, Moody's Investors Service, and Fitch Ratings to evaluate the default risk associated with both corporate bonds and municipal bonds. Compare to AAA Rating, BB Rating, B Rating; Junk Bond.

BOND CALENDAR A schedule of forthcoming bond issues.

BOND CERTIFICATE A printed document certifying a debt owed. A bond certificate typically includes the issuer's name, the face value, interest rate, maturity date the interest payment schedule.

BOND CONVERSION The process of swapping of a convertible bond for another asset, typically shares of common stock. The conversion terms are spelled out in the bond indenture.

BOND DISCOUNT The amount below face value (PAR) that a bond will bring on the open market (market value). Bond discount is usually expressed as a percent and is calculated by dividing the market value by the face value.

BOND DIVIDEND A dividend distribution that is paid to shareholders in the form of a bond instead of cash.

BOND POWER A form used in lieu of the assignment form to transfer ownership of a bond from one bond holder to another.

BOND PREMIUM The amount above face value (PAR) that a

bond will bring on the open market. The bond premium is usually expressed as a percent and is calculated by dividing the bond's face value by its market value. See Bond Discount.

BOND RISK PREMIUM The increased interest rate a bond issuer pays on a higher-risk debt instrument to attract investor interest. See Bond Rating; Junk Bond.

BOND SWAP An investment strategy in which a bond holder sells one bond while simultaneously purchasing another one. A bond swap is often used for tax purposes or to extend maturity dates.

C RATING A junk bond rating assigned to fairly speculative debt instruments. A C rating indicates an opinion that the issuer has the current capacity to meet the debt obligation, but investors face notable risk if business, financial, or economic conditions change measurably. Bond investors rely on bond ratings from organizations like Standard & Poor's, Moody's Investors Service, and Fitch Ratings to evaluate the default risk associated with both corporate and municipal bonds. Compare to Investment Grade.

CALL DATE The date at which the issuer of a callable bond has the right to retire the debt by repurchasing the bond before the maturity date. See Indenture.

CALL PROVISION Language in the bond indenture stipulating the terms under which a bond issuer can retire the debt by repurchasing the bond before the maturity date. See Callable Bond; Call Date.

CC RATING A junk bond rating assigned to fairly speculative debt instruments. A CC rating indicates the issuer is at greater risk of default than a CCC-rated issue and less than a C-rated issue if business, financial, or economic conditions change measurably. Bond investors rely on bond ratings from organizations like Standard & Poor's, Moody's Investors Service, and Fitch Ratings to evaluate the default risk associated with both corporate bonds and municipal bonds. Compare to Investment Grade.

CCC RATING junk bond rating assigned to fairly speculative debt instruments. A CCC rating indicates the issuer is at greater risk of default than a B-rated issue and less than a CC-rated issue if business, financial, or economic conditions change measurably. Bond investors rely on bond ratings from organizations like Standard & Poor's, Moody's Investors Service, and Fitch Ratings to evaluate the default risk associated with both corporate and municipal bonds. Compare to Investment Grade.

COLLATERAL Assets used to secure a loan.

COUPON RATE The interest rate paid on a bond. Also called the Yield Rate.

DEFAULT RISK The likelihood that a corporation or government bond issuer will fail to repay its debts. Bond ratings from services such as Standard & Poor's, Moody's Investors Service, and Fitch Ratings provide investors with a means of evaluating the issuer's creditworthiness and by extension the default risk for a given bond.

DUTCH AUCTION An auction system in which the price of an item offered for sale is incrementally reduced to establish the highest price at which a buyer will purchase it. The Dutch auction is used at U.S. Treasury auctions and sometimes to establish the offering price for an Initial Public Offering (IPO).

FACE VALUE The amount that a bond holder will receive from the issuer at redemption. The face value of a bond is only one factor determining the value of a bond on the secondary market. Investors will often pay more than face value for an existing bond with higher yield than is available on a new issue. See Par.

FALLEN ANGEL A bond that was previously rated investment grade but has fallen to junk bond status. See Bond Rating.

FITCH RATINGS A business credit research and ratings firm. Fitch Ratings issues creditworthiness opinions for the bond, Eurobond, and funds markets. Compare to Moody's Investors Service and Standard & Poor's. See Bond Rating.

FIXED RATE TAX A tax that is set at a certain amount and does not vary according to the value of the item being taxed. For example, U.S. consumers pay a federal tax on gasoline at the pump that is levied on a per gallon basis. Compare to Ad Valorem Tax.

GILT EDGED BOND An investment grade debt instrument issued by with rock-solid financials. Compare to Blue Chip Stock.

INVERTED YIELD CURVE A situation in which long-term debt instruments are returning a lower yield than short-term notes, resulting in a downward tilting yield curve. An inverted yield curve is generally seen as an indication that investors foresee an economic downturn. Compare to Normal Yield Curve.

LIMITED TAX BOND A municipal bond that is backed by a specific tax.

LOW GRADE BOND A bond at high risk for default. A low-grade bond is typically issued by a company experiencing financial difficulty or one that lacks sufficient history to prove itself creditworthy. See Investment Grade; Junk Bond.

MOODY'S INVESTMENT GRADE (MIG) A bond rating assigned by Moody's Investors Service to low risk, short-term bonds. Moody's investment-grade ratings are classified as MIG 1, MIG 2, or MIG 3, with MIG 1 being reserved for the most creditworthy bond issuers.

NET INTEREST COST (NIC) A calculation of the net cost of issuing debt. It is used most frequently by bond issuers to choose between competing underwriters.

NORMAL YIELD CURVE A situation in which long-term debt instruments are returning a higher yield than short-term notes, resulting in an upward tilting yield curve. Compare to Inverted Yield Curve.

ORIGINAL ISSUE DISCOUNT (OID) A discount from par issued at the time a bond is purchased. OID is treated as interest income for tax purposes.

REDEMPTION FEE A fee charged at the time a bond, mutual fund, or preferred stock is redeemed. Unlike the back-end load charged by some mutual funds, the redemption fee is used to cover operating costs and not paid to the broker.

REFUNDING RISK The risk to yield faced by a bond holder if the issuer calls back the debt prior to the maturity date and a similar interest rate cannot be secured in another investment. See Callable Bond; Called Date.

SENIOR DEBT A debt obligation that has priority for repayment over other debts in case of bankruptcy. See Junior Note; Senior Note.

SENIOR NOTE A promissory note that holds priority for repayment over other debts in case of bankruptcy. Also referred to as Senior Debt. Compare to Junior Note; Subordinate Debenture.

SINKING FUND PROVISION A requirement for certain bond issuers to buy back a portion of its debt at regular intervals. The bonds can be bought by the issuer on the secondary market or directly from bond holders. A sinking fund provision will be disclosed in the indenture. See Refunding Risk; Callable Bond.

UNSECURED DEBT A debt obligation that is backed only by the creditworthiness of the issuer and is not secured by a specific asset. See Convertible Debenture; Debenture; Subordinate Debenture.

WEIGHTED AVERAGE CREDIT RATING A method of assessing the risk level of a bond fund based on credit ratings of the holdings within the bond's portfolio.

YIELD CURVE A graph that plots the yield on a number of similar fixed income debt instruments with different maturity dates. See Inverted Yield Curve; Normal Yield Curve.

YIELD RATE See Coupon Rate.

CHAPTER TWENTY-ONE

Technical Analysis: Using the Past to Predict the Future

TECHNICAL ANALYSIS The use of price charts and statistical analysis to make assumptions about future price movements.

ADVANCE/DECLINE RATIO (A/D) An often quoted technical indicator that measures market breadth. The A/D ratio is calculated by dividing the number of advancing issues by the number of declining issues, with a ratio of 1 to 1 reflecting a neutral bias in the broader market. Technicians interpret any ratio that indicates that advances outnumber declines (2 to 1) as evidence of an overall bullish sentiment. Conversely, a technician would see a market in which declining issues outnumber advancing issues as having a bearish bias. Like the advance/decline line (A/D or AD), the periodicity in which an investor calculates the A/D ratio can vary from every few minutes (intraday) to daily, weekly, or longer.

ADVANCE/DECLINE SPREAD A market breadth indicator that is calcu-lated by subtracting the declining issues from advancing issues. See Advance/Decline Line; Advance/Decline Ratio; TRIN.

ADVANCING ISSUES The number of securities that have increased in price during a specified period of time, typically one day or one week. Technicians use advancing issues to calculate the advance/decline ratio and the advance/decline line. See Breadth-of-Market Indicator; Declining Issues; Market Bias.

ADVANCING VOLUME The number of shares traded on stocks that gained in price during a given period (intraday, daily, or weekly). Advancing volume is a technical indicator used to measure market breadth and calculate the upside/downside ratio. Compare to Declining Volume.

BEAR CORRECTION A temporary price retracement in a declining market. Compare to Bull Correction. See Bear; Bull; Correction; Market Cycle.

BEAR CYCLE See Bear Market.

BEAR RALLY A short-term rise in stock prices during a bear market. See Correction.

BEAR SQUEEZE A situation that occurs when sellers are trapped in a rising market. When the pressure from increasing losses mounts, they begin to buy their way out of their losing positions which fuels the upward price momentum and further panic buying among the shorts that are still in the market. A professional trader will sometimes try to take advantage of a bear squeeze by buying long into the upward price pressure and then selling short when the momentum begins to weaken. He will then ride the price back to a correction point, take his profit, and reenter the market as a buyer. Compare to Bull Squeeze. See Bear Trap; Bull Trap; Whipsaw.

BEAR TRAP A situation in which investors who sold short near the bottom of a down cycle find themselves trapped when the market unexpectedly reverses. As longs begin to enter the market, the shorts start buying their way out of their losing positions, which further fuels the upward price momentum and panic buying for the remaining short-sellers who are still in the market. When the short covering is complete, the upward momentum slows and the market often resumes its downward trend. Compare to Bull Trap. See Whipsaw.

BEARISH DIVERGENCE A situation in a bear cycle when two technical indicators move in opposite directions and signal a near-term turning point in the trend. Technicians often watch for divergence between the price of a security and its relative strength index. Compare to Bullish Divergence.

BETA A measure of price volatility relative to the broader market. A security with a beta above 1 indicates that it is more volatile than the

S&P 500. A beta below 1 indicates that it is less volatile.

BLOW-OFF TOP A topping out of the market created when a period of generally rising prices suddenly experiences a rapid increase in both price and volume followed by an equally rapid reversal. Compare to Capitulation. See Short Squeeze.

A Closer Look at a Blow-off Top

The blow-off is often triggered by news and is fueled by a sudden spike in buying when the short-sellers "give up" their bearish sentiment and accept that the price is going higher. It ends when the blow-off runs into selling created by profit-taking on the long side joining forces with a new surge in short-selling. A blow-off can take place in a single security or the market as a whole and is considered by technicians as one of the most reliable bearish indicators.

BOTTOM A range of trading at or near the lowest price within a market cycle before reversing and beginning an uptrend. See Correction; Cup with Handle; Double Bottom; Head and Shoulders; Reversal; Reverse Head and Shoulders; Rounded Bottom; Triple Bottom; V Bottom.

BOX SIZE The user-specified price-change that triggers the addition of an X or O on an existing column in a point and figure chart.

BREADTH-OF-MARKET INDICATOR A measure of the number of different securities being traded. Technicians watch a number of technical indicators that measure breadth of market in the belief that when the market moves up or down, the trend is likely to be more substantial and sustained if a large number of issues participate in the move.

BREAKAWAY GAP A blank space above or below the price bars on a price chart that is formed on a breakout from a major chart pattern and is accompanied by high volume. Technicians view a breakaway gap as signaling a major price move. See Exhaustion Gap; Gap Opening; Runaway Gap.

BULL CORRECTION A temporary price retracement in a rising market. Compare to Bear Correction. See Bear; Bull; Correction; Market Cycle.

BULL SQUEEZE A situation that occurs when buyers are trapped in a declining market. When the pressure from increasing losses mounts, they begin to sell their way out of their losing positions fueling the downward price momentum and further panic selling among the longs that are still in the market. A professional trader will sometimes try to take advantage of a bull squeeze by selling short into the downward price pressure and buying long when the momentum begins to weaken. He will then ride the price back to a correction point, take his profit, and reenter the market as a seller. Compare to Bear Squeeze. See Bear Trap; Bull Trap; Whipsaw.

BULL TRAP A situation in which investors enter long positions near the top of an up cycle. When the market unexpectedly reverses, buyers begin to sell their way out of their losing positions creating downward price momentum and panic selling among the remaining longs still in the market. When the selling complete, the market often resumes its upward trend. Compare to Bear Trap. See Bull Squeeze; Bear Squeeze; Whipsaw.

BULLISH DIVERGENCE A situation in a bull cycle when two technical indicators move in opposite directions and signal a near-term turning point in the trend. Technicians often watch for divergence between the price of a security and its relative strength index. Compare to Bearish Divergence.

CAPITULATION A bottoming out of the market created when a period of declining prices drops suddenly accompanied by high volume, followed by an equally rapid reversal. Compare to Blow-off Top; See Bull Squeeze.

A Closer Look at Capitulation

A capitulation is sometimes triggered by news and is fueled by a sudden spike in panic selling as investors "give up" their bullish sentiment and accept that a bear market trend is under way. It ends when the capitulation runs into buying created by profit-taking on the short side joining forces with a new surge of buying.

A capitulation can take place in a single security or the market as a whole and is considered by technicians as one of the most reliable bullish indicators because it typically precedes a reversal.

CLOSE The last price at which a transaction takes place in a trading session. Compare to Open. See Maximum Price Fluctuation.

CLOSING RANGE The highest and lowest prices at which trades occurred during the market close.

CONGESTION A period of trading that takes place in a relatively narrow range, without a significant increase or decrease in the price of the security or index. See Flat Market; Trading Range.

CONVERGENCE A price movement characterized by the narrowing of the difference between the futures price and the spot price of a commodity.

DECLINING ISSUES The number of securities that have decreased in price during a specified period of time, typically one day or one week. Technicians use declining issues to calculate the advance/decline ratio and the advance/decline line. See Breadth-of-Market Indicator; Advancing Issues; Market Bias.

DECLINING VOLUME The number of shares traded on stocks that declined in price during a given period (intraday, daily, or weekly). Declining volume is a technical indicator used to measure market breadth and to calculate the upside/downside ratio. Compare to Declining Volume.

DIVERGENCE A situation in which two technical indicators move in opposite directions. A divergence can signal a change in market strength and a potential reversal. See Bearish Divergence; Bullish Divergence; MACD; Relative Strength Index.

ELLIOTT WAVE THEORY A technical analysis theory developed by Ralph Nelson. Nelson believed that stock prices move in a cycle of five waves followed by a correction cycle of three waves. He believed that prices movements can be predicted by identifying the wave patterns on stock charts.

EXPONENTIAL MOVING AVERAGE (EMA) The price-weighted

moving average for the price of a security or an index for a given period of time. An EMA differs from a simple moving average in that it attaches more significance to recent data, making it more sensitive to early indications of a change to the current trend. Typically a 26-day or 12-day EMA is used for analyzing short-term trends and a 50-day or 200-day EMA is used for long-term trends. EMAs are used in a number of technical analysis tools, with the MACD being the most popular. Technical analysis programs calculate EMA automatically based on values input by the user.

FAIR VALUE The theoretical value of the S&P 500 futures after deducting the cost of owning the contract versus owning the physical stocks (compound interest and lost dividends). Fair Value is used to predict the direction of trading in the broader market during the first few minutes after the opening bell. When the S&P Futures trade above fair value, it indicates an initial bias toward a rise in stock prices. Likewise, when they trade below fair value, it indicates an initial bias toward a decline in stock prices. Fair Value is quoted on the Chicago Mercantile Exchange (CME).

52-WEEK HIGH The highest price at which a security traded during the previous year. Compare to 52-Week Low.

52-WEEK LOW The lowest price at which a security traded during the previous year.

FLAT MARKET A trend in which the trading range for the broader market does not move either higher or lower, but instead trades within the boundaries of recent highs and lows. A flat market signals lagging investor interest as market participants await an indication regarding the direction of the next move. See Congestion.

HIGH The highest price at which a trade occurred during a trading session.

INTRADAY TRADING Trading that takes place after the opening bell and before the closing bell of one trading day.

LOW The lowest price at which a trade occurred in a trading session.

MAX PAIN™ A trademarked technical analysis tool that calculates the point at which the maximum loss on an option contract would occur. It is based on the theory than 90 percent of all option contacts expire unexercised resulting in a loss for the option holder.

MOMENTUM The rate of change in the price or volume of a security or index. Some technicians believe that a move accompanied by increased momentum will continue until it runs out of buyers (long) or sellers (short). See Momentum Investor.

MOST ACTIVES A technical indicator that lists securities with the most number of shares traded in a given period of time. Most actives are usually tracked by the day and week.

MOVING AVERAGE (MA) The average price of a security or index for a given period of time, typically 50 or 200 days, although Bollinger Bands uses a 20-day moving average. MA can be calculated as an exponential moving average (EMA) or as a simple moving average calculated by adding together the closing price over "n" periods and dividing by "n." Each time the period advances, the calculation is updated to include the data from the most recent "n" periods. In common usage, unless EMA is specified, a simple moving average is assumed.

OPEN The price at which the first trade for a security takes place in a trading session. Compare to Close.

OPENING RANGE The highest and lowest prices at which trades occur during the market open.

OVERBOUGHT A condition in which the price of a security has risen to a higher point than can be sustained from a technical analysis perspective. A technician will typically expect a stock that is overbought to enter a correction cycle. Compare to Oversold.

OVERSOLD A condition in which the price of a security has fallen below a point than can be sustained from a technical analysis perspective. A technician will typically expect a stock that is oversold to enter a correction cycle. Compare to Overbought.

TECHNICAL ANALYSIS The use of price charts and statistical analysis to make assumptions about future price movements.

TECHNICAL INDICATOR A technical analysis tool for measuring and interpreting market behavior. Technical indicators can measure any number of factors, including the number of shares traded, the ratio of stocks rising to those declining, and the number of stocks making a new high or low.

THIN MARKET A market characterized by low volume and a wide spread between the best bid and best ask.

TICK INDEX A technical indicator that interprets market sentiment by subtracting the number of stocks trading on a downtick from the number of stocks trading on an uptick. A positive number reflects a bullish sentiment and negative number reflects a bearish sentiment.

TIGHT MARKET A market characterized by high volume and a narrow spread. A tight market is a sign of a highly-competitive market with strong participation by both buyers and sellers.

TRIN A market breadth indicator based on the relationship between the advance/decline spread and the volume of those stocks. It is calculated by dividing the advance/decline ratio by the upside/downside ratio. TRIN is an acronym for Trading Index and is also known as the Arms Index, named for its developer, Richard W. Arms, Jr.

A Closer Look at TRIN

TRIN measures the internal strength of market for a given period of time, typically the current trading day. It is recalculated on a minute-by-minute basis and is published on the Web site of the New York Stock Exchange and various financial news sites. To understand it better it is helpful to look at the calculation.

Advance/Decline Ratio ÷ Upside/Downside Ratio

[Where Advance/Decline Ratio = Advancing Issues divided by Declining Issues and

Upside/Downside Ratio = Advancing Volume divided by Declining Volume]

UPSIDE/DOWNSIDE RATIO A market breadth indicator that is calculated by dividing advance volume by declining volume.

VOLATILITY The tendency of the price of a security to make large, frequent moves. See Beta.

VOLUME The number of shares traded on a given exchange or in a single security or index. High volume is generally regarded as an indication of investor enthusiasm and low volume is taken as a sign of investor lethargy. Volume is a component of many technical analysis tools.

A Closer Look at Volume

Taken by itself high volume means little more than the presence of a healthy number of both buyers and sellers willing to enter the market. Low volume indicates a shortage of one or the other sometimes both. Factored along with price movement, high volume can be used to confirm the direction of a trend or detect a trend reversal. It can also entice traders into the dangerous waters of blow-off top, in which prices rise rapidly on high volume only to reverse just as rapidly when the market runs out of buyers.

CHAPTER TWENTY-TWO

Charting:
More Than Pretty Pictures

CHART A graph on which trading prices for a security index or commodity is recorded. Technicians use charts to analyze historical price performance and make assumptions about future price movements. See Bar Chart; Candlestick Chart; Point and Figure Chart.

ADVANCE/DECLINE LINE (A/D or AD) A widely used technical indicator that plots the difference between the number of declining issues and advancing issues for a specific period of time (intraday, daily, or weekly). It is calculated by subtracting the declining issues from advancing issues and adding the result to the previous day's number. Technicians use advance/decline line charts as a breadth-of-market indicator to detect early signs of a change in the market bias. See Advance/Decline Ratio.

A Closer Look at Advance/Decline Lines

The advance/decline line is a breadth-of-market indicator and is useful for establishing whether the trend of the market is rising or falling, how long the trend has continued, and if it is weakening, strengthening, or if it has reversed. Technicians also use the advance/decline line to detect early indications of a weakening in a trend signaled by a divergence between the AD line and a broader market index, such as the Dow Jones Industrial average or the S&P 500. An AD line comprised of daily data points is useful for following short-term trend. To follow long-term trends that span months or years, weekly data points are required.

ASCENDING TRIANGLE A trend continuation chart pattern in which the tops of the price bars remain relatively flat and the bottoms gradually rise. Lines drawn across the tops and along the bottoms of the price bars will eventually converge unless a breakout interrupts the increasingly restrictively trading range. Ascending triangles are viewed as a bullish pattern, but the short-term market direction will be confirmed by the direction in which the stock trades once the breakout occurs.

BAR CHART A graph used by technicians to analyze stock performance and make assumptions about future price behavior. It is comprised of a series of vertical lines called bars. The top and bottom of the bar represent the high and low for the periodicity selected. A tick on the left side of a bar indicates the open price and a tick on the right of the bar indicates the close. A bar chart uses time as the X-axis and price as the y-axis. Compare to Candlestick Chart; Point and Figure Chart.

BEAR FLAG A chart pattern named for the fact that its initial formation (the flag pole) takes place in a rapidly declining market. Once the pole is formed, a short period of consolidation results in a series of bars in which the highs and lows rise at the same rate, forming a parallel upward-sloping channel. Technicians view a bear flag as a neutral indicator and will place orders above and below trend lines drawn along the tops and the bottoms of the flag, then play the one that gets filled on the breakout. Compare to Bull Flag.

BOLLINGER BANDS A technical analysis tool that is comprised of three data points that together create an upper and lower trading channel (band) that are two standard deviations from the middle line, which measures mid-term trend. Price fluctuations between the upper and lower bands measure volatility and deviation from the 20-day simple moving average.

BREAKOUT A situation in which a security or index trades and closes above a resistance level or below a support level. A technician often interprets a breakout as a confirmation of a market trend and will typically expect the volume, volatility, and momentum triggered by the breakout to correlate with the importance of the resistance or support it penetrated.

BULL FLAG A chart pattern named for the fact that its initial formation (the flag pole) takes place in a rapidly rising market. Once the pole is formed, a short period of consolidation results in a series of bars in which the highs and lows decline at the same rate, forming a parallel downward-sloping channel. Technicians view a bull flag as a neutral indicator, so they will place orders above and below the trend lines drawn along the tops and bottoms of the flag and play the one that gets filled on the breakout. Compare to Bear Flag.

Figure 2 Bull Flag

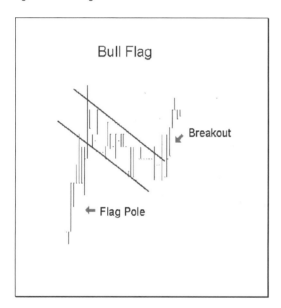

CANDLESTICK CHART A type of stock chart that shows the open, high, low, and close for a given periodicity with wide vertical bars, called the candlestick body, from which thin lines, called the shadow, extend above and/or below. Technicians use the height, width, and color of the body, along with the length and direction of the shadow to detect bullish and bearish signals for the stock.

CHART A graph on which trading prices for a security, index, or commodity is recorded. Technicians use charts to analyze historical price performance and make assumptions about future price movements. See Bar Chart; Candlestick Chart; Point and Figure Chart.

Figure 3 Candlestick Chart

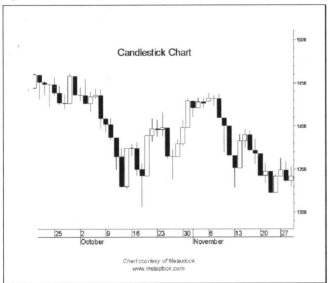

Figure 4 Candlestick Structure

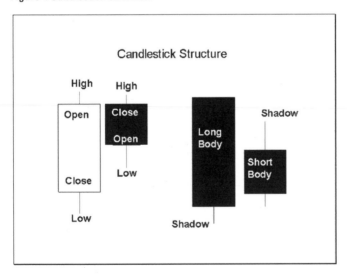

CHART PATTERN An identifiable shape, that is formed from bars or other marks representing the trading price on a chart. Technicians believe that the placement of a chart pattern and the shape it takes can be used as an indication of future market moves. See Bar Chart; Candlestick Chart; Point and Figure Chart.

CONSOLIDATION A period of trading in which the price bars remain within the boundaries of a chart pattern. Consolidation continues until a breakout occurs. See Technical Analysis.

Figure 5 Triple Top, Resistance, Consolidation, V Bottom, and Double Bottom

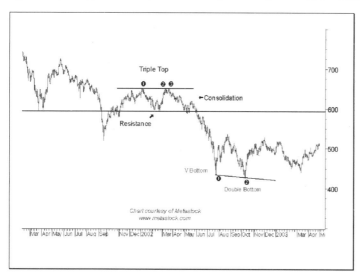

CUP WITH HANDLE PATTERN A chart pattern in which the price bars on a chart form a rounded bottom resembling a cup, followed by a short-lived price retracement. When the downward momentum slows and the price begins to rise again, it forms the handle pattern on the right side of the cup. Technicians believe that a price movement that breaks above the "rim" of the cup and handle will trigger a surge in volume and upward momentum. Compare to Double Bottom; Head and Shoulders; Reverse Head and Shoulders; Rounded Bottom; Triple Bottom; V Bottom. See Bottom; Trend; Technical Analysis.

DECLINING WEDGE A chart pattern characterized by rapidly declining highs that converge on more gradually decreasing lows, resulting in a downward sloping wedge formation. Technicians view a declining wedge as a neutral indicator and will place orders above and below the trend lines drawn along the tops and bottoms of the wedge and play the one that gets filled on the breakout.

DOUBLE BOTTOM A trend reversal chart pattern formed when the price of a single security or an index declines two times (either gradually or spiked) to roughly the same price level before reversing direction. Compare to Cup with Handle; Head and Shoulders; Reversal; Reverse Head and Shoulders; Rounded Bottom; Triple Bottom; V Bottom. See Trend.

A Closer Look at the Anatomy of a Double Bottom

A double bottom is comprised of three distinct reversals. The first is formed when the price declines to a point where the security or market as a whole runs out of downward moment. Depending on factors such as momentum and volatility either a bowl-shaped or "V" bottom will form at which point the longs and panicky shorts begin buying the stock, creating upward momentum. When the buying runs out of steam and the shorts re-enter the market, the second reversal is formed and the price begins to decline. The final reversal of a double bottom forms when the shorts fail to break through the previous low, convincing them that it's time to change direction or pull out and wait for the next down-cycle. At this point, the longs to regain control of the stock price for a period of time, setting the stage for an uptrend.

DOUBLE TOP A trend reversal chart pattern that is formed when the rises two times to roughly the same price level before reversing direction and beginning a downtrend. Compare to Bottom; Double Bottom. See Blow-off Top; Correction; Head and Shoulders; Triple Top.

EXHAUSTION GAP A blank space above or below the price bars on a price chart that is formed by a sudden price spike associated with panic buying or selling as a trend nears a reversal point. An exhaustion gap is typically created by panic buying or selling. See Gap; Breakaway Gap; Gap Opening; Runaway Gap.

FALSE BREAKOUT A situation in which a stock or index closes above or below a range defined by a short-or long-term trend line or other support or resistance level and then retracts to within the range again. False breakouts can take place for any number of reasons, including a response to news or from professional traders who are probing areas where they believe a number of stop orders may have been placed. See Stop-Running.

FIBONACCI RETRACEMENT A technical analysis model that calculates target retracement levels at 23.6 percent , 38.2 percent, 50 percent and 61.8 percent of the distance between the low and the high of the most recent price gain or loss.

GAP A blank space above or below the price bars on a stock chart left by a sudden spike upward or downward in trading. Gaps are created when the trading price of a security, index or commodity jumps above the high or drops below the low represented in the previous price bar. See Breakaway Gap; Exhaustion Gap; Gap Opening; Runaway Gap.

A Closer Look at Gap Openings

Gap openings often occur as a result of a knee-jerk response to a news event that causes the price of a security or an index to open above or below the previous day's trading range. When the temporary frenzy that caused the jump subsides, reason generally prevails and normal trading resumes but does not always return immediately to the previous trading level. Technicians believe that the upper and lower ranges of a gap act as resistance and support until they are penetrated in a subsequent retracement. How quickly that retracement takes place can vary, depending on its cause and over-all market conditions.

GAP OPENING A situation in which the first trade of the day for a security, index, or commodity takes place above the previous day's high or below the previous day's low, leaving a gap at which no trades took place. See Gap; Breakaway Gap; Exhaustion Gap; Runaway Gap.

Figure 6 Gap with Support

HEAD AND SHOULDERS PATTERN A common trend reversal chart pattern associated with a market top. Named for its resemblance to two shoulders with a head that rises above them in the middle, technicians believe that a breakout from a head and shoulders is one of the most reliable early indications of an uptrend end. See Neckline.

A Closer Look at the Anatomy of a Head and Shoulders Pattern

The start of a *left shoulder* begins when buying pushes a security to a new recent high. Once most of the available buyers are in the market, upward momentum slows, profit taking begins and the short-sellers come into play, causing the price to retreat somewhat. If it fails to make a new recent low, buyers will detect strength in the market and re-enter their long positions, pushing the price up again. A *head* is formed if the second rally pushes the price higher than the high established with the left shoulder and meets with selling that pushes it down for a second time. Provided the low of the head formation does not drop below the lowest point on the *right shoulder*, a third and final attempt to push the price to a new high will follow. If the third rally fails to match or break the new recent high, technicians will be watching for another price decline. A drop below the "neckline" of the left shoulder and head will confirm the end of the uptrend and the start of a new downtrend.

INCLINING WEDGE A chart pattern characterized by rapidly rising lows that converge on more gradually increasing highs, resulting in an upward sloping wedge pattern. Technicians view an inclining wedge as a neutral indicator and will place orders above and below the trend lines drawn along the tops and bottoms of the wedge and play the one that gets filled on the breakout.

Figure 7 Wedge Patterns

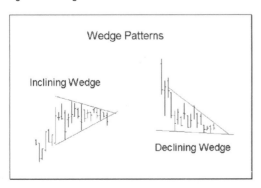

LINE STUDIES A technical analysis tool in which lines are drawn along or in relationship to data points on a chart. MACD, Fibonacci, and Relative Strength all employ line studies.

MACD (Moving Average Convergence/Divergence) A popular technical indicator that is used to signal trading opportunities and to detect overbought and oversold conditions, as well as early signs of an end to a market trend. To use the MACD to identify buying and selling opportunities, technicians overlay it with a nine-day exponential moving average (EMA) signal line and watch for one to cross over the other. A significant divergence between the MACD and the signal line can indicate an overbought and oversold condition and a divergence from the price of a security can signal the end of the current trend.

MCCLELLAN OSCILLATOR A technical analysis tool that measures overall market strength by plotting the difference between the 39-day and 19-day exponential moving average (EMA) of the advance/decline line for shares traded on the New York Stock Exchange.

NECKLINE A the lower trend line on a head and both shoulders pattern. The neckline touches both shoulders and the bottoms of the lowest bars comprising the head formation. For a reverse head and shoulders, the neckline is drawn along both shoulders and the tops of the highest bars comprising the head formation. A breakout from the trend line confirms a reversal.

PENNANT A chart pattern characterized by increasingly lower highs and higher lows. Technicians view a pennant as a neutral indicator and will place orders on both sides of the pennant and play the one that gets filled on the breakout.

Figure 8 Pennant with Breakout and Gap Opening

PERIODICITY The interval on the time axis of a stock chart. Technicians use a combination of periodicities of one week or less. A longer periodicity filters out much of the noise created by short-term price movements.

POINT AND FIGURE CHART A type of stock chart that plots price movement without a time axis. A point and figure chart is sometimes called an "X O" chart because it uses Xs to indicate an increase in the price and Os to indicate a drop in the price. The chart is built by adding one X above the next, as the price increases by a user-specified price interval (box size). When the price of the stock changes direction by a specified amount (reversal amount), a column of Os is begun to the right of the X column, with successive Os added below each previous one until the price reverses again and another column of Xs is begun. Point and figure charts are used to filter out minor price fluctuations and identify broader trends. Compare to Bar Chart; Candlestick Chart.

Figure 9 Point and Figure Chart

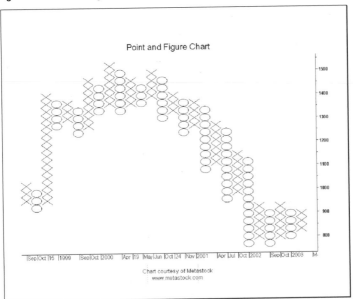

PRICE BAR The vertical marks on a bar chart that represent the trading range for a security, index, or commodity within a given periodicity. Compare to Point and Figure Chart. See Chart Pattern; Technical Analysis.

Figure 10 Price Bar

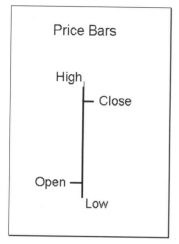

RELATIVE STRENGTH INDEX (RSI) A line study comparing the performance of a stock relative to the broader market. Relative strength is measured on a scale of 1 to 100. A stock with a relative strength index of 70, for example, has performed better than 70 percent of the stocks in the S&P 500. Technicians often watch for a divergence between the price of a security and its relative strength index.

Figure 11 Relative Strength Index

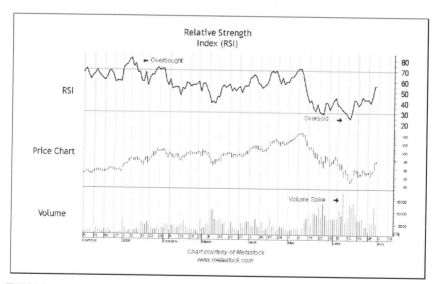

RESISTANCE A price or price range at which technicians expect the price of a security to bounce one or more times before breaking through to the upside. Resistance is typically caused by an abundance of sellers and a shortage of buyers at that price level. Technicians believe that the strength of a resistance point is determined by the significance of the trading that created it. For example a trading range that spanned many months will present more resistance to price penetration than the trading range for the previous day.

RETRACEMENT A temporary reversal. A retracement typically follows a rally or steep price decline, after which trading resumes in the direction of the overall trend. See Correction.

REVERSAL AMOUNT A user-specified criteria in a point and figure chart that determines how far a price can move in the opposite direction before a new column is added to the chart.

REVERSE HEAD AND SHOULDERS PATTERN A trend reversal chart pattern associated with a market bottom. Technicians believe that a breakout from a reverse head and shoulders is one of the most reliable early indications of an end to a downtrend. Also referred to as an Upside Down Head and Shoulders. Compare to Head and Shoulders Pattern. See Neckline.

RISING BOTTOM A chart pattern characterized by a period of trading in which the bottoms of the price bars gradually rise over time. Technicians view a rising bottom as a sign of market strength.

ROUNDED BOTTOM A trend reversal chart pattern formed when prices decrease gradually, trade for a period of time near their lowest levels, and then rise at roughly the same rate at which they declined. Compare to Cup with Handle; Double Bottom; Reverse Head and Shoulders; Triple Bottom; V Bottom. See Bottom; Trend.

ROUNDED TOP A chart pattern formed when prices rise gradually, trade for a period of time near their highest levels, and then decline at roughly the same rate at which they increased. Compare to Double Top; Head and Shoulders; Rounded Bottom; Triple Top. See Top; Trend.

Figure 12 Rounded Bottom, Cup with Handle and Breakout

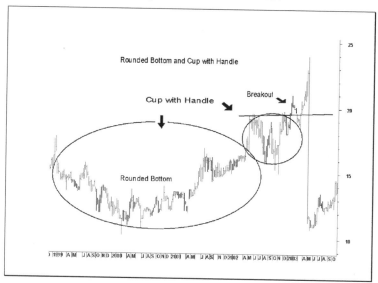

RUNAWAY GAP A blank space above or below the price bars on a price chart that is formed by a sudden price spike associated with market enthusiasm after a trend has been established. Some technicians believe that the overall length of a trend can be estimated by doubling the distance from the start of the trend to the beginning of the gap. See Gap; Breakaway Gap; Exhaustion Gap; Gap Opening.

SIMPLE MOVING AVERAGE The average price of a security or index for a given period of time, typically 50 or 200 days (20 days for Bollinger Bands). The simple moving average is calculated by adding together the closing price over "n" periods and dividing by "n." Each time the period advances, the calculation is updated to include data from the most recent "n" periods. Also referred to as the Moving Average (MA). Compare to Exponential Moving Average (EMA).

SPEED RESISTANCE LINES (SRL) Horizontal lines on a chart that divide a price movement into three equal parts. Technicians who use the speed resistance line model believe that each line reflects a resistance or support level.

STOCHASTIC OSCILLATOR A technical analysis model that suggests that the closing price of a security will increase relative its price range for a given period. The Stochastic Oscillator is comprised of a solid line (referred to as %K, which measures the relationship between a security's closing price and its trading range for a specific period) and a dotted line (referred to as %D, which is a simple moving average of %K). The oscillations of the two lines generate buy and sell signals, as they fluctuate within a scale of zero to 100. A result below 30 indicates an oversold condition and a result above 70 indicates an overbought condition.

SUPPORT A price or price range at which technicians expect the price of a security to bounce one or more times before breaking through to the downside. Support is typically caused by an abundance of buyers and a shortage of sellers at that price level. Technicians believe that the strength of a support area is determined by the significance of the trading that created it. For example a trading range that spanned many months will create more price support than then the trading range for the previous day.

SYMMETRICAL TRIANGLE A chart pattern characterized by increasingly lower highs and higher lows. A symmetrical triangle resembles a pennant, but typically is of longer duration and gentler slope. Technicians view a symmetrical triangle as neutral indicator and will typically place orders on both sides of the formation and play the one that gets filled.

TOP A range of trading at or near the highest price within a market cycle before reversing and beginning a downtrend. Compare to Bottom. See Blow-off Top; Correction; Double Top; Head and Shoulders; Triple Top.

TRADING CHANNEL A chart pattern in which trading takes place within two parallel trend lines. A channel can be horizontal or it can slope upward or downward. A trade above or below either trend line is considered a breakout. See False Breakout.

TRADING RANGE The upper and lower price boundaries for trading during a specific period of time. Some technicians interpret a breakout from a trading range as a buy or sell signal. After a breakout, the trading range becomes either support or resistance for future price movement. See Congestion.

TREND LINE A line drawn along the price bars on a chart. Technicians use trend lines to identify trends, mark the boundaries of chart patterns, to measure the degree and rate of change of price movements and to make assumptions about future price movements.

TRIPLE BOTTOM A trend reversal chart pattern formed at the end of a downtrend when the price of a single security or an index declines three times (either gradually or spiked) to roughly the same price level before reversing direction and beginning an uptrend. Compare to Cup with Handle; Double Bottom; Head and Shoulders; Reverse Head and Shoulders; Rounded Bottom; V Bottom. See Trend Compare to Double Top; Double Bottom. See Bottom.

Figure 13 Triple Bottom

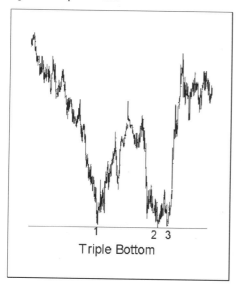

Triple Bottom

TRIPLE TOP A chart pattern formed at the end of an uptrend when the high rises to roughly the same level three times before reversing. Compare to Cup with Handle; Double Top; Head and Shoulders Pattern; Triple Bottom. See Top.

UPFLAG A chart pattern characterized by a steep rise in prices (the flag pole) followed by a period of more gradual but steadily increasing higher highs and higher lows (the flag). Many technicians believe that an upflag is a bullish indication because it indicates market strength.

Figure 14 Upflag

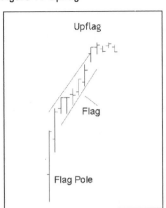

V BOTTOM A chart pattern associated with the end of a downtrend. A V bottom is a sharp price drop followed by an equally sharp reversal, resulting bars that resemble the letter V. Compare to Cup with Handle; Double Bottom; Head and Shoulders; Reverse Head and Shoulders; Rounded Bottom; Triple Bottom.

Figure 15 V Bottom

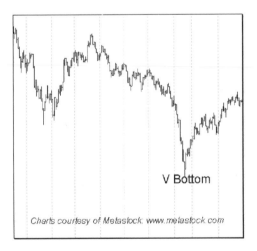

W BOTTOM A bottoming out of the market created when a security or the market as a whole declines two times to roughly the same price and reverses direction.

XO CHART See Point and Figure Chart.

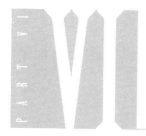

Investment Mechanics

Tools that Match Your Style: Starting With the Right Broker

HOUSE RULES Brokerage firm policies and procedures that govern the way customer accounts are handled.

ACTIVE INVESTMENT MANAGEMENT An investment strategy that involves buying and selling portfolio holdings to reallocate assets and improve returns. Active investment management requires extensive market analysis to screen and pick securities according to predetermined selection criteria and to make decisions about market timing. Compare to Passive Investment Management; Index Fund.

ARBITRAGE An investment strategy that involves purchasing a security, currency, or commodity in one market for immediate sale in a different market to take advantage of price disparities between the two.

A Closer Look at Arbitrage

Temporary price discrepancies can occur in securities, currencies, and commodities between the various markets on which they are traded. For example, the price of aluminum on NYMEX might briefly fall below the price at which it is trading on the London Metal Exchange. An arbitrageur might buy one or more contracts of aluminum on NYMEX and sell it immediately on the London Metals Exchange (LME). The difference between the purchase price and the selling price, less commissions, is the profit (or loss if the price of aluminum on the LME drops before the order to sell can be executed).

ASSET ALLOCATION An investment strategy in which an investor or fund manager adjusts portfolio holdings to maintain a predetermined balance between asset classes or sectors, for example. A fund's asset allocation strategy is disclosed in its prospectus. See Active Investment Management.

AVERAGE DOWN To buy additional shares in a long position as it moves down with the objective of reducing the average price per share. The wisdom of an average-down strategy is debatable. While many investors employ it as a means of lowering the breakeven price, some investment advisors caution against throwing additional money into a losing position. Compare to Average Up; Dollar Cost Averaging.

AVERAGE PRICE PER SHARE A method of calculating cost basis, in which the total cost for all shares of the same security is divided by the number of shares held. See Average Down; Average Up.

AVERAGE UP To buy additional shares in a long position as it moves up with the objective of reducing the average price per share and increasing profit in a successful trade. Compare to Average Down; Dollar Cost Averaging.

BACKTEST A system used to test a trading strategy in which a specially designed computer program is used to examine the success of a series of hypothetical trades after the fact. Backtesting programs apply user-defined entry and exit criteria to historical data and execute simulated trades from which detailed profit and loss statistics are generated.

BALANCED INVESTMENT STRATEGY An asset allocation strategy that seeks to moderate risk by including both income producing and growth investments in a portfolio.

BEAR SPREAD An options strategy in which an investor attempts to profit from a security's declining price. Compare to Bull Spread.

BLACK BOX TRADING A computer-based trading system for individual investors that uses a set of fixed, proprietary rules to generate buy and sell signals. Black box systems are named for the secrecy surrounding the methodology employed in the analysis.

BOX SPREAD An arbitrage strategy in which the profit in one position is locked in with an opposite position in another security. Boxing in can be accomplished with any asset class, but is most often employed with derivatives.

BULL SPREAD An options strategy, in which an investor attempts to profit from a security's rising price by simultaneously buying a put and a call in the same investment. If the price moves up as expected, the trader will close out the put option and let the call option run, presumably taking a profit that exceeds the small loss taken on the put. Conversely, if the price moves down, the profit on the put will offset the loss on the call. Compare to Bear Spread; Straddle. See Box Spread.

BUY AND HOLD A passive investment strategy in which a portfolio is comprised of quality stocks which are held for the long-term. Compare to Day Trading; Swing Trading; Market Timing.

BUY LONG To purchase a security or derivative contract with the intention of selling it at a profit when the price increases. Compare to Buy to Cover; Sell Short.

BUY THE RUMOR; SELL THE NEWS A market adage based on the belief that stock prices move in anticipation of news and rebound back when profit taking occurs after the news is released.

CALENDAR SPREAD An options strategy in which the investor buys one put option and one call option for the same underlying asset and strike price but with two different expiration months. See Bear Spread; Bull Spread.

CATCH A FALLING KNIFE A market idiom that warns of the danger of buying into rapidly dropping market.

CLOSED POSITION A completed investment in which both a buy and sell order has been executed, securing either a profit or a loss. The opposite of an open position.

COMMISSION A fee charged by a brokerage firm for executing an order to buy or sell an investment. Commissions can be based on the value of the trade or a flat rate fee.

COST OF CARRY The cost of owning an investment, such as

interest on the money borrowed to fund the purchase. In the case of a commodity, the carry also includes the cost of storage and insurance. See Negative Carry, Positive Carry.

CUSTODIAL ACCOUNT An account opened by a parent on behalf of a minor. Deposits to a custodial account are irrevocable and along with the earnings in the account become the permanent property of the minor. When the child reaches the age of majority (18 or 21, depending on the state) he or she assumes full control over the account and any assets in it.

DIRECT ACCESS TRADING (DAT) An Internet-based order entry and execution system offered by some brokerage firms that permits an investor to place trades directly with market makers and specialists, using an electronic communication network (ECN). Direct access trading can provide faster order fulfillment but also entails some extra risk because the order is not reviewed by a registered representative prior to submittal.

DISCRETIONARY ACCOUNT An account with a brokerage firm that authorizes the broker or another named individual to make decision on how funds in the account are invested without a requirement to consult with the account holder prior to execution. See Churning; Fiduciary; Managed Account; Prudent Man Rule.

DIVERSIFICATION The distribution of investment holdings into a variety of sectors or asset classes for the purpose of managing market risk. See Asset Allocation.

DIVIDEND REINVESTMENT PLAN (DRIP) A plan offered by certain companies that allows shareholders to use their dividend distribution to buy additional shares of the company's stock.

DOLLAR COST AVERAGING An investment strategy in which a set dollar amount is used to buy additional shares of a security or asset class at predetermined intervals. Advocates of dollar cost averaging believe that over time the market will rise higher than the average cost per share of the purchases and that attempting to use market timing to decide when to enter or exit the market increases risk. See Average Up.

EVENT RISK The risk to principal and profit created by unforeseen circumstances. Geopolitical changes, economic downturn, and adverse company news are examples of event risks. See Market Risk.

EXIT STRATEGY A plan for exiting an investment in a manner that will maximize profits or minimize losses.

FLAT A condition in which an investor holds no open positions.

FORMULA INVESTING An investment strategy designed to replace emotions in the decision-making process with a set of predetermined rules. See Black Box Trading; Buy and Hold; Dollar Cost Averaging.

GAMING To gamble on making money on investments by the continual issue of buy and sell orders at set intervals, typically less than 15 seconds. See IPO Halt.

GROSS YIELD Return on investment (ROI) before deducting the cost of the transaction, such as commission, margin interest, or management fees. See Cost of Carry.

HEDGE An investment strategy in which an individual or business makes an investment to protect against adverse price movement in another holding. See Bear Spread; Bull Spread; Calendar Spread; Commercial Hedger.

A Closer Look at Commercial Hedging

The cash price of a commodity can make the difference between making or losing money for a corporation or business person who uses that product to make a living. A spike in the price of jet fuel, for example, has the ability to put the entire airline industry in jeopardy, as does the price of steel for automobile manufacturers. Commercial hedging offers a way to lock in a favorable price, whether they are a consumer or a producer of the raw materials that keep the economy churning along with relatively stable prices. To understand how commercial hedging works, consider a soybean farmer who anticipates a bumper crop at harvest. On the surface a bountiful yield might seem like good news for the farmer. To protect himself against a potential loss, the farmer might buy a put option on a sufficient number of soybeans futures contracts to ensure the profit he stands to lose on the cash product. If the price of soybeans goes down, as he expects that it might, he can exercise his option at the lower price, pocketing the profit. If it goes up, the profit on the cash product he delivers to the market is reduced only by cost of the put, which he'll chalk up to cheap insurance against a wasted season.

HOUSE RULES Brokerage firm policies and procedures that govern the way customer accounts are handled.

INTEREST RATE The return on loaned money, expressed as a percentage of the principal. Companies that issue bonds, certificates of deposit, and other debt instruments pay a fixed or variable interest rate in exchange for the privilege of using an investor's money. Likewise, an investor pays a fixed or variable interest rate for the use of borrowed money when he or she uses margin or other debt strategies to fund or secure an investment. Interest rate is calculated by dividing interest paid by the principal.

LEG One trade in a straddle or spread strategy, where the investor holds simultaneous positions in the same or a related asset. See Bear Spread; Box Spread; Bull Spread; Option Spread.

LIFT A LEG A step in the execution of a spread strategy in which the investor closes one of two simultaneously held positions.

LIQUIDATION The process of converting property or investments into cash.

LIQUIDITY The ease at which an asset can be converted to cash. For investments, this refers to the degree to which supply equals demand. A shortage of either buyers or sellers in any market can result in substantial price swings resulting in an unfavorable fill for a market order or the inability to obtain a fill on a limit order. Conversely, high volume typically ensures an abundance of both buyers and sellers and greater liquidity.

MANAGED ACCOUNT An investment account established with a brokerage firm in which the account holder contracts with the stockbroker and pays a fee for account management services that includes investment selection and the transaction execution.

MARGIN Money borrowed from a brokerage firm to fund investment transactions.

A Closer Look at Margin

Regardless of the investment vehicle, margin always constitutes a loan toward the cost of the transaction, which is collateralized by the assets held in the account. If the investment returns a profit, the loan is repaid along with interest when the position is liquidated and the investor moves on to the next investment. Consider what happens, on the other hand, if the stock or futures position turns into a losing investment. Once the loss reaches a certain level, the investor will receive a margin call, at which time he typically has about three days to deposit sufficient money in the account to bring the balance up to the minimum margin requirements. Should the investor fail to meet the margin call, the broker is legally obligated to liquidate assets in the account to meet the call. One point that is lost on some investors, however, is that if the balance in the account still falls short, he is legally obligated to make up the difference – even if it means selling the homestead to do it. Under most circumstances, the position would be liquidated long before the losses reached that point, but sometimes it doesn't work out that way. Take a corporate bankruptcy, for example, in which the price of the stock drops dramatically overnight, producing a gap opening the next day, or a situation in which a futures contract locks limit up or down multiple days in a row. If an investor is stuck in the market in the wrong direction, the losses can be life-altering.

MARGIN ACCOUNT A brokerage account established for the purpose of borrowing money to fund investment transactions or for use as a performance bond when trading in derivatives. See Call Loan; Call Loan Rate; Call Money; Initial Margin; Margin; Margin Call; Maintenance Margin; Remargining.

MARGIN CALL A demand for the deposit of additional funds into a margin account to maintain the minimum margin requirements. If the account holder fails to meet a margin call, the broker has the right and legal obligation to liquidate account holdings to return the account to good standing. Also Maintenance Margin; Remargining.

MARGINABLE A stock that meets the requirements established by the Federal Reserve for being purchased on margin.

MARKET RISK The degree of risk that can be attributed to a market segment or the market as a whole. For example, a high rate of inflation can slow economic growth, impair consumer spending and stifle corporate profits, causing the broader market to decline. Market risk associated with one industry or sector can be reduced through sector diversification. Market risk associated with the market as whole, can be mitigated to some degree through asset allocation that includes multiple asset classes, such as bonds, stocks, cash, and ownership of actual commodities like gold and silver.

MARKET TIMING An investment strategy that employs analysis of current market conditions to decide when to issue a buy or sell order. Compare to Buy and Hold; Dollar Cost Averaging; Passive Investment Management. See Active Investment Management.

MARKETABLE SECURITY A security that is in sufficient demand to be easily converted to cash. See Liquidity.

MOMENTUM INVESTING A trading strategy that targets stocks with high volume and rapidly rising or dropping prices.

A Closer Look at Momentum Investing

Some technicians believe that a surge in volume accompanying a rapid price increase (or decrease) indicates an abundance of buyers (or short-sellers) for the security. Conversely, they believe that when the momentum begins to plateau, it reflects waning interest and foreshadows a reversal. Momentum investors enter the market on high momentum and attempt to exit at or near the peak of the momentum cycle with a profit.

NEGATIVE CARRY The cost of borrowing money to fund an investment that exceeds the profit earned. Compare to Positive Carry.

ODD LOT An order to buy or sell a security or bond in an amount that is not a multiple of the standard order unit (100 shares of stock or five bonds). Compare to Round Lot.

OPEN TRADE EQUITY See Paper Profit.

PAPER PROFIT Investment profit in an open position and that remains subject to risk of loss.

PASSIVE INVESTMENT MANAGEMENT An investment strategy that involves buying and holding a portfolio of securities that track the broader market. Index funds are an example of passive investment management, but individual investors who employ a buy and hold strategy use it as well. Compare to Active Investment Management.

PORTFOLIO Investment holdings by a single person, fund, or other institution.

POSITION A general reference to an investment holding. A position can be long or short, and it can be in any asset class, such as stocks, bonds, futures, or options. A position can be open (current) or closed (past), but in general use, unless a position is specifically referred to as closed, the assumption is that it references an open position.

POSITIVE CARRY The cost of borrowing money to fund an investment that does not exceed the profit earned. Compare to Negative Carry. See Margin.

PRINCIPAL The amount of money used to acquire an investment.

PROGRAM TRADING A computer-based trading system that uses a set of programmable rules to places orders to buy or sell investments based on market behavior. Institutions use program trading to manage the large volume of assets they manage. Less complex program trading software is also available for individual investors but is typically used by only sophisticated and experienced traders. Compare to Black Box Trading.

RANDOM WALK THEORY A market theory which holds that it is impossible to predict what stock prices will do in the future by looking at historical performance because market movements are purely random. Defenders of the random walk theory believe that attempting to outperform the market using technical analysis or fundamental analysis will fail over time and that the only way to profit in the market is to buy and hold stocks that are representative of the broader market. See Market Timing.

RATE OF RETURN A measure of investment performance expressed as a percentage of the principal invested. Calculated by dividing annual net profit by the principal. Also referred to as Yield.

RECAPITALIZATION A company's use of the proceeds from an Initial Public Offering (IPO) to pay down debt.

REMARGINING The process of depositing additional cash into a margin account for the purpose of meeting minimum margin requirements. See Margin Call.

RESTRICTED ACCOUNT A margin account in which the margin/asset ratio has fallen below the minimum margin requirements. See Margin; Remargining.

RETURN ON INVESTMENT (ROI) A measure of investment profitability, expressed as a percentage. ROI is calculated by dividing net profit on the investment by the principal. See Cash on Cash Equivalent.

RISK TOLERANCE The loss an investor is willing to endure in pursuit of profit.

A Closer Look at Factors Affecting Risk Tolerance

Temperament – Are you a risk taker or do you tend to play it safe?

Time – When will the money invested be needed for other purposes? Less than a year? More than five years? Not for 30 years?

Financial situation – Are you investing all of your money or a portion of it? Do you have other assets?

Job Security – Is your job likely to go away anytime soon? Are you in a high-demand field?

Investment experience/knowledge – Have you ever invested in stock? Bonds? Futures and options? How well do you understand the psychological and technical aspects of investing? Can you do your own analysis or are you dependent on your broker's recommendations?

Family/personal obligations – Are you single or are you contributing toward the support of other people, such as a spouse, children, or aging parents?

RISK-AVERSE INVESTOR A person with a low risk tolerance.

RISK-REWARD RATIO A measure of the degree of risk inherent in a given investment in relation to the potential profit associated with it.

ROUND TRIP COMMISSION A term that refers to the total commission costs for both sides of a trade: the order to buy and the order to sell.

RULE OF 72 A formula for calculating time it takes for the value of an investment to double at a specific compound annual rate of return. Calculated by dividing the number 72 by the annual rate of return. For example, the formula $72 \div 9 = 8$ shows that it will take 8 years for an investment to double if it earns a 9 percent compound annual rate of return.

SCALP A trading style that attempts to accumulate large profits by making a series of small profit-trades, typically capturing only a few cents of profit with each transaction. See Daytrader; In-and-Out Trader.

SCREEN A stock selection strategy in which an investor evaluates a company based on a set of fundamental analysis or technical analysis criteria. Stock screening can be done manually, with Internet-based tools or with specialized software available for that purpose.

SECTOR ROTATION The process of selling investments in one type of business to purchase holdings in one or more different types in which the investor sees greater profit potential. Sector rotation can be prompted by fundamental changes in the economy or within specific industries, or it can be part of a systematic investment strategy that follows cyclical or seasonal price patterns. See Asset Allocation.

SEGREGATED ACCOUNT An account in which a customer's funds are held separate from the funds of the brokerage firm.

SETTLEMENT The process by which a trade is finalized by the exchange of money, the delivery of certificates attesting to the transfer of ownership, and in the case of futures transactions sometimes delivery of the actual physical commodity.

SETTLEMENT DATE The date by which money and ownership of an asset must be exchanged to finalize an executed transaction. For securities, the settlement date is typically three days after transaction date. Compare to Transaction Date.

SIMULATED TRADING An Internet-based program offered by certain brokerage firms that allows an investor to practice placing buy and sell orders using real-time quotes, but without actual execution of the trades. Simulated trading can be beneficial as a training tool, but the profit and loss results can be misleading because the system cannot accurately incorporate the effect simulated trades would have had on a real-world trade.

SPECULATE To make a risky investment in anticipation of a major change in the future price or the asset.

STOCK PICKING See Screen Stocks.

STOCK SELECTION STRATEGY The method by which an investor establishes criteria on which to choose an investment.

STRADDLE A trading strategy in which an investor holds simultaneous long and short positions in the same or a related asset. See Bear Spread; Box-Spread; Bull Spread.

SWEEP ACCOUNT An account with a brokerage firm in which unused cash is automatically transferred (swept) into a money market fund or other short-term interest bearing investment.

TAKE A POSITION To enter the market by either buying long or selling short.

TIME VALUE OF MONEY A financial principle holding that a dollar earned today is worth more than a dollar earned at a future date. It is based on the assumption that today's dollar can begin earning compounded income immediately, whereas earnings on the future dollar are deferred.

UNREALIZED GAIN See Paper Profit.

UPSIDE POTENTIAL The difference between the current trading price of a security and the level to which it is most likely to rise in the short term.

WHIPSAW A loss incurred when a security makes a sudden reversal immediately after a position is initiated. See Bear Trap; Bull Squeeze; Bull Trap; Short Squeeze; Stop-Running.

YIELD A measure of the annual return on an investment, expressed as a percentage of the principal invested. Calculated by dividing annual net profit by the principal. See Rate of Return.

Orders, Quotes, and Fills:
Getting the Price You Want

SLIPPAGE The difference between the price at which an investor expects a market order to be filled and the actual price of the execution.

ALL OR NONE (AON) An order with an instruction attached stipulating that the order should be executed only if the entire order can be filled.

ASK The price a seller is willing to accept for a security or other financial instrument. Also referred to as an Offer. Compare to Bid, Best Ask.

ASK SIZE The total number of shares offered for sale at the current quote. Ask size is typically quoted in units of 100, where an ask size of three equals 300 shares offered. An ask size of 300 equals 30,000 shares offered. See Ask; Best Ask. Compare to Bid Size.

AT THE MARKET An order to buy a security at the best ask or to sell at the best bid. Also known as a market order. Compare to Limit Order. See National Best Bid and Offer (NBBO).

AWAY FROM THE MARKET A term that refers to a limit order that cannot be filled immediately because it is priced higher (for a sell order) or lower (for a buy order) than where the security is currently trading. Away from the market, orders are held until they are either filled or cancelled. Compare to Market Order. See Best Ask; Best Bid; National Best Bid and Offer.

BASKET ORDER One order that issues instructions for the

simultaneous purchase or sale of multiple securities. Professional investors often use basket orders for arbitrage and program trading, but some retail brokers offer basket order processing to retail customers through a direct access trading platform.

BEST ASK The lowest price at which competing market makers are currently offering to sell a security. A market order to buy is filled at the best ask, which increases and decreases continually in response to changes in supply and demand as buyers and sellers enter and exit the market. Compare to Ask; Best Bid; Bid. See National Best Bid and Offer (NBBO).

BEST BID The highest price at which competing market makers are currently offering to buy a security. A market order to sell is filled at the best bid, which increases and decreases continually in response to changes in supply and demand as buyers and sellers enter and exit the market. Compare to Ask; Best Ask; Bid. See National Best Bid and Offer (NBBO).

BID The price at which a buyer is willing to purchase a security, commodity, or option contract. Compare to Ask; Best Bid. See also National Best Bid and Offer (NBBO).

BID SIZE The total number of shares that all buyers are currently offering to purchase a security at the best bid. Bid size is typically quoted in units of 100, where a bid size of three equals 300 shares offered. A bid size of 300 equals 30,000 shares offered.

BLOCK TRADE A large lot of stocks or bonds traded in a single transaction. A securities transaction of at least 10,000 shares or a bond transaction of at least $500,000 is considered a block trade.

BROKEN LOT See Uneven Lot.

BUY An order to purchase a security or derivative contract. Compare to Buy to Cover; Sell. See Market Order; Limit Order; Stop Order.

BUY TO COVER An order to buy back shares that were sold short and close out the position. Compare to Buy Long. See Short Sale.

CANCEL An instruction to void a previously placed order that has not yet been filled. A market order cannot be canceled. In the case of an order that has been partially filled, an order to cancel will be applied to the unfilled portion of the original order.

COVER See Buy to Cover.

DAY ORDER An order that is good only for the trading session in which it was issued. Day orders are automatically canceled at the closing bell. Compare to Good until Canceled (GTC).

DELAYED QUOTE A stock or other quote that is reported some time after the transaction takes place, typically about 20 minutes. Delayed quotes are offered on a number of free investment Web sites. Compare to Real Time Quotes; Streaming Quotes.

DO NOT REDUCE (DNR) An instruction used to tell the broker how to handle a limit order to buy or stop order to sell on the record date for a security issuing a cash dividend. The price of a security is typically reduced by the amount of the dividend when the stock goes ex-dividend. Investors have a choice of reducing the price on a limit buy and sell stop orders by a commensurate amount or issuing a do not reduce order, in which case the order will stand as originally entered.

DOWNTICK A transaction that takes place at a lower price than the previous trade. Compare to Uptick.

EXECUTE To fill an order to buy, sell or short an investment instrument.

FILL See Execute.

FILL OR KILL (FOK) An instruction stipulating that the order should be cancelled if it cannot be executed in its entirety immediately. A fill or kill order does not allow for a partial fill. Compare to Immediate or Cancel (IOC).

FILLED An order that has been executed.

GOOD FOR DAY See Day Order.

GOOD UNTIL CANCELLED (GTC) An order that remains open and available for execution until a specific order to cancel it is issued. Compare to Day Order.

HIT THE BID An agreement by a dealer to sell a security at the highest bid offered by another dealer. For instance, when a dealer who is offering to sell a security at $23.54 agrees to accept the highest bid of $23.22, the selling dealer is said to hit the bid. Compare to Take the Offer.

IMBALANCE OF ORDERS A condition where the number of buy or sell orders is grossly mismatched, resulting in a wide spread between the bid and ask. An imbalance of orders can be caused by any source of investor nervousness but most frequently can be traced to news or a rumor affecting the security. Because order imbalances impair market liquidity, they can trigger a trading halt to prevent panic buying or selling.

IMMEDIATE OR CANCEL (IOC) An instruction stipulating that the order should be cancelled if it cannot immediately be filled in full or in part. Compare to Fill or Kill.

INSIDE MARKET The bid and ask prices at which securities are traded between market makers. The inside market is typically transacted at a higher bid or lower ask than where a market maker would be willing to sell the same securities to a retail customer.

INTERNALIZATION A process by which a retail broker chooses to fill a client's order from its on inventory rather than sending it to a market maker for execution. When a brokerage firm internalizes the execution, it makes money both from the commission it charges for the transaction and from the spread.

LAST The price at which the most recent transaction took place for a given security.

LEVEL I DATA A real time quotation service that provides current bid and ask prices for securities traded on NASDAQ and on the over-the-counter market.

LEVEL II DATA A real time quotation service that provides current bid and ask prices by market maker for securities traded on NASDAQ and on the over-the-counter market.

LEVEL III DATA A real time quotation service that provides current bid and ask prices by market maker and includes the ability to place orders with the individual market makers through a direct access trading platform for securities traded on NASDAQ and on the over-the-counter market.

LIMIT IF TOUCHED (LIT) An instruction to generate a limit order automatically to buy or sell a security if a trade occurs at a specific trigger price.

LIMIT ON CLOSE (LOC) An order to buy or sell a security at a specified price only if the stock trades at the limit price or better at the close and to cancel the order automatically if it cannot be filled. Compare to Limit on Open (LOO); Limit Order.

LIMIT ON OPEN (LOO) An order to buy or sell a security at a specified price only if the stock trades at the limit price or better when the market opens and to cancel the order automatically if it cannot be filled. Compare to Limit Order.

LOCKED MARKET A temporary condition in which the best bid is equal to the best ask, resulting in a zero spread.

LONG A trade in which the investor buys a security or futures contract seeking to sell it later at a profit. Compare to Short.

MARKET CENTER An order fulfillment point. For the securities industry, the market centers are comprised of the floor of a stock exchange (via a specialist), market makers and electronic communication networks (ECNs).

MARKET IF TOUCHED (MIT) An order to sell or buy a security at the best bid or ask if a trade takes place at a certain price level. A market if touched buy order is placed below the current trading price and a market if touched sell order is placed above the current trading price. Compare to Stop Order.

MARKET ORDER An instruction to buy or sell a security at the best ask or bid. The fill on a market order can vary dramatically from the price at which the security is trading at the time it is entered and the price at which the order is filled, depending on the number of shares available at the time it is received by the specialist or market maker. A market order generally cannot be cancelled. See Slippage.

NATIONAL BEST BID AND OFFER (NBBO) The highest bid and the lowest ask for a security at a given point in time for NASDAQ-traded securities.

OFFER See Ask.

OPEN ORDER An order that has not been executed and remains in the system available to be filled until an order to cancel it is received.

OPEN POSITION Any investment that has been entered into but not closed. For example, an investor who is long 100 shares of INTC has an open position until an order to sell those 100 shares has been placed and filled.

OR BETTER An instruction attached to an order requesting price improvement if possible. For example, an order to buy 100 shares of MSFT at $24.23 or better conveys an instruction to buy the shares at $24.23 or lower if possible. A sell order with the or better price improvement instruction means to sell it at a higher price if possible.

ORDER An instruction to buy, sell, or short an investment, stipulating the symbol, quantity, order type, and execution instructions. Depending on the broker, an order may be placed through an account representative or electronically, typically over the Internet. See Cancel; Order Ticket.

ORDER TICKET A form an account representative fills out conveying the transaction instructions. Order tickets

A Closer Look at Orders and Order Tickets

A *market order* has the simplest structure: "Buy 100 shares of MSFT at the market." Limit and stop orders, on the other hand, can be structured to convey a wide range of instructions by adding stipulations to a basic order, as this *limit order* with an *all or none* contingency instruction demonstrates: "Buy 100 shares of MSFT at 34.23, All or None."

A Closer Look at Orders and Order Tickets			
Order Essentials	Order Type and Triggers (Choose One)		Contingencies and Time in Force (Choose One)
Security	Market	Limit (Price)	Good Till Cancelled
Symbol	Market if Touched (Price)	Limit if Touched (Price)	Good for Day
Number of Shares			Fill or Kill
			All or None
Buy or Sell	Stop (Price)		Immediate or Cancel
Sell Short			Do Not Reduce
Buy to Cover	Stop Limit (Trigger Price & Limit Price)		Market on Open
			Market on Close
	Trailing Stop (Percent or Amount)		Limit on Open (Price)
			Limit on Close (Price)

PARTIAL FILL An order that is not completely executed. With a partial fill, a certain portion of the order has been completed and a portion remains in the system as an open order.

PRICE IMPROVEMENT A situation in which a market maker fills an order at a better price than the National Best Bid and Offer (NBBO). For a buy order, price improvement would mean filling the order at a lower price than the NBBO and for a sell order, it would mean filling the order at a higher price than the NBBO. Price improvement can be applied to both limit orders and market orders, but not all market makers provide it.

QUOTATION 1) The best bid or best offer as listed on the National Best Bid and Offer system. Also referred to as a Quote. See Delayed; Real Time Quote; Streaming Quote.

QUOTE See Quotation.

ROUND LOT A standard order unit for securities or bonds. Securities that are bought and sold in a lot of 100 or multiples of 100 are considered round lots, as are bond transactions placed in multiples of five. Compare to Odd Lot. See Odd Lot Dealer.

ROUTING The process by which an order passes from an instruction given by an investor to the market maker or specialist who fills it. Routing systems today are primarily electronic.

SELL An order offering to sell a security or commodity. See Market Order; Limit Order; Stop Order.

SELL SHORT A trading strategy in which an investor borrows shares of a security or futures contract (typically from a brokerage firm's inventory) and offers them for sale to other investors. If the price goes down, as the investor believes it will, he or she will buy the position back at the lower price and return them to the lender. If the price rises, the investor will be forced to buy the shares or contract back at a higher price to return them to the lender, resulting in a loss. In either case, the gross profit (or loss) on the trade will be the difference between the buy and sell price.

SHORT Holding or initiating a short sale. See Short Interest.

SHORT SALE See Sell Short.

SIZE See Bid Size; Ask Size; Order Ticket.

SLIPPAGE The difference between the price at which an investor expects a market order to be filled and the actual price of the execution.

A Closer Look at Slippage

Slippage is often tied to the volume of shares traded in a security. Volume equals liquidity. The inverse is also true, meaning that a large market order in a low volume market may be filled at a substantially higher (for a buy order) or lower (for a sell order) price than where the security was quoted when the order was placed.

SPREAD The price difference between what a buyer is willing to pay for a security and the what the seller is willing to accept. Specialists and market makers make their profits on the spread by purchasing the stock at the lower price and selling it at the higher one. See Bid; Ask.

STOP See Stop Order.

STOP LIMIT An order that acts as a trigger to generate a limit order when a security trades at a specified price, called the stop price. To place a stop limit order, a trader enters two prices: the stop, which triggers the automatic order and the limit price, which specifies the price at which the security should be bought or sold. Compare to Stop Order.

STOP ORDER An order that acts as a trigger to generate a market order when a security trades at a specified price. Also called a stop. Compare to Stop Limit. See Stop Price.

A Closer Look at Stop Orders

Stop orders can be used to enter a position or to exit one. To use a stop order to enter a position, an investor will place it at a point that confirms that a trend has been established. When the stop price is hit, it triggers the automatic generation of an order that initiates a position. After the investor has entered the market, a stop order can be used to manage risk and protect paper profits by placing the stop order at a price level that allows room for the security to fluctuate and yet coincide with the investor's risk tolerance. If the stop price is hit, an order will be automatically generated to exit the position, capturing a profit or minimizing the loss, depending on where the stop order was placed. See Stop Limit; Stop Out; Stop Running; Trailing Stop.

STOP OUT To exit a position through the use of a stop order. See Stop Running.

STOP PRICE The price at which a stop order generates a market order and a stop limit order generates a limit order.

SYMBOL A combination of letters that represents a security, derivative, or other financial instrument traded on an exchange or over-the-counter market. See CUSID.

A Closer Look at Symbol Formats for Common Stock Issues

	Exchange	Examples	
		Symbol	Company
Four-Letters	NASDAQ	MSFT	Microsoft
		INTC	Intel Corp.

A Closer Look at Symbol Formats for Common Stock Issues			
One, Two, or Three Letters	New York Stock Exchange & American Stock Exchange	C AA MER	Citigroup Inc.) Alcoa Inc.) Merrill Lynch & Co., Inc.)
Five Letters, ending in OB	Over-the-counter (OTC)	ONEV-OB	One Voice Technologies, Inc.

TAKE THE OFFER An agreement by a dealer to buy a security at the best offer quoted by another dealer. For example, a dealer who is bidding $23.22 agrees to buy it at the best ask of $23.54 is said to take the offer. Compare to Hit the Bid.

TICK A change in the price of a security, index, or commodity. See Downtick; Maximum Price Fluctuation; Minimum Price Movement; Uptick.

TIME IN FORCE See Time Order.

TIME ORDER An order that includes an instruction limiting the time when it should be issued and/or the duration it should remain in force before it is automatically cancelled. Also referred to as Time in Force. See Good For Day; Good till Cancelled; Market on Open; Market on Close; Limit if Touched; Market if Touched.

TRAILING STOP A type of stop order in which the stop price (trigger) moves with the trading price of a security. For example, a 10 percent trailing stop will generate a market order to exit a long position if the price of the security declines 10 percent from its high. Alternatively a trailing stop can be set to trigger a market order automatically if the price moves a certain fixed amount. For example, a trailing stop can be structured to generate a market order to exit a long position if the price of the security declines by $2 from its high. See Limit Stop.

UNEVEN LOT See Odd Lot.

UPTICK A transaction that takes place at a higher price than the previous trade. Compare to Downtick. See Short Sale Rule; Uptick Rule.

Recordkeeping and Taxes: Paying the Piper

COST A calculation of the cost of purchasing, owning, and selling a capital asset. Cost is used to determine the gain or loss on the subsequent sale of the asset.

BACKUP WITHHOLDING Funds required to be withheld from investment income to cover the tax liability associated with the transaction when the investor does not have a valid social security number on the account and on file with the IRS.

BASIS See Cost Basis.

BRACKET CREEP A situation in which a person's tax obligation increases over time due to the gradual move from a lower tax bracket to a higher one.

BUSINESS INCOME A classification used by the IRS for income generated from the operation of a business. Business income is reported on IRS Schedule C or C-EZ. Compare to Regular Income; Capital Gains.

CAPITAL GAIN Income derived from the sale of a capital asset, such as real estate, security or a mutual fund holding. Capital gain is calculated by subtracting the net selling price for the asset from the cost or cost basis. See Long Term Capital Gains; Short Term Capital Gains. Compare to Capital Loss.

CAPITAL GAINS TAX A tax on the net income derived from the sale of a capital asset such as real estate, securities, or a mutual fund holding.

CAPITAL LOSS A loss derived from the sale of a capital asset, such as real estate, securities, or a mutual fund holding. Capital loss is calculated by subtracting the net selling price for the asset from the cost basis. Compare to Capital Gain. See Capital Loss Carryover.

CAPITAL LOSS CARRYOVER A capital loss that cannot be deducted in the year it is earned because it exceeds the maximum $3,000 annual deduction. Excess losses are carried over and deducted in subsequent years until the full deduction has been claimed. See Capital Loss.

CONFIRMATION A printed or electronic statement provided by a stockbroker to an account holder confirming the details of a trade execution. Also referred to as a Trade Confirmation or Confirmation Statement. Compare to Purchase and Sale Agreement.

COST A calculation of the cost of purchasing, owning, and selling a capital asset. Cost is used to determine the gain or loss on the subsequent sale of the asset.

COST BASIS A method of establishing the cost of a capital asset that received as gift or inheritance. Cost basis is used to calculate the capital gains or loss from the subsequent sale of the asset. It is calculated by adding together the market value of the asset at the time it was gifted or inherited and any transaction expenses associated with ownership or sale. Compare to Cost. See Cost of Carry; Positive Carry; Negative Carry.

COVERDELL EDUCATION SAVINGS ACCOUNT (ESA) A tax-qualified savings account designed to accumulate savings to pay for education expenses. See 401(k) Plan; Coverdell Education Savings Account (ESA); Individual Retirement Account (IRA); Keogh Plan.

DEFERRED ACCOUNT See Tax-deferred Account.

DOUBLE EXEMPTION A tax benefit offered by certain bonds that qualify for exemption from both federal and state taxation. Municipal bonds, or munis as they are often called, are typically exempt from federal taxes and, depending on the state of issue, may also be exempt from state taxes, as well.

FORM 1099 A series of forms on which various forms of investment income are reported to the investor and the Internal Revenue Service.

A Closer Look at Form 1099	
Form	**Type of Income Reported**
FORM 1099-DIV	Dividends and Distributions
FORM 1099-INT	Interest Income
FORM 1099-OID	Original Issue Discounts
FORM 1099-B	Proceeds from brokerage Transactions
FORM 1099-MISC	Royalties and In Lieu of Dividend Distributions

401(k) PLAN An employer-sponsored, tax-advantaged, deferred compensation retirement plan. Under the rules that govern these accounts, plan participants can deposit deferred income into an employer-administered account. The plan administrator determines what latitude the account-holder has in making his or her own investment decisions, which in some cases are limited to employer-approved funds.

INDIVIDUAL RETIREMENT ARRANGEMENT (IRA) A savings account for individuals that provides for special tax treatment on savings set aside money for retirement. The most common types of IRAs are the Roth IRA and the Traditional IRA. See Qualified Account; Roth IRA; Tax-Qualified Account.

KEOGH PLAN A tax-qualified retirement plan for the self-employed. Keogh accounts operate much like a Traditional IRA, in that taxes on the annual contributions and income within the account are not payable until they are taken as distributions.

LONG TERM CAPITAL GAINS Income derived from the sale of a capital asset that has been held for more than one year. Long term capital gains are typically taxed at a lower rate than regular income. Compare to Short Term Capital Gains, Capital Loss.

MARK TO MARKET An accounting method that assigns (marks) the value of an open position as equal to its market price (close) at the as of the end of the trading session.

PURCHASE AND SALE AGREEMENT A statement provided to an account holder by a Commodities Futures Merchant (CFM) providing transaction details when a position is closed.

QUALIFIED See Tax-Qualified.

QUALIFIED DIVIDEND A dividend distribution paid by a U.S. corporation or certain foreign corporations that qualify for special tax treatment.

REGULAR INCOME A classification used by the IRS for income that does not qualify for special tax treatment, such as long term capital gains and business income. Regular income is reported on IRS Form 1040 or 1040-EZ.

ROTH IRA A tax-qualified savings account for individuals that allows the account holder to set aside money for retirement. A Roth IRA differs from a traditional IRA in that the contributions to a Roth IRA account are fully taxable at the time they are deposited and that both the principal and the income earned in the account are tax-free when they are withdrawn as distributions. See Individual Retirement Arrangement (IRA).

SCHEDULE D The IRS form used to reporting capital gain (loss).

SCHEDULE D-1 The continuation form to IRS form Schedule D, used for reporting capital gain (loss).

SHORT TERM CAPITAL GAIN Income derived from the sale of a capital asset that has been held for less than one year. Short term capital gains are taxed as regular income. Compare to Long Term Capital Gains; Capital Loss.

SUBCHAPTER M A reference to the Internal Revenue Service code that permits a regulated investment company or real estate investment trust (REIT) to avoid double taxation by passing along expenses (taxes on capital gains) and earnings (dividends and interest) to its account holders.

TAX PLANNING Investment decisions made to reduce a tax obligation. Capturing a loss at the end of the year so that it can be declared on the current tax return is an example of a tax planning strategy, as is investing in a tax-deferred account such as an IRA or 401(k).

TAX-DEFERRED ACCOUNT A tax-advantaged savings account in which the tax obligation associated with the contributions and/or investment earnings within the account are postponed until a later date. See 401(k) Plan; Qualified Account; Roth IRA; Traditional IRA.

TAX-EXEMPT SECURITY An investment on which the investor does not incur a tax obligation on the profit earned. U.S. government securities are an example of a tax-exempt security. See Double Exemption.

TAX-LOSS SELLING The practice of selling losing investments at the end of the year for the purpose of declaring the loss on that year's taxes. Tax-loss selling can result in a temporary drop in stock prices.

TAX-QUALIFIED An account that qualifies for favorable treatment from the IRS, typically in the form of deferred or reduced tax liability. Also referred to as a qualified account. See 401(k) Plan; Coverdell Education Savings Account (ESA); Individual Retirement Account (IRA); Keogh Plan.

TRADITIONAL IRA A tax-qualified savings account for individuals that allows the account holder to set aside money for retirement. A traditional IRA differs from a Roth IRA in that the contributions to a traditional IRA are tax-deductible at the time they are deposited and both the principal and the income earned in the account are taxed as regular income when they are withdrawn as distributions. See Individual Retirement Arrangement (IRA).

TRANSACTION DATE The execution date for a trade. Compare to Settlement Date.

WASH SALE RULE A reference to an IRS regulation that governs how a capital loss from an investment transaction is recognized. The wash rule requires a loss can be declared only if the investor waits 31 days before buying the identical security again. Also referred to as Wash Rule.

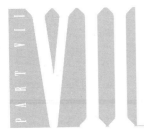

PART VII

Additional Resources

CHAPTER TWENTY-SIX

Investor Resources: Getting Help When You Need It

INVESTMENT ADVISER REGISTRATION DEPOSITORY A NASD-developed and operated system that maintains registration and disclosure information on registered investment advisors. On the Web at **www.iard.com**.

ADVISORY NEWSLETTER A publication that provides market commentary and investment recommendations. Most advisory newsletters are subscriptions services. See Hulbert Financial Digest.

AMERICAN ASSOCIATION OF INDIVIDUAL INVESTORS (AAII) A networking and education organization for individual investors. On the Web at **www.aaii.com**.

BARRON'S A weekly finance magazine published by Dow Jones, Inc. It is available in print format or an online subscription. It is available online at **www.barrons.com**.

BOND BUYER, THE A daily publication for the bond market that contains a comprehensive listing of municipal bond data. The Bond Buyer was established in 1891 and is also known as The Daily Bond Buyer. On the Web at **www.bondbuyer.com**.

BOND MARKET ASSOCIATION (BMA) A trade association comprised of banks, dealers, brokers, and underwriters of debt instruments. The BMA also provides educational services to individual investors. On the Web at **www.bondmarkets.com**.

CERTIFIED FUND SPECIALIST A financial professional who

possesses a certificate attesting to his or her qualification to advise clients on the selection of mutual fund investments.

COMMODITY TRADING ADVISOR A person who is registered with the Commodity Futures Trading Commission (CFTC) to provide, advise, and manage futures and options trading activity for another person.

COMPUSTAT A subscription service from Standard & Poor's that provides market information and fundamental data.

DUN & BRADSTREET (D&B) A business and finance research company that issues corporate credit ratings and maintains a database of financial information on corporations worldwide. A company's D&B rating can affect both its stock price and its bond rating. On the Web at **www.dnb.com**.

EDGAR ONLINE A publicly traded company that provides value added data services based on the Securities & Exchange Commission's EDGAR database of corporate filings. EDGAR Online trades under the symbol EDGR on NASDAQ and is online at **www.edgar-online.com**.

FEDERAL REGISTER A government publication that provides public notice of new regulations from the Office of Thrift Supervision, legal notices, presidential proclamations, executive orders, documents required by an Act of Congress, and other official documents of public interest. The Federal Register is published daily, Monday through Friday and is available on the Web at **www.gpoaccess.gov/fr/index.html**.

FITCH INVESTORS SERVICE The company that issues the Fitch Ratings for the bond, Eurobond, and funds market. Compare to Moody's Investors Service and Standard & Poor's. See Bond Ratings.

HULBERT FINANCIAL DIGEST A MarketWatch/Dow Jones subscription service that rates advisory newsletters by tracking and measuring their recommendations against actual performance. The digest is available by e-mail or U.S. Postal Service delivery. On the Web at **www.marketwatch.com**.

INVESTMENT ADVISER REGISTRATION DEPOSITORY A NASD-developed and operated system that maintains registration and disclosure information on registered investment advisors. On the Web at **www.iard.com**.

INVESTMENT ADVISOR A professional hired by an individual to provide financial and investment advice. See Registered Investment Advisor (RIA); Trailer Fee.

INVESTOR PROTECTION TRUST A non-profit organization that provides resources to help individual investors make informed investment decisions. On the Web at **www.investorprotection.org**.

INVESTORS BUSINESS DAILY (IBD) A daily financial newspaper and Internet-based investment news and information resource. On the Web at **www.investors.com**.

MOODY'S INVESTORS SERVICE A financial research firm opining on the creditworthiness of bond issuers. See Bond Rating. On the Web at **www.moodys.com**.

MORNINGSTAR, INC. An investment research and rating service for mutual funds, stocks, closed-end funds, Exchange Traded Funds, hedge funds, and other investments. On the Web at **www.morningstar.com**.

NATIONAL ASSOCIATION OF INVESTORS CORPORATION (NAIC) A networking and education organization for individual investors.

REUTERS A global business and financial news service. In addition to news content for media organizations, Reuters provides financial information products to businesses, financial professionals, and investors. One the Web at **www.reuters.com**.

STANDARD & POOR'S A market research firm that publishes credit ratings and financial reports used by individuals and institutional investors. It is also the originator of the family of S&P indexes, the best known and most closely watched of which is the S&P 500. On the Web at **www.standardandpoors.com**.

VALUE LINE, INC. An investment research firm with product offerings for individual, professional, and institutional investors. Value Line is known for the Value Line Investment Survey for stock analysis, but the company has similar products for mutual funds and options as well. On the Web at **www.valueline.com**.

WALL STREET JOURNAL, THE A financial news publication from Dow Jones & Company. It is available in print daily and online. The weekly and Sunday editions are delivered each Saturday morning and Sunday mornings, respectively. On the Web at **www.wsj.com**.

Acronyms

A/D	Advance/Decline Ratio
AAII	American Association of Individual Investors
ABS	Automated Bond System
ACE	American Stock Exchange
ACH	Automated Clearing House
ADR	American Depositary Receipt
ADS	American Depositary Share
AMBAC	American Municipal Bond Assurance Corporation
AMEX	American Stock Exchange
AON	All or None
APB	Accounting Principles Board
ASAM	Automated Search and Match
AUD	Australian Dollar
BBA	British Banking Association
BDK	Display Book
BEA	Bureau of Economic Analysis
BEX	Boston Equity Exchange
BIF	Bank Insurance Fund
BMA	Bond Market Association
BOD	Board of Directors
BOX	Boston Option Exchange
BOP	Balance of Payments
BSE	Boston Stock Exchange
CAPEX	Capital Expense or Capital Expenditure

CBO	Collateralized Bond Obligation
CBOE	Chicago Board Options Exchange
CBOT	Chicago Board of trade
CD	Certificate of Deposit
CDSL	Contingent Deferred Sales Loan
CEA	Council of Economic Advisers
CEO	Cash Flow
CFAT	Cash Flow after Taxes
CFE	CBOE Futures Exchange
CFO	Chief Financial Officer
CFPS	Cash Flow Per Share
CFRI	Cash Flow Return on Investments
CFTC	Commodity Futures Trading Commission
CH	Swiss Franc
CHX	Chicago Stock Exchange
CND	Canadian Dollar
CNY	Chinese Yuan
COGS	Cost of Goods Sold
COMEX	Commodities Exchange Inc.
COO	Chief Operating Officer
COT	Commitment of Traders Report
CPA	Certified Public Accountant
CPI	Consumer Price Index
CPS	Current Population Survey
CQS	Consolidated Quote System
CRD	Central Registration Depositary
CSCE	Coffee, Sugar, and Cocoa Exchange
CTA	Consolidated Tape Association
CTP	Consolidated Tape Plan
CTS	Consolidated Tape System
CUSIP	Committee on Uniform security Identification Procedures
DAT	Direct Access Trading
DCF	Discounted Cash Flow
DD	Due Diligence

DJIA	Dow Jones Industrial Average
DNR	Do Not Reduce
DPO	Direct Public Offering
DTD	Day to Day
ECN	Electronic Communication Network
ECN	Electronic Communication Network
ECU	European Currency Unit
EDGAR	Electronic Data Gathering Analysis and Retrieval
EMA	Exponential Moving Average
EPS	Earnings Per Share
ESA	Educational Savings Account
ETF	Exchange Traded Fund
EV	Enterprise Value
EV/EBITDA	Enterprise Value to EBITDA Ratio
FASB	Financial Accounting Standards Board
FBE	European Banking Federation
FCF	Free Cash Flow
FCM	Futures Commission Merchant
FCPA	Foreign Corrupt Practices ACT (FCPA)
FDIC	Federal Deposit Insurance Corporation
FHA	Federal Housing Administration
FHLBS	Federal Home Loan Bank System
FIBV	International Federation of Stock Exchanges
FIRREA	Financial Institutions Reform, Recovery, and Enforcement Act of 1989
FOCUS	Financial and Operational Combined Uniform Single Report
FOK	Fill or Kill
FOMC	Federal Open Market Committee
FOREX	Foreign Exchange Market
FTC	Federal Trade Commission
FWB	Frankfurter Werpapierborse Frankfurt (Stock Exchange)
FY	Fiscal Year
G10	Group of Ten

G24	Group of Twenty-four
G5	Group of Five
G7	Group of Seven
G8	Group of Eight
GBP	British Pound Sterling
GDP	Gross Domestic Products
GTC	Good until Cancelled
HKD	Hong Kong Dollar
HOLDRs	Holding Company Depositary Receipts
IASB	International Accounting Standards Board
IB	Introducing broker
IMF	International Monetary Fund
INR	Indian Rupee
IOC	Immediate or Cancel
IPO	Initial Public Offering
IRA	Individual Retirement Arrangement
IRS	Internal Revenue Service
ISE	International Securities Exchange
ISM	Institute for Supply Management
ISO	International Organization for Standards
ITS	Intermarket Trading System
JPY	Japanese Yen
KCBT	Kansas City Board of Trade
LEI	Leading Economic Indicators.
LIBID	London Interbank Bid Rate
LIBOR	London Interbank Offered Rate
LIFFE	London International Financial Futures and Options Exchange
LIT	Limit if Touched
LOC	Limit on Close
LOO	Limit on Open
LSE	London Stock Exchange
MA	Moving Average
MACD	Moving Average Convergence/Divergence
MBS	Mortgage-Backed Security

MID	Market Index Deposit
MIG	Moody's Investment Grade
MIT	Market if Touched
MRQ	Most Recent Quarter
MSRB	Municipal Securities Rulemaking Board
Mx	Montreal Stock Exchange
NAIC	National Association of Investors Corporation
NASAA	North American Securities Administrators Association
NASD	National Association of Securities Dealers
NBBO	National Best Bid and Offer
NEV	Net Asset Value
NEVPS	Net Asset Value Per Share
NFA	National Futures Association
NIC	Net Interest Cost
NMS	National Market System
NSTS	National Securities Trading System
NSX	Cincinnati Stock Exchange
NYBOT	New York Board of Trade
NYCE	New York Cotton Exchange
NYMEX	New York Mercantile Exchange
NYSE	New York Stock Exchange
OARS	Opening Automated Reporting System
OCIE	Office of Compliance Inspections and Examination
OID	Original Issue Discount
OPRA	Options Price Reporting Authority
OTC	Over-the-counter Market
OTCBB	Over-the-counter Bulletin Board
P&L	Profit and Loss Statement
P/B	Price to Book Ratio
PCAOB	Public Company Accounting Oversight Board
PBGC	Pension Benefit Guaranty Corporation
PCE	Personal Consumption Expenditures
PCX	Pacific Stock Exchange
PE	Price to Earnings Ratio

PERS	Post Execution Reporting System
PHLX	Philadelphia Stock Exchange
PIABA	Public Investors Arbitration Bar Association
PPI	Producer Price Index
REIT	Real Estate Investment Trust
ROA	Rights of Accumulation
ROE	Return on Equity
ROI	Return on Investment
RSI	Relative Strength Index
S&P	Standard & Poor's
SAIF	Savings Association Insurance Fund
SEC	Securities & Exchange Commission
SG&A	Sales, General & Administration
SIPC	Securities Investor Protection Corporation
SOES	Small Order Execution System
SOX	Sarbanes-Oxley Act of 2002
SPDR	Standard & Poor's Depositary Receipt
SRL	Speed Resistance Line
SRO	Self-Regulatory Organization
SSF	Single Stock Futures
STA	Securities Traders Association (STA)
SWX	Swiss Exchange
TRIN	Trading Index
TSE	Toronto Stock Exchange
TSX	Toronto Stock Exchange
TTM	Trailing 12 Months
UCC	Uniform Commercial Code
UIT	Unit Investment Trust
UPC	Uniform Practice Code
USD	U.S. Dollar
YOY	Year-Over-Year

Conclusion

Some investors manage to get through a lifetime with an investment vocabulary that doesn't go much beyond *buy, sell, market order,* and *capital gains tax.* Some of them even manage to make money. They would be the lucky ones. For the rest of us, making our money work for us means investing more than our money. It means investing time and effort into learning.

With more than 1,000 of the most frequently used finance investment terms defined in *Wall Street Lingo,* this reference can be a reliable partner as you delve ever more deeply into the investment opportunities that match your objectives and risk tolerance. It is, however, only one tool among the many you'll need.

Personally, I've found that the research tools available on the Internet and through a good broker to be invaluable. Libraries and book stores rank highly, as well. The answers are out there and they're not difficult to find. Becoming familiar with the basic vocabulary is the first step and you've just made it. Congratulations. Invest wisely, prosper always, and never stop learning.

Table of Figures

Access, Clearport eAccess, and COMEX are marks of NYMEX.

American Association of Individual Investors and AAII are marks of American Association of Individual Investors.

American Association of Individual Investors is a mark of the American Association of Individual Investors.

American Stock Exchange and Amex are registered trademarks of American Stock Exchange LLC.

ARCA, ARCAEX, ABS, Automated Bond System, SuperDot, Display Book, NYSE Group, The Big Board, NYSE, New York Stock Exchange, and NYSEArca are marks of the New York Stock Exchange.

Archipelago is a registered trademark of Archipelago Holdings, Inc.

Barron's, The Dow, DJIA, Dow Jones Industrial Average Display Book, DIAMONDS DJEuro, Stoxx, Stoxx50, and The Wall Street Journal are registered trademarks of Dow Jones & Company.

BBA Libor and BBA are registered trademarks of BBA.

BEL 20, CAC40, Euronext, and Liffe Connect are trademarks of Euronext.

BeX, BoX, and Boston Stock Exchange are marks of Boston Stock Exchange, Inc.

Bond Market Association is a copyright of The Bond Market Association.

CBOE, Chicago Board Options Exchange, Gas at The Pump, and LEAP are marks of the Chicago Board Options Exchange.

CBOT is a registered trademark of Chicago Board of Trade.

Chart Pattern Recognition is a trademark of John Murphy.

Chicago Business Barometer is a trademark of National Association of Purchasing Management Chicago, Inc.

Chicago Stock Exchange is a service mark of Chicago Stock Exchange, Incorporated.

CME, Chicago Mercantile Exchange, and Globex are registered trademarks of Chicago Mercantile Exchange Inc.

CNDX is a service mark of Canadian Venture Exchange.

Compustat, Standard & Poor's, S&P, S&P 500, Standard & Poor's Depositary Receipts, and SPDRs are marks of The McGraw-Hill Companies, Inc.

CUSIP is a registered trademark of the American Bankers Association.

D&B is a registered trademark of Dun & Bradstreet.

DAX, Deutsche Börse, Eurex US, and Xetra are registered trademarks of Deutsche Böerse AG.

Edgar is a registered trademark of the U.S. Securities & Exchange Commission (SEC).

Equis and MetaStock are registered trademarks of Equis International, a Reuters Company.

Fitch Investor Service and Fitch Ratings are marks of Fitch, Inc.

Fortune 500 is a registered trademark of Time, Inc.

Freddie Mac is a mark of Freddie Mac.

FTSE and FTSE 100 are registered trademarks of London Stock Exchange Plc. and The Financial Times LTD.

Ginnie Mae is a service mark of Government National Mortgage Association.

Hang Seng is a registered trademark of Hang Seng Data Services Limited Corporation.

HOLDRS and Holding Company

Depository Receipts are registered trademarks of Merrill Lynch & Co., Inc.

IARD is a service mark of NASD Regulation, Inc.

IASB is a trademark of International Accounting Standards Committee Foundation.

Instinet is a service mark of Instinet LLC.

Investor's Business Daily and IBD are trademarks of Data Analysis, Inc.

ISE and International Securities Exchange is a service mark of International Securities Exchange, Inc.

ISM, Report on Business, and the Institute for Supply Management are registered trademarks of the Institute for Supply Management.

ISO is a trademark of International Organization for Standardization.

KCBT and Kansas City Board of Trade are marks of Board of Trade of Kansas City, Missouri, Inc.

London Stock Exchange is a trademark of London Stock Exchange Limited.

Max Pain is a trademark of BCA Software.

Moody's, Moody's Investors Service, and MIG are proprietary marks of Moody's.

Morningstar, Inc., and Morningstar are registered trademarks of Morningstar, Inc.

MSRB is a trademark of Municipal Securities Rulemaking Board.

NASD is a registered trademark of National Association of Securities Dealers.

NASDAQ 100, NASDAQ Canada, NASDAQ Composite, Nasdaq National Market, NASDAQ, SOES, Supermontage, and the Nasdaq Stock Market are marks of the Nasdaq Stock Market, Inc.

National Association of Investors Corporation and NAIC are registered trademarks of National Association Investors Corporation.

New York Board of Trade and NYCE are registered trademarks of NYBOT.

Nikkei and Nikkei 225 is a trademark of Kabushiki Kaisha Nihon Keizai Shimbun Sha Corporation.

NSX and National Stock Exchange are marks of the National Stock Exchange.

PHLX and Philadelphia Stock Exchange are marks of Philadelphia Stock Exchange, Inc.

Pink Sheets is a registered trademark of Pink Sheets LLC and the National Quotation Bureau.

POSIT is a registered trademark of Investment Technology Group, Inc.

Reuters is a registered trademark of the Reuters group of companies.

Russell 2000 and Russell 3000 are registered trademarks of the Frank Russell Company

Sallie Mae is a service mark of Student Loan Marketing Association

SIPC is a service mark of Securities Investor Protection Corporation.

SWX is a trademark of SWX Swiss Exchange.

The Bond Buyer is a registered trademark of the Bond Buyer Online.

The Conference Board Help-Wanted Online Data Series is a registered trademark of The Conference Board, Inc.

The Conference Board is a trademark of the Conference Board, Inc.

The Hulbert Financial Digest is a registered trademark of Hulbert Financial Digest, Inc.

TSX, TSX Venture Exchange, and TSX Group are marks of TSX Inc.

Value Line and Value Line Investment Survey are registered trademarks of Value Line, Inc.

Wilshire 5000 is a trademark of Wilshire Associates.

Yellow Sheets is a registered trademark of Pink Sheets LLC.

Bibliography

Steven B. Archelis, *Technical Analysis From A to Z*, McGraw Hill, New York, 1985.

David L. Scott, *Wall Street Words*, Houghton Mifflin Company, Boston, New York, 2003.

Gretchen Morgenson and Campbell R. Harvey, Ph.D., *Dictionary of Money and Investing*, Tim Book, Henry Holt and Company, New York, 2002.

John Murphy, Chart Pattern Recognition, Equis International, Salt Lake City, 2000.

R.J. Shook, *Wall Street Dictionary*, Career Press, Franklin Lakes, NJ, 1999.

John Downs and Jordan Elliot Goodman, Dictionary of Finance and Investment Terms, Barron's Educational Series, Inc., Hauppauge, NY, 2003.

Burton G. Malkiel, *A Random Walk Down Wall Street*, W.W. Norton & Company, New York, London, 1990.

William J. O'Neil, *24 Lessons for Investment Success*, McGraw Hill, New York, 2000.

Donald G. M. Coxe, *The New Reality of Wall Street*, McGraw Hill, New York, Chicago, San Francisco, Lisbon, London, Madrid, Mexico City, Milan, New DelhiSan Juan, Seoul, Singapore, Sydney, Toronto, 2003.

Grant Noble, *The Trader's Edge*, McGraw Hill, New York, San Francisco, Washington, DC Auckland, Bota, Caracas, Lisbon, London, Madrid, Mexico City, Milan, Montreal, New Delhi, San Juan, Singapore, Sydney, Tokyo, Toronto, 1995.

Richard Roberts *T h e Economist Wall Street The markets, Mechanisms and players*, The Economist in Association with Profile Books Ltd, London, 2002.

Nilus Mattive, *The Standard & Poor's Guide for The New Investor*, McGraw Hill, New York, Chicago, San Francisco, Lisbon, London, Madrid, Mexico City, Milan, New Delhi, San Juan, Seoul, Singapore, Sydney, Toronto, 2004.

Internet Resources

Table 5

American Association of Individual Investors	http://www.aaii.com
American Stock Exchange	http://amex.com
Austin Coins	http://www.austincoins.com
Bank of England	http://www.bankofengland.co.uk
Barron's	http://www.barronsmag.com
BMA	http://www.bondmarkets.com
Boston Stock Exchange	http://www.bostonstock.com
Briefing.com	http://www.briefing.com
British Banking Association	http://www.bba.org.uk
Bureau of Economic Analysis	http://www.bea.gov
Bureau of Labor Statistics	http://stats.bls.gov
BusinessWeek	http://www.businessweek.com
Census Bureau	http://www.census.gov
Chicago Board of Trade	http://www.cbot.com
Chicago Board Options Exchange	http://www.cboe.com
Chicago Mercantile Exchange	http://www.cme.com
Chicago Stock Exchange	http://www.chx.com
Commodity Futures Trading Commission	http://www.cftc.gov
Cornell University	http://www.law.cornell.edu
Council of Economic Advisors	http://www.whitehouse.gov/cea/
Council of Institutional Investors	http://www.cii.org/about/

Daily Reckoning	http://www.dailyreckoning.com
Deutsche Bundesbank	http://www.bundesbank.de
Dictionary.com	http://www.dictionary.com
Dow Jones Company	http://dowjones.com
Dun & Bradstreet	http://www.dnb.com
Energy Information Agency	http://www.eia.doe.gov
Eurexchange	http://www.eurexchange.com
Euroclear	http://www.euroclear.com
Euronext	http://www.euronext.com
Export-Import Bank of the United States	http://www.exim.gov/
Facts on File	http://www.factsonfile.com
Fannie Mae	http://www.fanniemae.com
Federal Reserve	http://www.federalreserve.gov
Federal Trade Commission	http://ftc.gov
Find Law	http://library.findlaw.com
Fitch Investments	http://www.fitchinv.com
Freddie Mac	http://www.freddiemac.com
G10	http://g10.org/
G24	http://www.g24.org/
Ginnie Mae	http://www.ginniemae.gov/
GrowCo.com	http://www.growco.com
Hyperhistory.com	http://www.hyperhistory.com
Institute for Supply Management	http://www.ism.ws/
International Monetary Fund	http://www.imf.org
International Standards Organization	http://www.iso.org
Investionary.com	http://www.investionary.com
Investors.com	http://www.investors.com
Investorwords.com	http://www.investorwords.com
Kansas City Board of Trade	http://www.kcbt.com
Library of Congress	http://thomas.loc.gov/cgi-bin /bdquery/z?d098:HR00559:
London Metal Exchange	http://www.lme.co.uk

London Online	http://www.londononline.co.uk
MaxPain	http://65.108.12.28/cgi-bin/maxpain.cgi
Moody's Investors Service	http://moodys.com
Morningstar.com	http://morningstar.com/
Municipal Securities Rulemaking Board	http://www.msrb.org/msrb1/
NASD	http://www.nasd.com
NASDAQ	https://www.nasdaq.com
National Association of Investors Corporation	http://www.betterinvesting.org
National Cooperative Bank	http://www.ncb.coop/
National Futures Association	http://www.nfa.futures.org
National Stock Exchange	http://www.nsx.com
New York Board of Trade	http://www.nybot.com/
New York Stock Exchange	http://www.nyse.com
New York University	http://www.nyu.edu
North American Securities Administrators Association	http://www.nasaa.org
NYMEX	http://www.nymex.com
Office of Thrift Supervision	http://www.ots.treas.gov
Opra Data	http://www.opradata.com
PBGC	http://www.pbgc.gov/
Philadelphia Stock Exchange	http://www.phlx.com/
Pink Sheets	http://www.pinksheets.com
Princeton University	http://www.wws.princeton.edu
Public Broadcasting Service	http://www.pbs.org
Public Company Accounting Oversight Board	http://www.pcaobus.org/
Public Investors Arbitration Bar Association	http://www.piaba.org
Reuters	http://www.reuters.com
Securities & Exchange Commission	http://www.sec.gov

Securities Industry Association	http://www.sia.com
Securities Industry Automation Industry	http://siac.com
SIPC	http://www.sipc.org/
Standard & Poor's	http://www.standardandpoors.com
Stock Charts.com	http://stockcharts.com
Teach me Finance.com	http://teachmefinance.com
The Black Vault	http://www.blackvault.com
The Bond Buyer	http://www.bondbuyer.com
Toronto Post	http://www.torontopost.biz
Trading-glossary.com	http://www.trading-glossary.com
Treasury Department	http://www.publicdebt.treas.gov
TSX	http://www.tsx.com
U.S. Bankruptcy Court	http://www.uscourts.gov/
U.S. Department of Justice	http://www.usdoj.gov
U.S. Department of State	http://www.state.gov
U.S. History.com	http://www.u-s-history.com/
U.S. House of Representatives	http://uscode.house.gov/
U.S. Treasury Products	http://www.treasurydirect.gov
U.S. Trademarks Office	http://www.uspto.gov
University of British Columbia	http://fx.sauder.ubc.ca/ECU.html
University of California	http://www.law.uc.edu
University of Pennsylvania	http://www.law.upenn.edu
University of Toronto	http://www.g7.utoronto.ca
USA Today	http://www.usatoday.com
Value Line	http://valueline.com
Value Line	http://www.valueline.com/
Wall Street Journal Classroom	http://wsjclassroom.com
Washington Post	http://www.washingtonpost.com
Wikipedia	http://en.wikipedia.org
World Federation of Exchanges	http://www.world-exchanges.org/
Yahoo Finance	http://finance.yahoo.com

Index

Double witching week 142

Dow Jones & Company 59

Dow Jones industrial average 107

Downgrade 164

Downtick 239

Dual listed 117

Dual trading 24

Due diligence 164

Dun & Bradstreet 254

Durable goods 92

Durable goods orders 92

Dutch auction 195

E

E-commerce 77

Earnings 177

Earnings announcement 165

Earnings before interest 185

Earnings calendar 165

Earnings per share 185

Earnings surprise 186

Earnings warning 186

Economic contraction 77

Economic cycle 77

Economic expansion 77

Economic indicator 74, 77

Economic recovery 77

Economist 50

EDGAR (electronic data gathering analysis and retrieval) 69

EDGAR online 254

Efficient market theory 77

Electronic communication network (ECN) 24

Electronic trading system 25

Elliott wave theory 202

Embargo 34

Emerging market fund 125

Employment report 92

Employment situation report 93

Enterprise value 186

Enterprise value to EBITDA 186

Enterprise value to revenue 186

Entity 34

Equities 117

Equity 117, 177

Equity fund 125

Equity linked note 134

Equity unit investment trust 117

Eurex 15

Eurex US 16

Euro 78

Eurobond 134

Euro CD 134

Euro certificate of deposit 134

Euroclear 45

Eurocurrency 78

Eurodollar 78

European banking federation (FBE) 69

European central bank (ECB) 51

European currency unit 78

European option 143

European union (EU) 51

Event risk 228

Ex-dividend 165

Ex-dividend shares 165

Ex-food and energy 78

Exchange fee 125

Exchange traded fund 117

Execute 239

Exercise 143

Exhaustion gap 212

Existing home sales 93

Exit strategy 228

Exotic currency 148

Expense 177

Expiration date 143

Expiration month 143

Exponential moving average 202

Export-import bank of the United States 51

Export/import prices 94

Extended blue room 25

Extended hours trading 25

F

Face value 195

Factory orders 94

Fair disclosure regulation 34

Fair value 203

Fallen angel 165, 195

False breakout 212

Family of funds 125

Farm credit bank 51

Farm credit system 51

Fed 51

Federal deposit insurance corporation (FDIC) 51

Federal funds rate 78

Federal home loan bank 51

Federal home loan bank system (FHLBS) 51

Federal home loan mortgage corporation (Freddie Mac) 59

G

H

I

O

P

Q

R

S